The Subversive Seventies

The Subversive Seventies

MICHAEL HARDT

OXFORD
UNIVERSITY PRESS

OXFORD
UNIVERSITY PRESS

Oxford University Press is a department of the University of Oxford. It furthers
the University's objective of excellence in research, scholarship, and education
by publishing worldwide. Oxford is a registered trade mark of Oxford University
Press in the UK and certain other countries.

Published in the United States of America by Oxford University Press
198 Madison Avenue, New York, NY 10016, United States of America.

Library of Congress Cataloging-in-Publication Data
Names: Hardt, Michael, 1960– author.
Title: The subversive 70s / Michael Hardt.
Other titles: Subversive seventies
Description: New York, NY : Oxford University Press, [2023] |
Includes bibliographical references and index.
Identifiers: LCCN 2023006107 (print) | LCCN 2023006108 (ebook) |
ISBN 9780197674659 (hardback) | ISBN 9780197674666 |
ISBN 9780197674673 (epub) | ISBN 9780197674680
Subjects: LCSH: Protest movements—History—20th century. |
Social movements—History—20th century. |
Neoliberalism—History—20th century. | Nineteen seventies.
Classification: LCC HM883 .H373 2023 (print) | LCC HM883 (ebook) |
DDC 303.48/40904—dc23/eng/20230413
LC record available at https://lccn.loc.gov/2023006107
LC ebook record available at https://lccn.loc.gov/2023006108

DOI: 10.1093/oso/9780197674659.001.0001

Printed by Sheridan Books, Inc., United States of America

Contents

PART IV: STRATEGIC MULTIPLICITIES

PART V: ENCAMPMENT AND DIRECT ACTION

PART VI: THE CONTINUATION OF WAR BY OTHER MEANS

1

Introduction

The Subversive Seventies

> That we have had nothing to do with terrorism is obvious. That we have been "subversive" is equally obvious. Between these two truths lies the key issue at stake in our trial.
>
> —Militants of Autonomia awaiting trial in
> Rebibbia Prison, Rome, 1983

The 1970s was a decade of subversives. Politicians and their generals, police chiefs and secret service agents, conservative journalists and intellectuals saw "subversives" everywhere, challenging authority, laying siege to the established order, undermining the time-honored way of life. This mentality was so flexible it could designate as subversive indigenous peasant armies and gay liberation organizations, self-organized industrial workers and antinuclear activists, revolutionary feminists and Black liberation militants. Every corner of the Left was fertile ground for subversive elements, which the forces of order had to root out and destroy—a project they pursued with zeal and brutality. The battle against subversives in the 1970s legitimated extreme forms of repression and opened the counterinsurgency playbook for use against a range of domestic enemies. Police and military repression of the Left rose to extreme levels and took a wide variety of forms with varying degrees of lethal and nonlethal force, including disinformation campaigns, surveillance, infiltration, extralegal incarceration, targeted assassinations, mass "disappearances," and torture.[1]

It is tempting, given all the mystifications it evokes and the violence it justifies, simply to discard the term "subversive." But it is more useful to approach the term from the other side and embrace it. After all, those engaged in the progressive and revolutionary movements of the 1970s were in fact (and understood themselves to be) subversives. Instead of working within the system, they aimed to undermine the bases of established authorities and transform the fundamental structures of society. These activists were not satisfied with limited social and political reforms or partial alleviation of the suffering and exploitation of the subordinated if this meant leaving the foundations of the established order intact. Liberation was the core principle that guided a wide spectrum of movements, from women's liberation and the liberation of colonized peoples to Black liberation, gay liberation, and proletarian liberation. Subversion and liberation thus go hand in hand, and only together can they make another world, a better world, possible. I propose to return to the subversive seventies, then, not from the perspective of those in power desperately clinging to the established order but rather from that of those striving to change it.

Many books have been written (and many more are still needed) about the regimes of domination that emerged in the 1970s: brutal military dictatorships in Latin America, Turkey, and South Korea; the birth of neoliberalism along with the attack on labor unions and the dismantling of welfare structures; the oppressive authority of state socialisms; and much more. This book is about the other side.

In the following chapters, I select and analyze social and political movements that are subversive in a double sense: they seek to dismantle and overthrow the social structures of domination while, at the same time, constructing the bases for liberation. These are, in fact, the ones most relevant for our contemporary political situation, in part because they challenged political and economic structures that were emerging at the time and still rule over us today. The subversive seventies constitute a first *essai* to confront our current conjuncture, a first test of the terrain.[2] They offer us, in other words, not only initial analyses of today's structures of economic and political domination, and not only effective forms of critique and resistance against them, but also experiments with alternative social and political relations on the path to liberation.[3]

The Decade When Nothing Happened

Many of the progressive and revolutionary projects of the seventies remain today relatively unknown. They are often obscured or discounted in relation to conventional images of the politics of the 1960s. Clarifying and repositioning the relation between the two decades, then, is a prerequisite for appreciating the political accomplishments of the seventies and revealing their importance for us today.[4]

Most standard accounts cast the progressive and revolutionary movements of the sixties in a brilliant and rosy light. Iconic images that celebrate the decade's struggles for peace, justice, and freedom are shared touchstones of cultural memory. Students occupying courtyards of the Sorbonne and administrative buildings at Columbia University; new leaders declaring independence in Algeria, Kenya, and other former colonies; Black marchers in Selma, all dressed in their Sunday best, maintaining their solemn poise and commitment to nonviolence even under brutal police attack; Mexican student demonstrators at Tlatelolco massacred by government snipers; Prague protesters facing off with Soviet tanks; young people in the streets across the world protesting the US war in Vietnam—these are some of the snapshots in a collective photo album.

Such representations, as many authors have rightly demonstrated, are often sanitized to white out the most radical and troubling elements of the global sixties.[5] One consequence of such distortions is to obscure the political developments of the subsequent years. Todd Gitlin, for example, after having celebrated progressive US political culture in the sixties as an era of innocence and hope, laments that by the end of the decade it all came to an end. "By the early Seventies," he claims, "the upheaval was over—as mysteriously as it had appeared, and as worldwide." The powerful tide of revolution that flooded the sixties, Gitlin continues, now swept back out just as ferociously (1987, 13, 407).[6]

To maintain that nothing happened in the 1970s, however, requires strategic blindness.[7] To some extent, that blindness has to do with "how." Many of the most prominent movements of the sixties—industrial workers' movements, feminists, national liberation and anti-imperialist struggles, antiracist movements, student and youth rebellions, indigenous struggles—continued in the seventies, in many cases in greater numbers and with greater intensity than before. The fact that they could become invisible (at least for some) was due to the fact that they took on very different characteristics, radically altered forms of organization, and new objectives, which did not fit into acceptable narratives. Nanni Balestrini and Primo Moroni, for example, referring to 1968 and 1977, the signal dates of movement activity in Italy, maintain that whereas dominant society could comprehend and digest, so to speak, the forms of protest that characterized the sixties, the militancy of the seventies proved indigestible. "This is why," they maintain, "we have the 'official' versions of good old '68 and bad '77. In fact, whereas '68 was recuperated, '77 was annihilated" (Balestrini and Moroni 2021, 535–536, translation modified). The seventies movements were wiped from memory, then, in part because they had become unrecognizable from (or politically unacceptable to) the "official" narrative.[8]

The strategic blindness is even more apparent, however, regarding "who," because the seventies landscape of progressive and revolutionary activity included movements by populations that previously had not been active or had not been widely recognized, notably feminist struggles, gay liberation movements, movements of the poor and unemployed, indigenous struggles, and various racial and ethnic rebellions.[9] "The media says that nothing happened in the 70's," Bernice Johnson Reagon told a feminist audience at the 1981 West Coast Women's Music Festival in San Francisco, "and most of us get up on stage and we talk as if that in fact is the case, and it's a lie. The only way it will be true is if you believe them and do not take the next step" (1983, 368). As if hidden by an invisibility cloak or screened from view by an optical filter, the intense political activity that emerged in the seventies remains unseen from the dominant perspective. Nothing to see here. Move along. The first challenge, then, is simply to remove the blinders and "see" the seventies, to take stock of the intense and widespread political activity that actually took place.

The Decade When Everything Went Wrong

A more significant challenge to interpreting the seventies is posed by the "good sixties/bad seventies" paradigm, whereby radical and revolutionary activity did continue but took on increasingly dark and destructive characteristics. Two influential histories of the era, for example, use their subtitles to designate the decline and degeneration from one period to the next: the subtitle of Hervé Hamon and Patrick Rotman's two-volume set contrasts "the years of dreams" (1958–1968) and "the years of powder," meaning gunpowder (1968–1975).[10] And the subtitle of Todd Gitlin's book distinguishes the "years of hope" (the early and mid-1960s) from the "days of rage" (roughly after 1968).[11] In both histories, the image of youthful innocence and nonviolence in the former period, with its hope and dreams, is contrasted with the image of destructiveness in the latter. The periodizations do not neatly line up, of course, but a shared standard view is that after the late 1960s the Left was destroyed—or, even worse, destroyed itself.[12]

There are several versions of this argument. Each identifies a different cause of the destruction, and each has a kernel of truth, which is what makes this argument so challenging. One version of what went wrong focuses on the internal conflicts and, especially, the erosion of unity on the Left.[13] Progressive and revolutionary organizations were profoundly shaken in the seventies by internal challenges to the hierarchies that constituted them. This was the era in which feminists refused to continue to serve, in Shulamith Firestone's memorable phrase, as the "ladies' auxiliaries of the Left," contesting the patriarchal structures and sexist attitudes within student, labor, and antiracist movements (Firestone 1979, 31); Black workers rebelled against white-dominated union hierarchies; feminists of color and lesbians challenged racial and sexuality hierarchies and exclusions within feminist movements; Black nationalists challenged the racism of white allies; gay liberation movements and the Stonewall generation decried the homophobia of the Left; third world militants criticized the provincialism and complicity of first world activists; and much, much more. To many it seemed the Left was imploding, tearing itself apart through separatism and identity politics. To others, of course, this reckoning was long overdue, and any nostalgia for unity was just a means to mask subordination. It was essential to reveal hierarchies within the movements themselves, they maintained, and understand that liberation projects must attack multiple forms of domination (defined by race, gender, sexuality, class, and more) both inside and outside the Left. Here one can easily recognize the positive effects of internal conflicts and an example of the demand for multiplicity in action.

A second version of the "everything went wrong" argument (as well as the "good sixties/bad seventies" paradigm) highlights the numerous defeats the Left suffered in the seventies. A long list comes quickly to mind. The 1973 US-supported coup d'état in Chile dashed the global hopes that had been raised by Salvador Allende's election. Military dictatorships in Brazil, Bolivia, Uruguay, and Argentina, plus military coups d'état in Thailand (1976) and Turkey (1980), strangled all forms of leftist political action and expression. Vibrant social movements, such as the Italian extraparliamentary Left and the South African Black Consciousness Movement, were defeated by state repression and mass arrests. The industrial labor movement, too, suffered pivotal, generation-defining defeats, with mass firings of workers; these extended into the next decade, culminating in, for example, the 1980 Fiat

strike in Turin, the 1981 US air controllers' strike, and the 1984–1985 UK
miners' strike. These defeats, each more tragic than the last, piled up like so
many mangled vehicles in a highway accident.[14] We certainly do have to face
clearly every defeat and its terrible consequences, but simply focusing on victory or defeat misses what is most politically significant and useful. Robin
D. G. Kelley rightly laments that "too often our standards for evaluating social movements pivot around whether or not they 'succeeded' in realizing
their visions rather than on the merits or power of the visions themselves"
(2002, ix). Those visions remain alive and strong beyond defeat: the long history of revolutionary movements teaches us that a defeat, however devastating, is never an endpoint. Future projects of liberation begin from where
it ended, taking its achievements and the power of its vision as the point of
departure for new struggles.

   A third version of the "everything went wrong" argument highlights
the political violence of the seventies, sometimes with the (misleading) assumption that the sixties were characterized by peaceful, nonviolent protest.[15] This is a complicated story that does not allow for easy, unqualified
political judgments. In this version of the "good sixties/bad seventies" paradigm, the Left lost its way and destroyed itself through the violent actions
of organizations that conducted clandestine armed struggle, including
the Red Brigades, the Japanese Red Army, Germany's Red Army Faction,
Black September, the Popular Front for the Liberation of Palestine, the
Provisional Irish Republican Army, the Montoneros, and numerous other
such militarized formations. Some of these groups committed horrifying
acts that should unequivocally be condemned morally and politically, and in
the course of the book I will offer some analyses and critique of them. Before
engaging such judgments, though, one must first contend with the context
of extreme repression in which these groups operated. Although state suppression of leftist political activism in the 1960s had not been peaceful—far
from it—in the 1970s the intensity of state and police violence, sometimes in
conjunction with fascists, death squads, and other right-wing groups, rose
exponentially. Ever greater numbers of demonstrators were beaten and shot;
counterintelligence schemes proliferated, along with unfounded legal pro-
ceedings against activists and unjustified imprisonment. Second, one must
distinguish among different modes of deploying weapons and different
strategies of self-defense, some of which, I will argue, were appropriate and
necessary for protecting innovative, democratic political movements. In particular, some organizations developed a dual strategy by which they were

able to defend the movements from repression while developing democratic social projects. Finally, focusing on armed struggle must not be allowed to eclipse other, often more significant political movements that did not deploy weapons. The spectacular and frequently tragic robberies, bombings, kidnappings, and assassinations garnered extraordinary attention at the time and still today occupy an outsized position in historical memory—vastly disproportionate to the small numbers of militants involved in these groups. I will thus try to quarantine discussions of armed struggle, civil war, and terrorism toward the end of the book in order elsewhere to allow for undivided attention on other movements.

The 1970s are undoubtedly a troubling decade that defies simple, unqualified judgments. Jaime Pensado and Enrique Ochoa, thinking primarily about Mexico, note the dual nature of what they, too, call "the subversive seventies": "on one hand, . . . the emergence of a distinct spirit of utopia and revolution and, on the other, . . . a novel rhythm of despair and political violence" (2018, 7). Such divided, ambivalent, even contradictory assessments of the 1970s are probably necessary. "What, then," asks Dan Berger, in line with Pensado and Ochoa, "are we to make of the 1970s? It was a deeply ambivalent and contentious moment, simultaneously moving in multiple directions" (2010, 3). I will highlight these characteristics in the following chapters, but it is worth noting from the outset that the complexities and the ambivalence of the seventies should be not lamented but recognized as a virtue. Even in such a fraught political context, facing unresolvable problems and the threat of brutal repression, these movements were able to navigate through the dangers and forward projects of liberation.[16]

Concepts Generated in the Movements

The array of progressive and revolutionary movements across the globe in the seventies was extraordinarily varied, and each should be appreciated and evaluated in its own singular context. And yet, if one takes a step back to view the broad international landscape, some coherent patterns emerge, which are particularly evident in the concepts that are produced by and circulate among the movements. I propose to interpret the movements in terms of their concepts, but by that I am not referring primarily to what intellectuals had to say about them. We need to cast aside the false assumption of a division of labor by which intellectuals think and activists act, and to recognize the value of theorizing advanced collectively in the movements themselves. Part of the work of political movements, especially revolutionary ones, in fact, is to invent concepts.

Autonomy is one concept that characterized the aspirations of a wide range of progressive and revolutionary movements of the seventies. Radical industrial workers, for instance, while taking control of their own struggles, declared their autonomy not only from the factory bosses but also from the leadership and dictation of the dominant unions. Industrial workers in a range of national contexts created collective decision-making structures to determine themselves when to begin a strike and when to end it, whether to occupy a factory and how to manage it, and even when to take up arms to defend themselves. (The early 1970s were a high point of industrial class struggle in many countries in terms of both the intensity and number of strikes.) The claim to autonomy was also a strong component of the many movements that employed the strategy of encampment, designed, in most cases, to block large infrastructure projects—an airport, a military base, or a nuclear reactor—by occupying the land, for months in some cases and for years or even over a decade in others. Each encampment effectively declared autonomy from the state and refused the state's authority to make unilateral decisions over these infrastructure projects. Autonomy in all these cases indicated not only a refusal of authority but also a refusal of structures of representation, claiming decision-making power for those involved regarding the most important issues affecting their lives.

Multiplicity is another conceptual touchstone that runs through the movements, emerging especially clearly from feminist debates. A precondition for the political conception of multiplicity was the recognition, increasingly widespread by the middle of the decade, that the centrality of industrial workers in the revolutionary struggle had come to an end. This was not the end of class struggle or its importance, of course, but the end of the assumed priority of industrial workers and the belief that a workers' vanguard could lead and unify the revolutionary movement as a whole. (This complex and contrasting development of the peak of industrial workers' power and the end of their centrality in revolutionary movement will be explored in depth in Part III.) What emerged instead were parallel conceptions of multiplicity: an analysis of power and a strategic proposal. Activists and theorists in the seventies formulated an analysis of power characterized by intersecting identities and multiple structures of domination (capitalist, racial, imperialist, and patriarchal), which anticipated in some respects the notion of intersectionality that developed a decade later. Correspondingly, they forwarded a strategic proposal that feminist, antiracist, anti-imperialist, and anticapitalist struggles be articulated together without priority among them. Similar proposals of strategic multiplicity were also formulated in multiracial political projects, under the banner of "people of color" in the United States, for instance, and within the Black Consciousness Movement in South Africa. In these cases, too, the strategic multiplicity can only function, as we will see below, so long as none of its component parts is given priority over the others.

Democracy is a third concept that resonated widely in the struggles. The notions of revolutionary democracy that proliferated not only stood opposed to authoritarian government and capitalist control but also rejected the established structures of liberal democratic regimes. In summary terms, one could say that this democracy prioritizes participation over representation: universal participation in political decision-making rather than existing schemes of representation that leave power in the hands of the few. Revolutionary movements experimented with investing power in a vast array of commission structures so as to institutionalize democratic participation: work commissions in factories, rural village commissions, neighborhood commissions, and more. And, in some cases, movements found effective means to scale up local decision-making structures to the metropolitan and national levels.

Liberation, finally, may be the concept that links together all the others and serves as the master concept for the era. Activists were convinced that, through organized struggle, it was possible to change everything, to reinvent society from the ground up. Liberation is not just emancipation—that is, releasing people from their chains in order to participate in the existing society. Liberation requires, in addition, a radical transformation of that society, overturning its structures of domination and creating new institutions that foster freedom. But even that is not enough, because for liberation not only the structures but also the subjects must change, initiating a process of collective subjective transformation. The seventies may be the last period in which numerous large-scale social and political movements had the audacity and confidence to aim unequivocally at liberation and put in practice the means to achieve it.

I know that these concepts presented so briefly remain at an abstract theoretical level. The investigations of the movements in the following chapters, however, will elaborate them in more specific and concrete terms, and, in turn, the concepts will guide my analysis of the political developments. This conceptual approach is particularly appropriate, as I said, because the activists themselves were theorizing collectively, generating these and other concepts as beacons to guide and understand their own struggles.

History of the Present

What most significantly divides the progressive and revolutionary movements of the seventies from those of the sixties are their different relations to the present. Simplifying a great deal, the sixties were a crucial historical turning point that marked the *end* of an era. The coincidence and accumulation of struggles in that decade, sometimes referred to as the "global 1968"—including anticolonial and anti-imperialist struggles, revolts against state socialist regimes, insurgencies against racial domination, industrial worker rebellions against factory discipline, and more—made the ruling global framework of power as well as disciplinary regimes in each country increasingly ungovernable, and precipitated a series of social, economic, and political crises in the early 1970s.[17] We can certainly learn from the movements of the sixties, then, both those that were victorious and those that were vanquished—but, fundamentally, they belong to a past world, not ours.

The 1970s, in contrast, mark the beginning of our time. It was a decade of great tectonic shifts in the structures and mechanisms that rule the social order, which scholars have tried to capture from a variety of angles with various terms. Postindustrial society, for instance, took form in the seventies: it was, perhaps paradoxically, as I said, the peak of industrial workers' power as well as the beginning of its decline. Simultaneously, labor and wage regimes shifted from Fordist to post-Fordist models, initiating an era of increasingly precarious and informal forms of employment. At the same time, neoliberal policies set a course of privatizing public goods, undermining welfare structures, and increasing the gap between rich and poor, while making the state less responsive to social demands and progressive reforms.

Progressive and revolutionary projects adapted to this new context in myriad ways. Since protest had become less effective, for instance, due to the state's being less responsive to social demands and imposing higher levels of repression (a condition I will later refer to as "the end of mediation"), activists had to move beyond protest and invent new forms of organization and ac- tion. At the same time, there was a proliferation and increased visibility of diverse forms of liberation struggle, including those along lines of gender, race, sexuality, and multiple forms of labor. This was due in part, as I said, to the fact that industrial workers could no longer function as vanguard and central protagonist of a unified movement. Activists began to develop modes of articulation among these multiple movements to address these new needs and organize strategically.

These are just some of the ways in which the progressive and revolu- tionary struggles of the seventies should be recognized as first experiments to challenge our contemporary structures of power and to discover, in these conditions, paths toward liberation. In the chapters that follow, then, I highlight some continuities with the present, emphasizing instances in which movements of the seventies invented early forms of practices and strategies that have blossomed and become central in twenty-first-century movements. I will also indicate some instances in which movements of the seventies were actually ahead of those today, deploying practices of contes- tation and liberation that did not continue widely in the subsequent decades and have become subterranean currents, which have the potential to spring forth once again.

In the end, then, whether we consider the movements of the seventies in- spiring or troubling, they are fundamentally *ours*. The history of our present begins there. My interest in returning to the seventies is thus not really his- torical. My aim instead is to use the seventies as a vantage point from which to see more clearly what liberation movements can be and do today.

Addendum

This is the kind of book that will remain forever incomplete and thus invites additions (as well as corrections and critiques). Although my selection cri- terion for subversive movements is clear—I have chosen, as I said earlier, struggles that challenge or overthrow structures of domination while constructing projects of liberation—decisions for selection in the following chapters are not always straightforward. The selections are inevitably con- ditioned by the limits of my knowledges, intellectual abilities, and linguistic capacities. Take this book, then, as an initial endeavor to discover what the subversive seventies have to teach us.

PART I
TO REMAKE THE WORLD FROM THE GROUND UP

2

Revolutionary Democracy

We found that people could not liberate themselves unless they were active participants in the process of liberation.

—Samora Machel

Rebels against Portuguese colonial rule in Mozambique, Angola, and Guinea-Bissau made democracy and popular power central watchwords in the 1960s and 1970s. Far from the standard view that democratization among the colonized and subordinated nations must follow behind the democratic models of the dominant countries, crafting poor copies of their representative institutions, electoral systems, and the like, in the course of the revolutionary movement the insurgents in Portugal's African colonies invented concepts and practices of revolutionary democracy and popular power that far outstrip what conventionally passes for democratic governance.

The specific conditions of the Portuguese colonies were key to these developments. The weakness and rigidity of the Portuguese government with respect to other European colonial powers was a curse for the liberation movements in its African colonies but also presented a unique opportunity. Whereas most British and French colonies in Africa achieved independence in the sixties, anticolonial movements in Mozambique, Angola, and Guinea-Bissau were still struggling for freedom in the seventies. Portugal held on to colonial rule not because it was stronger than the other European powers but, on the contrary, because it was weaker. Since it was incapable of the political reforms and economic restructuring necessary to create a neocolonial arrangement, Portugal's fascist dictatorship carried out protracted wars, relying on military might and repression to maintain the colonial regime (*Lutte* 1973, 14; Davidson 1981, 120).[1] Portugal did not have the "luxury" of practicing neocolonialism, and thus what resulted in all three countries was, according to Boaventura de Sousa Santos, "a decolonization process almost totally free from neocolonialist features" (Santos 1982, 263). This is one reason that, despite their numerous differences, the anticolonial movements in Portuguese Africa—the African Party for the Independence of Guinea and Cape Verde (PAIGC) in Guinea-Bissau, the People's Movement for the Liberation of Angola (MPLA) in Angola, and the Liberation Front of Mozambique (FRELIMO) in Mozambique—shared significant characteristics.

The comparative weakness of Portuguese rule also meant that the colonial regime established few governmental structures that the liberation movements could adopt or appropriate for themselves. "The colonial rulers had left behind them no political or cultural baggage or furniture that could be of any use at all," maintained Basil Davidson, creating a "political void" (2009, 105; see also 1979, 130; 1976a, 25). Liberation movements in the Portuguese colonies therefore could not, like those in other colonies, Davidson claimed, follow a reformist model and appropriate for their own use the institutions of the colonial state.

This is where the curse of Portuguese colonialism presented an opportunity. In the midst of protracted wars and severe hardships, the liberation movements had to confront the political abyss before them. Without the possibility of copying European political institutions or reviving traditional African forms of authority, they sought to invent new social relations and political institutions, filling the void left by the colonizers with revolutionary democracy and popular power.

Revolutionary Democracy

Amilcar Cabral, who was not only the leader of the PAIGC in Guinea-Bissau but also the most widely recognized intellectual of all the movements against Portuguese rule in Africa, articulated a program of radical democracy in very practical terms. Although Cabral often advocated using "the weapon of theory" and argued passionately that theory was a necessary part of revolutionary struggle—"nobody," he declared, "has yet successfully practiced revolution without a revolutionary theory" (1980b, 123)—he was not given to abstract theoretical arguments and had no formal philosophical training. He had earned a degree in Lisbon as an agricultural engineer, and in the revolutionary struggle he maintained an engineer's sense of practicality, addressing concrete, immediate problems. Some of Cabral's most interesting and theoretically rich texts took the form of lessons delivered orally to relatively uneducated party members in liberated zones and subsequently transcribed. Think of these lessons as theory on the ground, for which the reader has to construct, since there are no citations or footnotes, the relation to other currents and developments in political theory.

During one set of lessons delivered in 1964, Cabral put forward a series of "watchwords" (*palavras de ordem*) to party cadres. One of them was revolutionary democracy, which, he insisted, needed to be put into practice throughout the struggle. He was under no illusion, of course, that, given the characteristics of the colonized population, universal self-rule was immediately achievable. The greatest weakness of African liberation struggles, he declared, was their lack of ideology, "which is basically explained by ignorance of the historical reality which these movements aspire to transform" (Cabral 1980b, 122). Almost universal illiteracy—only 1 percent of the population could read—was merely one obstacle preventing the colonized from understanding their history and grasping adequately their political situation. Maria Poblet rightly explains that, for Cabral, this state of poverty was the only realistic point of departure. Cabral understood well, she writes, "that oppression and exploitation rob people of the capacity to self-govern, both structurally and psychologically, and that building that capacity is a core task within the revolutionary struggle, and not after" (Poblet 2013, 241). Revolutionary democracy, then, has to be a process that takes the population's poverty and illiteracy as its point of departure and builds from there a capacity for self-governance.

The first component of revolutionary democracy Cabral elaborated, then, was simply transparency, which also implies a realistic assessment of the state of the struggle: "Do not hide anything from the mass of the people, do not lie, fight against lies, do not disguise the difficulties, errors and failures, do not believe in easy victories, nor in appearances" (Cabral 1980a, 249). Speaking truth to others, in effect, corresponds to speaking truth to oneself and thus not fooling oneself that the situation is better than it is. The second component of Cabral's revolutionary democracy, and the more important one in my view, involves opening to as many as possible the power of decision-making. "Do not be afraid of the people," he counseled, "and persuade the people to take part in all the decisions which concern them—this is the basic condition of revolutionary democracy, which little by little we must achieve in accordance with the development of our struggle and our life" (Cabral 1980a, 250). Revolutionary democracy in this scenario, perhaps paradoxically, still involves hierarchy: a party cadre with superior knowledge and capacities who goes to the people to aid, educate, and inspire them. But really this should be understood as a process that points toward the elimination of such hierarchies, which aims to result, eventually, in equal and universal structures of collective decision-making. That is the goal of the process, however, not the present reality.

Cabral offers another approach to this process in terms of what he calls collective leadership, which should be applied at all levels of the party. "Do everything possible in order that the leadership bodies of the Party may operate genuinely, not on the basis of one, two or three persons, but of all their members, men and women. . . . To lead collectively, in a group, is to study questions jointly, to find their best solution, and to take decisions jointly, it is to benefit from the experience and intelligence of each and all so as to lead, order and command better" (Cabral 1980a, 247). The practice of collective leadership, like that of revolutionary democracy, is a progressively expansive procedure. Not only does it aim to destroy the monopoly of decision-making, but also it serves as a training ground for those who do not yet have the capacity of self-governance. Like revolutionary democracy, collective leadership cannot immediately be instituted in full form, but by putting it into practice, even imperfectly, we open the road toward its realization.

Popular Power Creates Its Own Conditions of Possibility

The need to create "popular power" (*poder popular*) is a common refrain in the discourse of the revolutionary leaders in all three Portuguese colonies. "The question of popular power," proclaimed Samora Machel, leader of FRELIMO and first president of independent Mozambique, "is the essential question in our Revolution" (1985b, 12). The concept of popular power was primarily developed not through theoretical elaborations but in practice by the revolutionary movements themselves. Popular power had already been implemented in Mozambique's liberated zones, Machel claimed, which "serve as laboratories of our experience and centers from which our political line and its practical results are spread" (1985b, 3, translation modified). The practices of popular power are material, institutional correlates to Cabral's notions of revolutionary democracy and collective leadership, and thus the relation among these concepts helps us to understand them all more concretely.[2]

Popular power in the early 1970s was practiced primarily in the zones that revolutionary forces had liberated from Portuguese rule. Among the few published accounts of life in the liberated zones are those of Basil Davidson, a British journalist, a historian, a tireless advocate for the liberation struggles, and someone who had the confidence of revolutionary leaders. Davidson, echoing Cabral, emphasized that the Portuguese colonizers, because of their political weakness and reliance on military force, left an institutional and political void in the colonies, which the revolutionary movements had to fill. And they did this without any return to traditional precolonial African social relations, such as "rule by elders" or "rule by chiefs," but instead by inventing new institutions, conceived in terms of popular power (Davidson 1976c, 71–72; 1981, 165).

Since the liberated zones were primarily in rural areas, the first key to popular power was to increase political participation in village society. "To get the process going," Davidson writes with regard to FRELIMO in Mozambique, needs "structures of political participation at every level of social life and within every significant class or grouping (structures such as the committees and networks of *poder popular*, of people's power)" (2009, 106). As Cabral emphasized, however, the population, especially in the rural areas, was not intellectually and socially prepared for self-governance, lacking the necessary habits and traditions. To address this lack, the PAIGC in Guinea-Bissau invented forms of *educação militante* (militant education) that, as Sonía Vaz Borges (2019) explains, were integrated into the liberation struggle as essential components. At the same time, and this is perhaps another facet of the same process, the practice of popular power had to be itself an educational process, developing the capacities of the population. "Transforming support or sympathy into active and voluntary participation by rural multitudes implied, essentially," Davidson reported, regarding the PAIGC in Guinea-Bissau, "the building of new political and social institutions of self-government" (1981, 163). And, at the same time, the people to populate those institutions had to be created. In effect, popular power had to create its own conditions of possibility.

In practice, local decision-making institutions, such as village "action committees," tasked with addressing the immediate needs of the population, were the basic units of popular power (Davidson 1976b, 103). Once formed, these local committees were expected to be set in motion and to expand along two axes: along one, they needed to include ever larger portions of the population in decision-making regarding ever more issues of common social and political concern, and along the other, they had to scale up to address ever larger questions of regional and national concern.

After being hosted by revolutionaries on a four-week tour of southern liberated areas of Guinea-Bissau at the end of 1972, Davidson elaborated the expansive process along the first axis, as more people were empowered to decide over more issues. "This was achieved in three stages: first, the promotion of representative committees of local self-government; secondly, the development of an elective assembly-delegate structure as practice improved; and thirdly, again with further practice, the devolution to these committees of increasing powers and duties" (Davidson 1981, 163). Only with time—"as practice improved," Davidson said—do the committees include more people and receive more responsibilities.

Regarding the scalar expansion of democratic institutions from the local to the national, Samora Machel maintained, regarding Mozambique, that in the liberated zones the people must exercise democratic participation simultaneously "at different levels" (Machel 1975, 94). First, there are local councils (*conselhos*), which delegate representatives to district councils, which delegate to provincial councils, and finally the national level. "This structure is democratic," Machel continued, "because at all levels the members are democratically appointed, which allows the exercise of popular power through representatives chosen by the masses" (Machel 1975, 96). Davidson reports a similar pyramidal structure in the liberated zones of Guinea-Bissau.[3] One fact that Davidson's reports, however enthusiastic, make clear is that during the revolutionary struggle, although popular power was the order of the day in the liberated zones and increasingly in cities still under colonial rule, it was by no means a finished product or realized achievement, but an aspiration and a process.

In Chapter 6 we will see that in several instances during the Portuguese Revolution—for example, in the formation of the Comité de Luta in Setúbal in 1975—there was a similar process of local democratic commissions progressively enlarging their scope and scaling up. Some observers report, in fact, that Portuguese soldiers deployed in the African colonies learned the lessons of popular power from the liberation forces and then brought them back to Portugal. Such accounts are difficult to verify, but the revolutionary projects do share important aspects; moreover, there is something poetic and satisfying about the idea of the colonizers learning revolutionary democracy from the colonized.[4]

Revolutionary Movements and Authoritarian States

Many contemporary readers may find it difficult to give serious consideration to the liberation movements' claims of revolutionary democracy and popular power given that in the almost half century since independence the postcolonial states of Guinea-Bissau, Mozambique, and Angola have shown little signs of democratic institutions, revolutionary or otherwise. How can we square the democratic promise of the revolutionary movement with the misery of the postrevolutionary state? I am not able to diagnose adequately the pathologies of Africa's postcolonial states here, but in my view that is not necessary in order to appreciate and evaluate the revolutionary movements.[5] In the Introduction I cited Robin D. G. Kelley's claim that movements should be judged on the power of their visions rather than on some standard of success or failure. I would reformulate that to say that we need to analyze and appreciate revolutionary movements, even ones that "succeed," relatively independently from the resulting outcomes. (I will make this argument again in Chapter 4, for instance, regarding the revolutionary movements in Iran and Nicaragua.) If revolutionary movements are held responsible for all that comes after and if the movements are seen through the lens of those results, including all the ways their processes were defeated, distorted, and betrayed, we will miss the extraordinary wealth they have to offer.

That said, it is not difficult to identify some of the main factors that plagued both the revolutionary process and the postrevolutionary states. The revolutionary leaders were well aware of the internal weaknesses and impediments of the movements, and sought to overcome them. One set of obstacles that I already mentioned—namely, the poor educational and social level of the population as well as the lack of habits and traditions of democratic practice prior to the anticolonial struggle—were thought to be addressed in part in the process of struggle through political education.

A second set of obstacles was posed by those within the anticolonial movements who sought to restore traditional African political and social forms. At the 1968 congress of FRELIMO, for instance, there was a conflict between two factions: a traditional African nationalist faction versus one with "a national liberation philosophy that argued for an inner struggle for women's equality, participatory democracy and an end to economic exploitation—in sum *poder popular* (people's power). The latter, the revolutionary current, led by Samora Machel, finally emerged triumphant in 1970" (Munslow and O'Keefe 1984, 17; see also Newitt 2017, 142). Traditionalist currents were not completely vanquished, however, and reappeared during the revolutionary struggles and the postcolonial states in various guises, sometimes supported by foreign powers.

A third set of internal obstacles was posed by the leaders themselves, most of whom, Cabral maintained, came necessarily from the petty bourgeoisie, the only class of Africans with adequate education.[6] The danger he foresaw for postcolonial states was that these leaders, after eliminating foreign rule, would strive to establish themselves as a new ruling class that profits from the bureaucratic and commercial arrangements of the neocolonial state. The petty bourgeoisie are thus, according to Cabral, faced with two options: either "to betray the revolution or to commit suicide as a class" (1980b, 136). Whether or not Cabral's notion of class suicide of the native petty bourgeoisie has any practical value, it does rightly identify a stubborn political problem. The extreme aggregation of powers in the hands of the state has certainly been a plague in each of these countries since the conquest of independence.[7]

These internal obstacles, however, although themselves dangerous and difficult to resolve, were dwarfed by the external obstacles, which proved after independence to be overwhelming and insurmountable: military interventions from all sides, cold war proxy conflicts, economic blackmail and sabotage, assassinations, and much more. It is certainly important to investigate what alternative avenues would have allowed the postcolonial states better to defend their independence and realize the democratic objectives promoted during the revolutionary struggle, especially to the extent that can be relevant for contemporary political initiatives. But, as I said, we must not allow this to prevent us from the potential they have to offer.

Uneven and Combined Political Development

With that in mind, one should marvel at the fact that these movements, especially given the hardships and poverty of their situation, were able to invent and implement such original concepts and practices of democracy. A contributing factor is the fact, which I mentioned at the outset, that the peculiarities of Portuguese colonialism created, in addition to great suffering, a political opportunity: namely, a political void that allowed for a new political imaginary.

This opportunity presents, in effect, a *political* translation of the theory of uneven and combined development, elaborated by Leon Trotsky and others.

The economic theory was meant to counter, first of all, standard notions that "undeveloped" economies necessarily advance through the same stages through which the developed economies previously passed. Instead, their development combines traditional technologies and methods with the most advanced ones. Moreover, the "privilege of historical backwardness," as Trotsky calls it, is the potential to make a leap forward when faced with something like an economic and social void, "free" of the encrusted, conservative economic traditions and social structures that are resistant to change.[8]

The political void created by the Portuguese colonial regime—the lack of usable political baggage or furniture left behind by the colonizers, as Davidson puts it, as well as the refusal on the part of the revolutionaries to resurrect traditional African systems of authority—is in some respects a political analogue to Trotsky's "privilege" of economic backwardness. Being unencumbered by the ballast of established political institutions resistant to change allows for a leap forward, beyond what could be achieved in the more "developed" political democracies.

The concepts of popular power, revolutionary democracy, and collective leadership elaborated in these liberation struggles provide a guide for revolutionary change well beyond the colonial context. They form the outlines of something like the "real democracy" that protesters who filled the squares of Spanish cities in 2011 demanded instead of the sclerotic political structures we are taught to revere as democratic. Moreover, these concepts posed not only the goals to be realized but also the educational processes needed to prepare the way, which are equally important today. Colonial populations, after all, are not alone in being unprepared for institutions of robust self-rule. In all contemporary societies, just as much as a half century ago, a project for revolutionary democracy has to create its own preconditions by transforming the political capacities of the population through some kind of militant education. Only then would we be prepared for a leap toward a revolutionary democracy.

3

Gay Liberation

How can a relational system be reached through sexual practices? Is it possible to create a homosexual mode of life?

—Michel Foucault

With respect to gay liberation, the 1970s can be dated precisely: the decade began in June 1969 (at the rebellion at New York's Stonewall Inn) and ended in June 1981 (with the first reported case of what would later be known as AIDS). Between these two events was an extraordinarily active and varied set of social and political movements under the banner of gay liberation, especially in North America and Europe. In some respects, however, the decades prior and subsequent to the seventies pose obstacles to understanding and appreciating their significance. At the latter end, the AIDS pandemic, along with the grief, mourning, outrage, and activism in response to it and the government's inaction, looms so large that it seems difficult to see beyond it. After the advent of AIDS, the demands, freedoms, excitement, and achievements of the seventies seem to belong to a distant and lost past. On the other end, a focus on notions of sexual revolution and sexual liberation that were typical of the 1960s encourages a skewed and mystified view of gay liberation in the seventies, which was, I argue, not so much a sexual revolution as a political one. We have to clear away obstacles posed by both the sixties and the eighties, then, in order to grasp the potential of gay liberation in the seventies.

Sexual Revolution

Gay liberation in the seventies was not about sex. Although that statement, as we will see, is only partly true, it is nonetheless a good starting point. The standard view, of course, is that gay life and gay liberation in those years were *all* about sex. No doubt, in cities like New York, after the Stonewall

Rebellion had lessened somewhat the danger of police violence against gay men, a lot of men were having a lot of sex with a lot of different partners in relatively public spaces. The 2005 Joseph Lovett documentary film *Gay Sex in the 70s* is one of many celebrations of how gay men in New York took advantage of their newly found sexual freedom through relatively anonymous (and yet intimate) encounters. On the abandoned Chelsea docks and behind parked freight containers, in the dark rooms beneath bars and in the parks, in porn theaters and in bathhouses, and in many other places, men met with strangers or relative strangers for sex. One of the men interviewed in the film fondly recalls that during those years, anytime he wanted he could leave his apartment, go down to the street, and have sex within twenty minutes.

It is thus understandable to assume that in the seventies gay men in some cities had finally realized the calls for sexual revolution and free love that had caused so much excitement and anxiety among heterosexuals in the 1960s, from the intellectual invocations of the work of Sigmund Freud and Wilhelm Reich to the clichéd media images of hippies and Woodstock. The sex practices of gay men in this period, after all, were not only less vulnerable than previously to homophobic violence (at the hands of the police and others) and not only freer than others from the social powers and traditional institutions that govern and restrict sexual behavior (regarding monogamy, fidelity, and the like) but also relatively free from internal, psychic complexes and inhibitions regarding sex. The image, then, which is at least partially true, is that gay men in these specific urban contexts could have sex whenever they wanted, with whomever they wanted, with relatively little guilt and relatively few regrets. From this vantage point, gay liberation was the liberation of gay men's sexual urges—libido unbound. Thus the gay liberation movements of the seventies appeared to be, as Jeffrey Weeks puts it, "the last major product of late 1960s euphoria" (1990, 206), a kind of belated appendage of the previous decade.

Part of a Revolutionary Movement

I am not suggesting that one should separate gay liberation movements from sex, but understanding the movements and their aims solely in terms of sexual practices and sexual freedoms is clearly inadequate. "Sex was only part of what had mattered to gay men," writes Jim Downs, "as they began to make gay liberation meaningful in their lives" (2016, 4).To better understand the movements, then, and to grasp how they were revolutionary, one has to supplement sexual revolution with their other parts.

One means of recognizing the expansive political agenda of gay liberation movements is to highlight their relations to other movements of the era. The Gay Liberation Front (GLF), explains Jeffrey Weeks, "which crystallized in America in 1969, immediately identified itself as part of 'The Movement,' claiming solidarity with other oppressed groups" (1990, 186). The fact that many activists came to gay liberation with extensive experience working in other New Left movements certainly facilitated these connections and solidarities both practically and ideologically. "We want a new society," proclaims the Third World Gay Revolution's 1970 manifesto, "a revolutionary socialist society." Gay liberation movements thus participated as one element in the wide constellation of the radical left, oriented toward a comprehensive revolutionary project in which homosexuals and their liberation played one part. The London GLF argued in its 1971 manifesto that gay liberation must go hand in hand with the abolition of patriarchal and racist structures as well as class society. The manifesto goes on to argue that the abolition of the institution of the family and its replacement with cooperative communes is one example of a project that weaves together gay liberation with feminist and proletarian struggle, and indeed several gay communes were established in London, often by people squatting in unoccupied buildings (Walter 1980, 21–22; Weeks 1990, 202). The New York GLF, similarly, coupled its actions in defense of gay and lesbian rights with active participation in antiwar protests, Black Panther rallies and conferences, and radical feminist actions. The Groupe de Libération Homosexuelle (GLH) in France similarly maintained constant political interactions (and conflicts) with Marxist groups and the workers' movement more generally. French gay liberation militants participated in a wide variety of demonstrations of the radical Left and advocated a necessary complementarity among struggles: "No socialist revolution without a sexual revolution, no sexual revolution without a socialist revolution," for example, was a common slogan (Girard 1981, 129). The San Francisco gay liberation and lesbian feminist organizations of the seventies may have been the most dedicated to and successful in forming connections and alliances across the Left. Emily Hobson analyzes in detail how new formations of gay politics in San Francisco were inspired and influenced by Black liberation movements, Third World radicalism, and antiwar politics. As a result, the San Francisco GLF, to give just one example, "linked a remaking of gender expression with anti-capitalist and anti-racist goals" (Hobson 2016, 28). In all these cases, then, sex was only part of what interested gay liberation activists in the sense that they were also intent on solidarities with other movements and contributing to a larger revolutionary struggle.

One should note, however, that although gay liberation organizations tried to create and reinforce relations of solidarity, the response of other groups on the Left was decidedly mixed. Several organizations of the British New Left, especially the Marxist parties and groups, were not open to forming alliances and cooperating politically (Walter 1980, 28). Although some Marxist groups in France were somewhat supportive of gay liberation, there remained widespread discourses about homosexuality being a bourgeois concept: since the source of oppression is class hierarchy, according to a persistent argument, "seeking to better the condition of homosexuals was simply bandaging the wounds of a sick society that needed, instead, to be destroyed" (Girard 1981, 128–129). One should recognize, however, Emily Hobson insists, that the hostility toward gay liberation and lesbian feminism expressed by New Left and other radical organizations "was complex and contested, not monolithic and unchanging" (2016, 8). One of the most notable and consequential overtures was Huey Newton's call in a series of statements in August 1971 for the Black Panther Party and others on the radical Left to recognize the revolutionary nature of gay liberation and women's liberation movements and to form alliances with them (Bloom and Martin 2012, 306–307). The failures of some sectors of the Left to reciprocate and to recognize gay liberation as part of a revolutionary process, however, do not negate the fact that gay liberation organizations were dedicated to being part of a larger movement in which many different liberation movements participated.

The Revolutionary Potential of a Homosexual Mode of Life

A different way of understanding that sex was only part of what mattered to the gay liberation movements requires that we view sex as intrinsic and essential to a revolutionary project and yet not its ultimate aim, something like a means rather than an end.[1] To discover how homosexuality can threaten the dominant social order, Michel Foucault claimed in a 1981 interview with the French magazine *Le gai pied*, one has to get beyond the 1960s ideology of the sexual liberation for which more and freer sex is the goal (Foucault 1997, 138). There is nothing subversive or troubling for dominant society about same-sex desire or homosexual acts, he maintains. In fact, Foucault continues, the standard image of homosexuality as immediate pleasure, since it focuses merely on sexual desire and sex acts and reinforces standard canons of beauty, loses any possibility of being disturbing (*perd toute virtualité d'inquiétude*) (136).

Moreover, not only does the focus on gay sex lack any subversive power on its own, but it actually undermines or masks what is truly subversive: it "cancels everything that can be troubling [*inquiétant*] in affection, tenderness, friendship, fidelity, camaraderie, and companionship, things that our rather sanitized society can't allow a place for without fearing the formation of new alliances and the tying together of unforeseen lines of force. I think that's what makes homosexuality 'disturbing': the homosexual mode of life, much more than the sexual act itself. To imagine a sexual act that doesn't conform to law or nature is not what disturbs people. But that individuals are beginning to love one another—there's the problem" (Foucault 1997, 136–137). Foucault's argument in this passage is challenging. First of all, it should be clear that he is not proposing that there are two discrete options: either sex or a mode of life defined by affection, friendship, love, and so forth. No, the latter can only be realized via the former: the subversive and revolutionary homosexual mode of life, he claims, is "a relational system" that must "be reached through sexual practices" (137). Gay sex is only part of what gay liberation can be, then, in the sense that it is a vehicle for creating a new mode of life.

More challenging still is to understand why the homosexual mode of life should be any more troubling than the dominant, heterosexual mode—or, indeed, why it should have any more potential for change. After all, have not all of the affects and bonds of Foucault's list—affection, tenderness, friendship, fidelity, camaraderie, and companionship—long been part also of the heterosexual mode of life? When people begin to love one another, he claims, a subversive power arises—but what is new about people loving one another?

The unstated assumption that grounds Foucault's argument, it seems to me, is that the homosexual mode of life is relatively unburdened of the deadening inertia, routinized habits, and norms of dominant society. A rather distant analogy can clarify this point: the revolutionary potential for gay liberation is something like the promise to create a revolutionary democracy of the anticolonial forces in Guinea-Bissau, Angola, and Mozambique that I analyzed in Chapter 2. The Portuguese colonizers had left them no political or cultural baggage or furniture, so to speak, with which to fashion a copy of European liberal democratic society. Amilcar Cabral, however, from within the revolutionary struggle in Guinea-Bissau, recognized this absence as an advantage: in that political void they had the opportunity to transform the meaning of democracy, build it from the ground up, and give it a profoundly revolutionary direction.

Gay life post-Stonewall faced a similar political and cultural void. "To be 'gay,' I think," Foucault explains, "is not to identify with the psychological traits and the visible masks of the homosexual," conforming to the identity and norms of either the dominant society or the inherited subculture (1997, 138). Like the anticolonial revolutionaries in Africa, they were forced to face a void, with no access to the dominant institutions that structure hetero-sexual society, such as marriage and family. This void, however, is a form of poverty that is really—or "virtually," as Foucault says—a great wealth. Void here, in other words, implies potential autonomy and opportunity for inven-tion. Just as the revolutionary democracy that Cabral proposed could not copy existing European institutional forms, so too the bonds and affects of the homosexual mode of life do not reproduce those of the dominant so-ciety. They create a new array of attachments and affects. And, ultimately, in the void they have the potential to create new social relations. The homo-sexual mode of life thus not only troubles or disturbs dominant society. To be "gay," Foucault maintains, means "to try to define and develop a mode of life," which must be, obviously, a new, different, autonomous mode of life (1997, 138, translation modified).

In important respects, however, the notion of facing the void is not an ad-equate figure for the position of gay liberation. In Foucault's estimation, the homosexual mode of life is powerful not because it is outside but because it is already inside the dominant social formation. "Homosexuality," by which I understand him to mean the homosexual mode of life of the 1970s, post-Stonewall, "is a historic occasion to reopen affective and relational virtualities, not so much through the intrinsic qualities of the homosexual, but because the 'slantwise' position [en biais] of the latter, as it were, the diag-onal lines he can lay out in the social fabric allow these virtualities to come to light" (Foucault 1997, 138). One revolutionary stream of the Italian workers' movement, which I will analyze later, located the proletariat as "within and against" the capitalist order. Foucault positions "the homosexual" similarly inside, but "the diagonal lines" are autonomous, pointing elsewhere, rather than being directly against.

But how could such a new mode of life and its "affective and relational virtualities," however new and different they are, be revolutionary? Foucault's catalogue of attachments and bonds that characterize the homosexual mode of life, to which I have already returned several times, resembles a list in Marx's "Economic and Philosophical Manuscripts" of the senses (meaning the human organs of interaction with the world) that will be transformed in communist society: "seeing, hearing, smelling, tasting, feeling, thinking, contemplating, sensing, wanting, acting, loving" (1975, 351). The path toward communist society requires that we transform all of our relations to each other and the world, which in capitalist society are construed in terms of possession and consumption. There is a strong resonance between the new "relational system" that characterizes for Foucault the homosexual mode of life and the new sensorium, the redefinition of the entire catalogue of affects and bonds, that for Marx grounds a communist society. Thinking through Marx's conception of a transformation of the senses as an essential step toward communist revolution, admittedly itself a difficult argument to grasp, provides one means to understand how Foucault can see the new affects and attachments of the homosexual mode of life having a similarly revolutionary potential.

Gay Sex and Liberation

I left hanging earlier the question of the role of gay sex in this revolutionary context, specifically how, as Foucault says, the homosexual mode of life and its relational system must "be reached through sexual practices" (1997, 137). The key is to understand what "through" means here, which suggests that gay sex is not the end goal but an essential means toward new social relations.

Another list in Marx's "Economic and Philosophical Manuscripts" provides some help in understanding the role of gay sex here. Among socialist workers in his time, he claims, was developing a "need for society" that supplants or recasts the dominant set of human needs and reorients activities that previously aimed at either personal pleasure or individual gain in the existing social structure. "Smoking, eating and drinking, etc.," Marx writes, "are no longer means of creating links between people," by which we must understand means of reproducing the dominant social relations and seeking advantage within its hierarchical structure. His emphasis that these activities are no longer means does not, however, imply that they become ends in themselves—smoking for the pleasure of smoking, and so on. "Company, association, conversation," he continues, "which in its turn has society as its goal, is enough for them" (1975, 365). Marx's vision in this passage, as elsewhere in these manuscripts, is obviously not fully fleshed out, but it is clear that contact, conversation, and interchange with others, because the socialist workers are relatively free from capitalist social norms, can be reoriented so that they do not simply reproduce the existing social structure with its norms and hierarchies but instead create a new one. He is grappling, then, with the challenge to understand how a future communist society (or what Foucault calls a new relational system) can be achieved through social encounters and practices that are oriented differently. Common practices (smoking, eating, drinking) and basic affects (feeling, wanting, loving) can be diverted from their position in the dominant order and reoriented so as to sustain alternative social relations.

Samuel Delany helps close the loop between Marx and Foucault and brings us back to our point of departure, that is, gay sex in the post-Stonewall era. Delany recounts his experiences, primarily in the seventies, in the sex movie houses in New York's Times Square, theaters that showed straight porn and permitted (or encouraged) gay sex in the audience. In the place of Marx's socialist workers who smoke, eat, and drink together, Delany and other gay men have sex in relatively public places. In the seats of the movie theaters around Times Square, Delany explains, gay men would masturbate on their own, or offer oral sex to strangers or acquaintances, or have intercourse. Money was sometimes exchanged but usually not. Even the men in the theater who were not gay sometimes participated in the intimate and collective encounters. Delany narrates, for example, that a good-looking straight man repeatedly came to one of the theaters to masturbate while watching the film. He would refuse offers of blow jobs and ask the other men not to sit directly next to him, but nonetheless he was not bothered (and seemed relatively content) that while he was masturbating watching straight sex on the screen, several other men would masturbate watching him (Delany 1990, 20–22).

"Contact" is the key term that Delany employs to understand these encounters: contact "blooms in and as 'casual sex'" (1990, 123). But this contact has a potential not present in encounters in the dominant society. Delany emphasizes, in particular, the multiplicity of encounters and relations formed: cross-class and interracial contacts are possible through public sex in the theaters. He encounters and befriends homeless men and wealthy men of various races through the course of his visits to the theaters. "These *were* relationships," he insists, lasting and intimate relationships, but clearly relationships qualitatively different from those dictated by heterosexual society (1990, 40). In the theaters, through the shared practices of casual sex, Delany discovered a space relatively independent of capitalist and racial hierarchies and norms, where new contacts and encounters were possible. In a Whitmanesque mode, Delany declares that a democratic metropolis needs such spaces for casual sex—or, really, it needs modes of encounter that are autonomous, independent of the ruling social hierarchies (1990, 127). And this revolutionary possibility is reached, as Foucault says, through sexual practices.

Virtuality

Foucault uses "virtuality" several times in his essay to emphasize the power and significance of the homosexual mode of life, and one can assume that he has in mind the technical use of the term developed by several French philosophers during this period. The virtual, Gilles Deleuze often repeats, especially in his analyses of Henri Bergson and Marcel Proust, is real without being actual. Whereas the virtual is often oriented toward the past (Proust's madeleine and his relation to memory is a prime example), Foucault's use here is directed toward the future (like the specter of communism in the *Communist Manifesto*). Just as the past is not really dead, the future is already alive. It just has not yet been actualized.

Foucault in this way poses the homosexual mode of life in the passage quoted earlier as being able "to reopen affective and relational virtualities" and allowing "these virtualities to come to light" (1997, 138). The future these virtualities refer to is not specified, but it is already entirely real in the new affective modes, social relations, and attachments being created in homosexual life. José Muñoz, inspired by the cultural production and political projects around the time of the Stonewall Rebellion, conceives this link between queerness and virtuality in an even more general frame: "Queerness is essentially about the rejection of a here and now and an insistence on potentiality or concrete possibility for another world" (2009, 1). For Muñoz, as for Foucault, queer practices can reveal the virtualities of fundamentally different social relations that are already real in the present.

The homosexual mode of life is thus subversive in the double sense that I proposed in the Introduction: it both undermines the dominant order and proposes a project of liberation that founds a new society. The revolutionary character of the homosexual mode of life is fully within the current society, virtual although not realized—less like seeds that will one day sprout than specters that already walk among us.

4

Liberation Theologies

Vos sos el Dios de los pobres, el Dios humano y sencillo, el Dios que suda en la calle, el Dios de rostro curtido, por eso es que te hablo yo así como habla mi pueblo.

You are the God of the poor, the human and simple God, the God who sweats in the street, the God with a weathered face, that's why I speak to you the way my people speak.
                    —Carlos Mejía Godoy, Nicaraguan peasant Mass

The revolutions in Nicaragua and Iran are seldom grouped together, despite several similarities: the regimes of Shah Pahlavi and Anastasio Somoza were both brutal dictatorships supported by the United States and were overthrown by anti-imperialist insurrections just six months apart—the shah escaped Iran in January 1979 and Somoza fled Nicaragua in June. It is true, of course, that the political situations of the two countries were vastly different: Nicaragua's geographical proximity to the United States made it subject to different political and military pressures; Iran's oil wealth gave it a more prominent position in the geopolitical hierarchy; and so forth. Moreover, the two governments that resulted from the revolutions, the Islamic Republic led by Ayatollah Khomeini and the socialist Sandinista government, bore little resemblance to each other.

One characteristic that the Iranian and Nicaraguan uprisings shared, however, is the way they wove together theology and Marxism, sometimes through coalitions between separate religious and communist groups but often within single organizations. I want to highlight specifically how these liberation theologies provided the bases for new forms of community and the orientation for rebellion and liberation. The radical political projects to emerge generated new political imaginaries and found the means both to remake the world and to transform themselves.

Crises of the Shah's Regime

In the late 1970s, when the shah was suffering from cancer, his regime was confronted with economic crisis and significant international pressure regarding abuses committed by the police, the army, and the security forces. As tensions and protests rose, increasingly brutal attacks on demonstrators certainly played a role in accelerating opposition to the regime. One of the most pivotal massacres, which took place in September 1978, came to be known as "Black Friday." On the Eid al-Fitr holiday, which marks the end of Ramadan, large crowds in every city celebrated with public prayers, as is traditional, but this year the celebration was mixed with protests against the shah. The holiday passed without incident, but when protests continued in the following days, drawing enormous crowds, the government banned street demonstrations and declared martial law in Tehran and other cities. On Friday, September 8, the army attacked the demonstrators with tanks and helicopters, firing live rounds, notably at Jalal Square in Tehran. Official sources reported 87 dead and 205 wounded, but the opposition declared that many thousands had been killed (Abrahamian 1982, 515–516). In the following months, as unrest grew, labor strikes put increasing pressure on the government: in October government and oil workers went on strike, and in November a nationwide general strike was called.

Instead of focusing on these immediate causes, however, I want to approach the insurrection by exploring the social forces at two deeper layers. Crucial to the overthrow of the regime, first, were the activities of guerrilla organizations that had been active since the early 1970s. Investigating this layer will highlight the Marxist nature of the revolutionary process. These groups inflicted symbolic and material damage on the shah's regime, but they did not have deep roots in the population and were relatively separate, vanguard organizations. The guerrilla organizations would not have succeeded—and this is the second layer—without the mass movement, and investigating this will highlight the Islamic role in the revolutionary process. But although this division of ideological orientations at the two levels, separating the secular and the religious, provides a helpful mode of presentation, it gives a false impression. I want to emphasize, as I said, the extent to which the Marxist and Islamic components were intertwined, in various ways and to different degrees, throughout the revolutionary movements.

The Trajectory of Iranian Marxist Revolutionaries

Focusing on the revolutionary movement, distinct from the results of the revolution, allows us to recognize the central role played by Marxist revolutionary organizations. Marxists were prominent among the militant and clandestine organizations that opposed the regime throughout the 1970s; they were a key component of the insurrection that toppled the shah; and in the first years after the revolution they remained a major political force with considerable prestige (Moghadam 1987, 17). This perspective thus seems to reveal a narrative, which I will complicate below, in which Islamic clerics hijacked the revolution, completely casting aside the Marxists who had been central to winning the fight.

To understand the actions and influence of Marxist organizations in Iran in the 1970s requires at least basic knowledge of political developments earlier in the twentieth century because, like in other countries in the region, there is, on the one hand, a long and complex tradition of communist and socialist political organizations and, on the other, constant interventions by imperialist powers—and the histories of the two, of course, are deeply intertwined. The decade following World War II has special significance in this regard, with resonances still strongly felt throughout the 1970s revolutionary period. The stage is set by the August 1941 British-Soviet invasion of Iran, which forced Reza Shah of the Pahlavi dynasty, who had supported the Axis powers in the war, to abdicate in favor of his son, Mohammad Reza Shah. A period of political opening ensued in which various political forces and power centers could newly participate; in particular, this allowed communist movements, which had been crushed in the 1920s, to form again. The Tudeh Party, which was the most significant Marxist organization in Iran in the 1940s, was formed in part by communists released from prison subsequent to the overthrow of Reza Shah. The party could now participate in the constitutional system, enjoying substantial popular support and electoral success.[1]

As fruit of this relatively open political period in Iran, Mohammed Mossadeh, a reformist and nationalist politician (by no means a communist) with a long record of government service, was nominated as prime minister in April 1951, and almost immediately nationalized British oil interests in Iran, an action popular with the general public and, by and large, supported by the Tudeh Party (although this greatly simplifies complex political developments). The British government, however, was predictably enraged by being deprived of its access to Iranian oil. After more than two years of overt and covert political machinations, the United Kingdom convinced the United States to engineer a CIA-led coup d'état in August 1953, deposing Mossadeh, consolidating authority in the hands of the shah, and restoring British oil rights. Unsurprisingly, after the coup the shah's government granted a majority of oil rights to US companies.[2] Political opponents of the shah were systematically arrested, tortured, and executed, and, along with other progressive and communist organizations, the Tudeh Party was virtually destroyed. During the subsequent two decades, Iran experienced a political situation not unfamiliar to anyone with basic knowledge of US foreign interventions in the twentieth century, from Latin America to Southeast Asia: an authoritarian regime set in place by a coup d'état, open access for the United States and other imperialist powers to natural resources, and brutal repression of all expression of political opposition.

The Tudeh Party, then, due to the repression it had suffered, did not play a significant role in the revolutionary movement in the 1970s. By that point, in fact, the Tudeh Party had a stronger organization outside of Iran, largely in Europe, than within the country (Behrooz 1999, 76–77). The communist organizations that did play central roles in the revolutionary process, instead, were clandestine armed groups. The Organization of Iranian People's Fadai Guerrillas (Fadai) was the most active of these in the 1970s. "The Fadaiyan," writes Maziar Behrooz, "engaged the Shah's forces in intense, mostly urban, guerrilla activity which included assassination of those engaged in repression, bank robbery and the bombing of centres of the regime's power" (1999, 62). They bombed offices of US oil companies, for example, in the early seventies; kidnapped a factory owner who had called in security forces against striking workers in 1974; and, also in 1974, assassinated a notorious torturer who worked for SAVAK, the intelligence and security forces (Behrooz 1999, 62–63). Although the Fadai, which was composed largely of university students, was not a mass organization and did not have strong connections to the general population, militants believed that their "little motor" of armed attacks would set in motion the "big motor" of general insurrection (Vahabzadeh 2019, 223). Despite the fact that the Fadai suffered intense repression and more than once its leadership group was arrested or assassinated, and also that it endured numerous internal conflicts, expulsions, and splits, the group managed to survive and continue its military operations throughout the revolutionary period.

With the victory of the revolution in 1979, the Fadai and the other communist groups seemed to be in an excellent political position. They had succeeded in their primary objectives: the overthrow of the shah's regime, including dismantling the hated police, SAVAK, and the army; and the definitive expulsion from the country of imperialist forces, most importantly the United States. Furthermore, according to Behrooz, "the movement as a whole, and the guerrilla groups in particular, found prestige and popular support after the revolution. This development made the communist movement a force to be reckoned with during the two years after the 1979 revolution" (1999, xiv). Finally, industrial workers exerted considerable power in the postrevolutionary period, organized in *shuras*, or factory councils, which conducted waves of strikes (Bayat 1987; Jafari 2019). And yet, despite these propitious conditions, by the mid-1980s the Fadai along with all the other communist and socialist organizations had been entirely eliminated.

Obviously, this reversal had nothing to do with the typical cold war script in which the CIA and other US covert and overt agencies conspire to eliminate communist leaders and movements. In postrevolutionary Iran the annihilation of Marxist movements was accomplished by several overlapping factors. Ruthless state repression certainly played a role, but more important may have been that Islamic political actors, including Khomeini himself, outmaneuvered the Marxists politically, in particular with the proposition of the March and December 1979 referenda to approve the creation of, respectively, an Islamic republic and a new constitution. Many historians trace the primary cause to weaknesses of the communist organizations themselves. Some highlight the fact that the communist revolutionaries never succeeded in gaining popular support and becoming a mass movement (Vahabzadeh 2019). Others emphasize the divisions on the Left, not only among the various groups but also within each. The Fadai, for instance, which was perhaps the most powerful opponent to the Islamic Republic in 1979 and 1980, was divided into a radical "minority," which maintained a revolutionary agenda, and a conservative "majority," which was conciliatory toward the Islamic regime. The division allowed the reactionary Islamic forces to recuperate elements within the Fadai compatible to their project and to destroy the others (Behrooz 1999, 105).

One ideological position, in particular, played a significant, revealing role in this drama. Anti-imperialism was a defining position for all Iranian Marxist groups, but precisely on this issue the Islamic regime completely outflanked them. Khomeini, the clerics, their student supporters, and militants in the Islamic movements were extraordinarily vocal and well organized in opposition to US domination. "Episodes such as the capture of the US Embassy in Tehran in 1979," claims Behrooz, "confronting US interest in the region, and numerous other examples of anti-imperialist sentiments proved the IRI [Islamic Republic of Iran] to be, in its own way, as anti-imperialist as the Marxists, if not more so" (1999, 138). The Islamic regime's anti-imperialism, even though deployed as part of a reactionary politics, completely took away a primary ideological pillar that had distinguished the Marxists, leaving them little means to appeal to the population and to contest the Islamic regime effectively.

Peeling away the first layer of assumptions, then, has revealed the central role of Marxists in the revolutionary movement and how after the victory those communists and socialists were outplayed politically and subsequently massacred by Islamic clerics. They appear, from this perspective, in the role in which Marx had cast the proletariat in France's 1848 revolution: the first to the barricades to win the fight against the monarchy and then (in the "June days") the first to be sacrificed by the new ruling powers.

Islamic Liberation Theology: The Mujahedin and Ali Shari'ati

Although that narrative is helpful for highlighting the role of Marxist organizations in the revolutionary movement, which tends to remain unknown to casual observers of Iran, it obscures, in turn, the role of popular and revolutionary Islamic organizations, assuming a clear separation between secular and religious political forces. This is a second layer of assumptions that needs to be peeled away, because political Islam functioned in the revolutionary movement as a liberation theology, deeply interwoven with Marxist and anti-imperialist principles.[3]

This blurring of boundaries between secular and religious and the mixture of Marxist and Islamic elements are evident in the People's Mujahedin Organization of Iran (Mujahedin), a clandestine armed organization that, like the Fadai, conducted its first guerrilla actions in 1971 and continued with attacks throughout the decade despite fierce repression, including the assassination and imprisonment of its leadership and large numbers of members. The Mujahedin's repertoire of targets was also consistent with the Fadai: its militants assassinated a general in SAVAK, for instance, and killed two US military advisors (Behrooz 1999, 73). Although the Mujahedin was dedicated to Islamic principles, "its revolutionary interpretation of Islam produced an ideology not very different from that of the Marxist Feda'i," based primarily in anti-imperialism and anticapitalism (Abrahamian 1982, 492). Indeed, the leading theorists of the organization in the early 1970s saw Marxism and Islam as compatible political orientations. In 1975, a rift in the Mujahedin with respect to the relative importance of Marxism and Islam resulted in two organizations, each of which put the accent on a different side, creating a Marxist Mujahedin and an Islamic Mujahedin (Abrahamian 1982, 494). The split, however, is less important for my argument than the general agreement regarding the intersection of Marxist and Islamic ideas among the Mujahedin in the earlier periods, which is indicative of a broad band of the popular movements against the shah's regime.

This theoretical interweaving of Marxism and Islam is best articulated in the writings of Ali Shari'ati, who, although he died before the revolution, was in many respects the most innovative Iranian thinker of the period and the most significant intellectual reference for the revolutionary movement. Shari'ati went to study in Paris in 1959 and stayed for five years, earning a doctorate in sociology under the direction of Georges Gurvitch, a strong opponent of the French colonial regime in Algeria. Shari'ati, too, participated in French anticolonial circles, and he translated into Persian some of Frantz Fanon's writings.[4] In 1964 Shari'ati returned to Iran and, after a brief period in prison for "advocating 'Islamic Marxism,'" he took up teaching positions (Kanaaneh 2021, 47). His lectures in Tehran in the early 1970s "became the meeting ground of a new generation of young, otherwise Marxist, Muslim intelligentsia" (Ghamari-Tabrizi 2004, 512). Although Shari'ati had no political affiliation, his lectures were extraordinarily popular among both the communist and Islamic armed struggle organizations such as the Fadai and the Mujahedin.[5] His most widespread influence, however, came after his death in June 1977. Although Shari'ati died of heart failure, those in the Iranian revolutionary movement, as happens in many such cases, believed he had been martyred by the regime (Rahnema 1998, 36). "It was Shari'ati's death and his subsequent resurrection on the streets," claims Ghamari-Tabrizi, "as the *martyred educator* that defined him as *the* revolutionary ideologue of the movement" (2000, 106). During the revolutionary movement, Shari'ati's lectures and writings served as essential inspirations for both educated and uneducated streams of the revolutionary movement.

The version of Islam that Shari'ati preached was radical in the sense that he advocated a return to the roots. He claimed that the original and authentic Islam, which he called "the Islam of Ali," is an insurrectionary movement of the people that stands opposed to the corrupt Islam that has subsequently come to predominate, "Safavid Islam," characterized by the domination of the clergy and the ruling class. Clearly, although Shari'ati does not pose it in these terms, he is advocating class struggle through Shi'ite theology. Part of his rhetorical genius was to renew the meaning of the most traditional elements of Islam in the context of contemporary political struggles. His lectures conducted "a general assault," according to Rahnema, "on all existing institutions[:] the shah's regime, relations of dominance and dependence fostered by imperialism, the prevalent capitalist economic system, the class-ridden social system, the domination of Western liberal culture, the prevalent traditional and clerically defined concept of Islam and finally the clerical institution" (1998, 299).

Shari'ati's poetic revolutionary style and his combination of political ideologies are illustrated by the series of names he deploys for "the triangle of domination." These are different ways of identifying the triple power—economic, political, and ideological—that currently rules over us and must be annihilated: *zar-zoor-tazvir* (jewel-coercion-deceiving), *estesmar-este'mar-estehamr* (exploitation-colonization-deception), *mälek-malek-mulla* (gentry-majesty-clergy), and *tigh-tala-tasbih* (sword-gold-rosary) (Ghamari-Tabrizi 2000, 107n2). Note the linguistic similarity he establishes in the Farsi terms, largely through alliteration, in each set of three. The verbal correspondences reinforce the idea that these different structures of domination are really united, a combined enemy. Struggles against capitalism, monarchy/imperialism, and clericalism are thus really one struggle. In this way, Shari'ati marked out the coordinates of the revolutionary movement that weaves together Marxism, anticolonial-Fanonian thought, and Shi'ism. "Thanks to Ali Shari'ati's legacy," Ghamari-Tabrizi maintains, "for many years Muslim and Marxist revolutionaries alike regarded themselves as comrades in arms holding the same ideals, albeit with different ideologies" (2016, 78). It should not be surprising, then, that Iranian revolutionaries influenced by Shari'ati were able to maintain a kind of theoretical fluidity, freely crossing boundaries among political paradigms and, more generally, between political and theological frameworks. Furthermore, the political vision that mixed Islam and Marxism in this way, of which Shari'ati's was one example, not only spoke to students and educated classes but also resonated with the knowledges, beliefs, and practices of the uneducated poor, allowing them to grasp their current political situation, understand the nature of their oppression, and envision the path toward liberation. It was thus a profound basis for the mass mobilization against the shah's regime.

Peeling away this second layer of assumptions, then, regarding the opposition between the secular and the religious, the Marxist and the Islamic, helps reveal the political and theoretical innovations of the revolutionary movement, especially as articulated by thinkers like Shari'ati. "The revolutionary movement in Iran," Ghamari-Tabrizi asserts, "offered a world-historical possibility to move away from a binary Islamist/secular politics" (2016, xii). In the revolutionary struggle, a liberation theology was developed and mobilized that confounds such divisions.

All of this is revealed, I should repeat, by distinguishing the revolutionary movement from the results of the revolution. It is important to be able to recognize and analyze the innovative political concepts and organizations even when they were defeated, distorted, or co-opted by the victors.[6] Appreciating the dynamism and originality of the revolutionary movement in Iran, furthermore, does not mean in any way legitimating the repressive theocratic regime that came to power after the revolution. On the contrary, perhaps the best way to challenge it is to reveal what its rule has effectively kept hidden.

The Sandinista Revolution

The Nicaraguan insurrection of the 1970s, like that in Iran, has to be situated with respect to imperialist interventions earlier in the century. A brief sketch is sufficient to paint a familiar picture. Because of its strategic importance, partly in relation to a planned Nicaragua canal, the United States occupied the country with Marine battalions from 1909 to 1933. Beginning in the late 1920s, Augusto Sandino led an armed rebellion against the US occupation, and once the US forces had left, Sandino vied for power with Anastasio Somoza, a political leader loyal to US interests. In 1934, Somoza invited Sandino to negotiations at the presidential palace in the capital, Managua, and there had him assassinated by the National Guard. The Somoza family subsequently led an authoritarian dictatorship, consistently friendly to the US government, for over four decades.

The Sandinista National Liberation Front (FSLN) is reported to have been founded in the early 1960s by Carlos Fonseca, Tomás Borge, and Silvio

Mayorga, but it did not succeed in mounting significant political or military operations until the 1970s. The organizational orientation of the FSLN generally followed the Cuban model, with a predominantly peasant guerrilla force that controlled rural areas and periodically made swift attacks in urban centers. The FSLN should also be situated in the specific Central American traditions of peasant liberation struggles, notably those in Guatemala, that mixed anticolonial and anti-imperialist elements (Grandin 2011).

Like the Marxist guerrilla organizations in Iran, such as the Fadai and the Mujahedin, the FSLN made daring attacks on the regime, which brought them prestige, recruits, and funds. Two of its most spectacular assaults on the Somoza government, which serve to mark the beginning and end of the revolutionary movement, stand out. In December 1974, when the FSLN was still relatively unknown, eight armed Sandinista revolutionaries raided a Christmas party of many close Somoza allies at a private house, timing the strike for just after the US ambassador left, so as not to provoke US involvement. They took the thirty attendees hostage and, in exchange for their release, the FSLN made three demands, which were swiftly met: a $1 million payment, a one-time broadcast slot on radio and television, and the release of numerous political prisoners (Clos 2012, 22). The 1974 Christmas party attack effectively announced the entry of the FSLN into the national political scene.

Another bold exploit, four years later, marked the beginning of the final insurrection. In August 1978, twenty-five Sandinista commandos took control of the entire National Palace, holding hostage nearly fifteen hundred government officials, including all members of Congress. Again they negotiated for the release of hostages, receiving a cash payment of $5 million, the release of eighty-three political prisoners, including Tomás Borge, and the publication of a Sandinista communiqué (Kinzer 2003, 40–42; Weber 1981, 44). The FSLN took power less than a year later.

From Christian Base Communities to Insurrection

The successes of the guerrilla movements and the popularity they achieved are roughly similar in Nicaragua and Iran, but the shared element I want to emphasize is the role religious communities played in the two uprisings and the way that Marxist and theological frameworks were interwoven. The role of religious participation in the Nicaraguan Revolution was widely noted at the time. "Although there have been progressive Christians in other Latin American countries," asserts Margaret Randall, "Nicaragua is the first country where Christians as a group played a decisive role in all aspects of the political and social conflict up to and including armed struggle" (1983, 11). And the practical engagements of Christians in armed revolutionary struggle was matched at the theoretical level: the "convergence of Marxism and Christianity," maintains Andrew Reding, "is perhaps the most extraordinary development of the Nicaraguan revolution" (1987, 2). The boundaries between the secular and the religious, the Marxist and the Christian, vanished, or at least ceased to be significant for many of those in the revolutionary struggle.

In Nicaragua and other Latin American countries a wide array of theorists elaborated this revolutionary theology. Undoubtedly, developments outside of Nicaragua, such as the 1968 statement of the Council of Latin American Bishops affirming the preferential option for the poor, along with the writings of liberation theologians such as Leonardo Boff and Gustavo Gutierrez, were significant supporting factors.[7] But most important were the practices of base Christian communities in Nicaragua and the theological developments that emerged from them.

In Solentiname, on a remote archipelago at the southern tip of Lake Nicaragua, for example, the Catholic priest Ernesto Cardenal founded a religious and political community in which peasants together interpreted the gospels according to their own experiences. "In their discussions on the weekly gospel," explains Andrew Bradstock, "the Solentiname campesinos unself-consciously and almost empathetically identified their own conditions with those of first-century Palestine, drawing parallels, for example, between the 'atmosphere of terror and repression' which they believed provided the context for Jesus' ministry and their own situation under Somoza (Herod) and the 'gringo ambassador' (Pilate)" (1987, 14; on Solentiname, see also Randall 1983, 39–40; Hodges 1986, 282–288; Cardenal 1976). The theological orientation of the members of the base Christian community was radical in much the same way that Ali Shari'ati's "Islam of Ali" was—that is, as a return to beginnings. Against the theology of the clerics and the ruling classes, the poor interpreted scripture and the life of Jesus as a guide to liberation for their own lives. Many of those in the Solentiname community subsequently joined the revolutionary struggle. Cardenal explains their motives for taking up arms in purely religious terms: "They did it for one reason alone: out of their love for the kingdom of God. Out of their ardent desire to establish a just society, a true and concrete kingdom of God here on this earth" (1979, 12–13). According to the readings of the community, the lessons of the gospel led them directly to armed insurrection.

The community, however, did not survive to see the victory. In October 1977, revolutionaries from Solentiname attacked and took control of a military garrison in the nearby town of San Carlos. The National Guard responded swiftly and brutally, killing all those at Solentiname suspected of sympathizing with the FSLN and destroying the community.

The experiences of many other base Christian communities among the poor in Nicaragua similarly moved from liberation theology to revolutionary action, including the San Pablo community, organized by the Spanish priest José de la Jara; the Barrio Riguero community, led by the Jesuit priest Uriel Molina; and Barrio OPEN 3, established by Maryknoll nuns (Randall 1983, 123–129; Foroohar 1989, 127–135; Kirk 1992, 69–76). "What few outside observers realized," claims Michael Dodson, referring to experiences like these, "was that the pathway leading many of the poor into the revolutionary movement had its origin in a religious awakening. Thousands of Christians, acting through grass-roots Christian organizations and communities, participated in all phases of the Popular Insurrection" (1986, 38). Whereas outside observers were often puzzled by the close collaboration of Christians and communists in the FSLN, for those inside the intersection was natural and immediate (Foroohar 1989, 132). As in Iran, the mixture of Marxist theory and theology was fertile soil for the growth of a massive popular in-surrection, giving both the educated and uneducated the means to under-stand the structures of domination that ruled over them, and the road to collective liberation.

The fluid combination of Marxism and Christianity became strained, however, especially at the official level, after the revolutionary victory. In the first years of the Sandinista government, several Catholic priests were named to central positions, including Ernesto Cardenal as minister of culture and his brother Fernando as minister of education. It is worth remembering that in Iran, too, although the political dynamics were very different, in the first months after the victory, before the referenda on the creation of an Islamic republic and a new constitution, a mix of clerics and Marxists held govern-mental positions. In Nicaragua, this cohabitation in government exacerbated a long-lasting conflict between the religious hierarchy and the popular movements. Whereas a large portion of the base of the Catholic Church in Nicaragua supported and participated in the revolutionary process, the bishops had maintained an ambivalent position, which became increasingly hostile after the formation of the Sandinista government (O'Shaughnessy 1986, 7). The base Christian communities that had functioned as an incubator for revolutionary activity, along with the priests and nuns who organized them, had always been viewed by the hierarchy as a threat to its authority. It should be no surprise that the Catholic hierarchy could not recognize (or refused to accept) the combination of communism and Christianity in the mass uprising and the claims of those militants that revolutionary action was the fulfillment of their religious vocation. The archbishop of Managua, Miguel Obando y Bravo, the highest-ranking Catholic official in the country, for instance, declared that the base Christian communities "have absolutely nothing religious about them: they are a façade to breed Marxism-Leninism" (cited in Kirk 1992, 98). The conflict came to a head in 1983 when Pope John Paul II, a devout anticommunist and dedicated opponent of liberation theology, visited Nicaragua and openly chastised the priests in the Sandinista government. I should halt the historical narrative at this point, however, because, as I said earlier, my interest in this chapter lies with the revolutionary processes in the two countries more than with the results of the revolutions.

Foucault in Solentiname

Michel Foucault visited Iran twice in 1978 on assignment as a kind of philosopher-correspondent for the Italian newspaper *Corriere della Sera*. On each occasion he wrote a series of brief articles, which not only described in simple and direct terms the political and economic crisis of the country, denouncing the brutality of the shah's regime, but also praised the popular uprising. "Given what the Shah's regime was," he explained in an interview after returning to Paris, "its political and economic oppression, its exploitation of the population and its masked imperialism, etc.—well, that an entire people should revolt against this regime is a good thing" (Sassine and Foucault 2018, 331). Much of what is valuable in Foucault's analyses, however, has been obscured by political passions regarding Islam and the actions of the postrevolutionary theocratic regime.[8]

Imagine if *Corriere della Sera* had dispatched Foucault to Nicaragua instead of Iran and he had been assigned to visit the base Christian community at Solentiname (which had been destroyed by the National Guard by that time). It is, in fact, not difficult to substitute the names of places and political figures while reading Foucault's articles, since the primary elements are so similar: the brutal dictator with US backing, the anti-imperialist uprising, liberation theology animating the popular insurrection, and so forth. Reading Foucault's writings diagonally, in this way, allows us to see his arguments more clearly and, in the process, cast a new light on the revolutionary movements themselves.

Repeatedly in his articles, Foucault seeks to de-exoticize for European readers the intersection of religion and politics. Do not dismiss the revolutionary power and liberatory nature of the movement in Iran, he implores his readers, simply because the uprising is conducted in theological terms. Numerous times in the past—Foucault cites the Anabaptists in sixteenth-century Germany and the Presbyterians in seventeenth-century England—revolutionary thought and practice have taken place primarily on a religious terrain, or, said differently, theology and religious practices have served as idioms of revolutionary struggle and media of popular mobilization (Foucault 2005c, 201). Foucault is not really interested here in religion per se or even religious experiences but rather in what he calls "political spirituality," which includes religion but extends well beyond its bounds. In fact, he maintains, political spirituality is an essential characteristic of modern revolutionary movements in general, including the Bolsheviks. "All of the great political, social, and cultural disruptions," he claims, "couldn't have taken place in history without originating in a movement of spirituality" (2020, 124). Insofar as they address political spirituality, then, Christian and Islamic uprisings in Nicaragua and Iran, like secular movements, touch on the core power of the revolutionary process.

Political spirituality, for Foucault, is aimed at subjective transformation. "We shouldn't be looking for" the will to rise up in Iran, he claims, "in a political ideology like Marxism," which he associates here primarily with the effort to transform social and economic structures. Political spirituality, instead, requires "becoming other than what one is" (2020, 122, 124). This is what, following Foucault's notion, the popular movements in Iran and Nicaragua found in Islam and Christianity. "Religion for them," Foucault asserts, "was like the promise and guarantee of finding something that would radically change their subjectivity" (2005b, 255). In order to understand political spirituality and subjective transformation as Foucault intends them here, one must keep in mind several aspects of these notions that are not immediately evident. First, it is worth repeating that political spirituality is not necessarily religious, despite the Islamic context of the examples he uses in these texts. Second, subjective transformation is not an individual process or a personal practice but a collective, social endeavor. Third, the transformation of subjectivity he affirms should not be counterposed to and does not exclude structural transformation. Instead, Foucault theorizes collective subjective transformations, both secular and religious, as means to realize structural change. The Shi'ite religion in the Iranian uprising, according to Foucault—and this is certainly equally true of Christianity in Nicaragua—forges from the poor and their myriad forms of indignation, yearning, hatred, and despair "a force" capable of collective action, transforming not only themselves but also their world (2005c, 202–203). "Everything was really changed in beliefs, ways of life, social relations, forms of political obedience, hierarchies within society, economic practices—everything was altered" (2020, 125). What Foucault finds most important, in other words, is how new *dispositifs* and biopolitical apparatuses—that is, transformed ways of speaking and acting, new modes of life, and novel ways of being together—are deployed in the service of liberation. The base Christian communities in Solentiname, San Pablo, Barrio Riguero, and Barrio OPEN 3, which I described earlier, aimed precisely at such new forms of life, which were then activated in insurrection.

I find Foucault's concept of political spirituality clarifying and inspiring, but I think he suffers from a blind spot that is manifest in both his historical and theoretical analyses. At the historical level, while affirming the Islamic nature of the uprising in Iran, he neglects its communist components. Earlier I criticized the narrative that religious forces hijacked the Iranian Revolution, stealing it from secular, leftist movements, because it neglects the Islamic character of much of the revolutionary movement. It is equally mistaken, of course, to ignore the Marxist character of the movements and see only their Shi'ite face. Foucault is unable to grasp, in other words, the strong overlap that existed in Iran (like in Nicaragua) of religious and communist struggles. As I said earlier, what was most interestingly shared by the Iranian and Nicaraguan revolutionary movements, taking place simultaneously on opposite sides of the globe, was the way religious and Marxist struggles, theological and political mentalities, were so intimately intermeshed. The liberation theologies permeating the movements are recognizable not only in the writings of intellectuals such as Ali Shari'ati and Ernesto Cardenal but also and more importantly in the practices and beliefs widespread among the poor who animated the popular uprisings.

At the theoretical level, this blind spot is manifest in relation to structures and structural change. It is too simple to say that by taking aim at subjectivity Foucault ignores structures, as if political spirituality were to refer solely to transformation of the former and Marxism that of the latter. It is more accurate to pose the difference as one of priority and sequence. Whereas political spirituality, according to Foucault, begins with a change in subjectivity in order then to arrive at a comprehensive social transformation, Marxism (or at least some versions of it) could be posed symmetrically as moving from the other point of departure but toward the same goal—that is, as starting from the change of social and economic structures in order then to alter subjectivity and finally to achieve a thorough revolution of society. What Foucault misses is that it must be both at once: just as empirically the movements were both religious and Marxist, the theoretical project must simultaneously aim to transform both collective subjectivity and structures of domination, each side of the struggle providing the conditions of possibility for the other.

The conclusion of this analysis should not be that we need today a new liberation theology, either Islamic or Christian. This was certainly not Foucault's view when he affirmed the Shi'ite popular uprising in Iran and highlighted the importance of political spirituality in revolutionary struggle. He recognized in the popular uprising in Iran (and could have found, equally, in Nicaragua) an attempt to create a new political imagination and a new mode of revolutionary practice. To combat the forms of domination we confront today, he maintained, we need to break old orthodoxies and invent new modes of thought and social practice. The key that his analysis helps us recognize, it seems to me, is a concept of liberation that pursues at once both subjective and structural transformation, a radical change of ourselves and our world. In Iran and Nicaragua this was developed on religious terrain, but it could equally well be constructed in purely secular terms.

PART II

POPULAR POWER

5

Two Versions of Popular Power

If I give the OK to this [the workers' autonomous decision to occupy the Yarur cotton factory], there is going to be another and another and another.

—Salvador Allende

Chilean society was a cauldron of political innovation from Salvador Allende's electoral victory on September 4, 1970, to the military coup d'état on September 11, 1973. I am most interested in experiments with novel forms of popular power that created participatory structures of decision-making and developed original schemes to share and manage social wealth—things that tend to be obscured from view in most accounts of the period. To reveal the dynamics of popular power, one has to first work through standard ways of framing the significance of the revolution, which highlight major political figures and dominant political forces.

Anticommunism and Anti-imperialism

The first frame of interpretation highlights how revolutionary Chile threatened the imperialist world order—cursed for this by some and celebrated by others. Henry Kissinger, for instance, then US national security advisor, was obsessed with Chile. Since Allende's election was a victory for the other side, he reasoned, one that set a dangerous precedent for other countries in the region, even more menacing than the model of Cuba, it had to be destroyed (Grandin 2006, 60; 2015, 147). In this cold war anticommunist frame, it mattered little that Allende was democratically elected and that his government attempted to achieve its policy goals exclusively through legal means, in accordance with the Chilean constitution—this made the precedent all the more dangerous. The fact that Allende's governing Popular Unity coalition included the Communist Party and that Allende promised and enacted socialist policies such as nationalizing industries and banks was more than enough for cold war anticommunists to dedicate themselves to its destruction.

The "anti-imperialism" frame is not exactly the flip side of the anticommunist frame, because, at least as deployed by Allende, it was not tied to the Soviet perspective and, in effect, ran diagonal to the cold war binary, evoking more strongly the project of the nonaligned nations. (The Allende government maintained good relations with countries on both sides of the cold war divide.) This frame has the virtue of capturing a political stance shared by all revolutionary forces in Chile at the time, as well as those throughout the continent and beyond. "Chile is squarely in line," Allende affirmed early in his presidency, "with the worldwide struggle against imperialism" (Debray 1971, 123). This frame also accurately names the forces outside the country that were intent on destroying the revolution. In his December 1972 speech at the UN, Allende accused International Telephone and Telegraph (ITT) and other transnational corporations of trying to foment civil war in his country, and declared that Latin America had become the principal field of US imperialist action (Allende 2000a, 8, 10–11). All of this proved to be true, of course: the Allende government was undermined throughout its duration and was overthrown by a concert of imperialist forces, including the US government and corporations such as ITT.

The overthrow of the Allende government sent shock waves across the globe, and interpretations of "the lessons of Chile" varied widely among different leftist organizations. For some parties that were pursuing "the democratic road to socialism," for example, the demise of Allende emphasized the need to avoid the wrath of imperialist and anticommunist powers, and thus tempered progressive ambitions even further. Enrico Berlinguer, then leader of the Italian Communist Party, writing just weeks after the coup, interpreted the lesson of Chile to be that legality and electoral victory are not enough: given the global relations of force, even gaining a majority of votes, he maintained, would not guarantee a Communist Party–led government's ability to function and survive. The events in Chile reconfirmed his view that his party could enter government successfully only by achieving a "historic compromise" in collaboration with the center-right Christian Democratic Party (Berlinguer 1972, 4–5). The lessons drawn by radical organizations, in contrast, reinforced the need for more revolutionary action in various directions, as we will see in later chapters. Two examples indicate the range of responses: in Portugal, when in 1975 the return of fascism seemed a real danger, "Portugal will not be the Chile of Europe" was a prominent slogan in support of the government and the continuing revolutionary process;[1] and in Germany the first attack of the Revolutionary Cells (Revolutionare Zellen) struck ITT facilities in West Berlin and Nuremberg in response to the corporation's active role in the Pinochet coup (Gerhardt 2018, 118).

The Traditional Left Versus the New Left

The anti-imperialist frame, although it highlights important aspects of the Chilean experience, sheds little light on the tensions, conflicts, antagonisms, and alliances among the various political forces within Chile. A second frame, which allows us better to see these dynamics, centers on the contest between what in Latin America was known as the "traditional Left" and the "New Left"—a division that does not correspond to Old Left/New Left divisions as understood in Europe and North America. Whereas the traditional Left, which in most Latin American countries included the Communist Party, generally participated in electoral politics and sought gradual reforms of national political and economic systems primarily through legal means, the New Left, following the Cuban model, focused primarily on armed revolt and guerrilla struggle aimed at insurrection with an internationalist or at least continental vision.[2] The relationship between the traditional Left and the New Left was not exclusively antagonistic, of course, but rather alternated between competition and collaboration—and this was certainly the case in Chile.

From this perspective, Allende appears as a paradigmatic figure of the traditional Left. His Popular Unity (UP) won power completely legally, without firing a shot. In his first annual address to the Chilean Congress in May 1971, he affirmed that "legality is the governing principle today in Chile" and that his government would realize "our revolutionary task while respecting the rule of law" (Allende 2000b, 96, 97). In this respect, his electoral success served as a confirmation of the traditional Left's strategies, just as the Cuban victory validated the New Left—setting up a contrast, both within Chile and on the international scene, between two paths to socialism.

In Régis Debray's book-length interview of Allende in early 1971, conducted a few months after his election, the two men play out faithfully the two roles in this drama. Debray, a close confidant of Fidel Castro and

faithful chronicler of Cuban revolutionary thought, would have been immediately recognized by readers, especially in Latin America, as a representative of the New Left, and thus a foil to Allende's conviction that "the Chilean
path to socialism" could succeed while honoring the results of elections and
maintaining the legal, constitutional order, without violence. When Debray
remarks that the Chilean example has been interpreted by some as an invali-
dation of the Cuban path, Allende retorts, with his typical modesty and mod-
eration, that different paths are equally valid and should be chosen based on
the national political situation.

DEBRAY: You know how in the overall picture of Latin America your image is
    being used as a counter-balance to those of Fidel and Ché. What do you
    think of those who say that what has just happened in Chile gives the lie
    to the thesis of the people's war, to the validity of the armed struggle, shall
    we say, elsewhere?
ALLENDE: I said it just before our victory. The revolutionary struggle
    may be found in the guerrilla *foco* or in urban insurrection; it may
    be the people's war and it may be an insurgence through the polling
    booths; it depends on the content it is given. In some countries, there
    is no alternative to the armed struggle: where there are no parties, no
    trade unions, where there is dictatorship, who is going to believe in
    the possibility of an electoral victory? There, elections offer no hope.
    And those people, these revolutionaries, have to reach their objective
    (Debray 1971, 127).

Debray, however, is not convinced by Allende's ecumenical response and
does not accept that, as Allende claims, the different paths are equally valid,
depending on circumstances. In his introduction to the interview, in fact,
Debray declares, "In the last analysis, and until further notice, power grows
out of the barrel of a gun." He seems to regard Allende as a noble figure—
perhaps, we could say, the best version of the traditional Left—but someone
who is ultimately naive about political realities and the possibilities for
peaceful transformation.[3]

This traditional Left/New Left frame has the virtue of revealing one important distinction among the revolutionary forces within Chile. Whereas
Allende and the UP exemplified the traditional Left, the New Left was
represented in Chile primarily by the Revolutionary Left Movement (MIR),
which stood as foil to the strategy of electoral politics and legality and as

standard-bearer of the Cuban path. The MIR, formed in 1965 and especially strong among students, peasants, and workers, conceived of itself as a Marxist-Leninist and Guevarist vanguard party aimed ultimately at armed insurrection, although its political activity during the Allende years primarily involved organizing campaigns with social movements and labor struggles.[4] At its peak in 1973 MIR counted approximately ten thousand members.

The actual relationship, however, between the MIR and the UP—and, indeed, between the MIR and Allende himself—did not conform neatly to the traditional Left/New Left divide. Their interactions and alliances were complicated and shifting in different periods and with respect to specific events. In the 1970 electoral campaign, for instance, the MIR chose not to join the UP coalition but did actively support its election efforts. And throughout the subsequent three years of the Allende government, the MIR's actions at times challenged but often coincided with government policies. We thus need a more nuanced view of the traditional Left/New Left divide in this case, one that focuses on difference of degree rather than difference of kind. The MIR is best seen as a sympathetic fellow traveler that, often in conjunction with peasant or worker movements, attempted to pull the UP further to the left and to accelerate the process of transition to socialism.

In the aftermath of the 1973 coup and in the years since, readings of the traditional Left/New Left divide during the Allende years have tended to shift and take on a darker aspect. "In the literature on the Allende years," Marian Schlotterbeck affirms, "the Chilean MIR is typically presented as the troublesome Far Left that remained outside of the governing Popular Unity coalition and that pushed Salvador Allende so far that the coup was inevitable" (2018, 3). By pushing the government to move too fast and by undermining the unity of the Left, the thinking goes, the MIR and other political forces of the New Left unintentionally contributed to the conditions of defeat.

Although in each of these versions the traditional Left/New Left frame, whether configuring the two sides as fellow travelers or antagonists, illuminates important dynamics of the political forces in Chile, it really only shines light on the uppermost echelons of the political scene, that is, the political leaders and their parties. It effectively leaves in the dark the dynamics of political struggle below. And to illuminate that netherworld we will need yet another frame.

Representation Versus Participation

This third frame highlights the distinction between centralized political powers and popular participation, emphasizing the tension and separation between the power "from above" deployed by the political parties and leaders, those of the traditional Left and New Left alike, and the power "from below" of autonomous, democratic political initiatives.[5] Viewed in this light, the UP and the MIR, the traditional Left and the New Left, are more linked by what they share than separated by their differences. The New Left parties, even though they often acted on the side of the popular struggles, were generally characterized by rigid internal hierarchies and centralized control, as were the traditional Left parties. In contrast, what was really new during the revolutionary period emerged in the projects and institutions organized on principles of participation and democratic decision-making—projects and institutions that sometimes collaborated with and sometimes conflicted with the centralized parties. We can begin to see this novelty by investigating some specific events that highlight the differing conceptions of popular power and social property—not just differences of degree but differences of kind.

During the Allende years, calls for popular power were ubiquitous, but were divided into those that meant greater representation and those aimed at greater participation. The program of Popular Unity, for example, promised to replace the two chambers of Chile's Congress with a People's Assembly, which would be more representative, with delegates subject to recall, and to create similar assemblies at the local level to decentralize and democratize power, although the government did not manage during its three years in power to act on this proposal (Winn 1986, 64). In practice, for the Allende government popular power meant that the government pledged faithfully to represent the interests of the people and the people should, in return, support its policies. Although the MIR was certainly closer than the government to the base of social movements and peasant and worker struggles, the forms of popular power it enacted shared this representative character: the party sought to speak for and guide the popular struggles.[6]

Outside the parties and their centralized structures, a different notion of popular power developed. "To Chile's workers, peasants, and *pobladores*," Peter Winn claims, "the election of a 'Popular Government' was a signal for them to take the revolution into their own hands and fulfill their historic aspirations through direct action from below" (1986, 140). In these contexts,

popular power came to require new schemas for people's autonomous participation in politics.

The Yarur *Toma*

One specific conflict that emerged during a 1971 factory occupation brings
into sharper focus the differences between these two conceptions of popular
power. The Allende government had planned gradually to nationalize selected
industries in order to create a "social property area" to function alongside the
"private property area" as core components of a mixed national economy. In
April 1971, by which time the government had already nationalized several
firms in important industries and sectors, such as mining and banking, the
roughly two thousand workers at the enormous Yarur cotton mill in Santiago
seized the factory. (In Chile at the time *una toma*, literally "a take," was the
term used for such a seizure, which in today's English political lexicon might
be called an occupation.) Yarur was the first factory seized by the workers
themselves—and it was done against the government's wishes.

Peter Winn describes in detail, with the aid of oral histories conducted with
participants, how the *toma* of the textile factory created an immediate rift between the workers and the government. In the lead-up to the events, the government and the other leftist parties had instructed the workers to wait, to be
patient. The workers justified their action by detailing the history of brutal
working conditions and persecution by the owners, the Yarur family; furthermore, they saw their actions as extending the government's own project of
socializing industries. The government, however, had different calculations
in mind. It was true that this plant fit one of the UP's criteria for nationalization: the Yarur factory had a virtual monopoly over the production of certain
cotton goods, and the UP had designated monopolies as candidates eventually for nationalization. And yet the government, which had so far focused
nationalization efforts on foreign corporations, was not prepared to challenge domestic industry owners. "In early 1971," Winn explains, "the Allende
government was not ready—neither politically or administratively—for 'the
expropriation of the national bourgeoisie' and the creation of a social property area" (1986, 148). The government, furthermore, wanted to take the time
to ensure that seizing a Chilean-owned business was legal under the Chilean
constitution.

Allende was reportedly furious when he heard that workers had seized the factory. The political decision had been taken out of the government's hands. Most revealing about his response was his inability to understand or to accept that the workers played an autonomous role in the events.[7] After receiving the news, Allende first summoned to the Presidential Palace veteran socialist and communist labor leaders and demanded they explain why they had supported or allowed the factory seizure. When they responded that the unions had not planned this and indeed had counseled against the action but the workers had taken the decision on their own, Allende refused to accept this explanation, and he summoned the Yarur workers' factory representatives. When the workers confirmed that they had taken the action autonomously, having come to a decision in participatory assemblies in the factory, the president again refused to accept it. "You are not going to convince *me* that the whole thing was spontaneous," he responded. "There was work beyond the scenes on this," referring presumably to manipulation by union or party leaders. After recounting these meetings, Winn concludes, "The conflict between revolution from above and revolution from below was all too clear" (1986, 185–186). This conflict is also expressed in terms of what can and cannot be seen: from above, Allende was able to grasp the situation only in terms of the contest between union and party leaders, blind to the fact that the workers had organized and decided autonomously.

The workers, disappointed and dismayed by the president's disapproval, had, in fact, taken the government at its word regarding popular power and acted on it—not popular power as representation, but popular power as participation.[8] Once workers had established their control of the Yarur factory, they created institutions for democratic participation. "This was the first industry to have a council," one of the Yarur workers proudly claimed, "the first to have a coordinating committee, the first to hold a general assembly" (Winn 1986, 209). They were developing a thoroughgoing concept of popular power and constructing the institutions to support it.

And the Yarur workers were certainly not the only ones. Throughout Chile, assemblies and councils were being established for participatory decision-making—not just in factories but also in housing occupations, peasant organizations, and other sectors. In effect, a layer of participatory activity developed beneath and relatively autonomous of the actions of the government and the parties. Marian Schlotterbeck recounts how a "people's assembly" organized in Concepción in July 1972 illustrates both the widespread development of participatory structures and the ways that histories of the period have generally been blind to them. The date of the people's assembly was chosen to commemorate the beginning of the Cuban Revolution, and the MIR, which was particularly strong in Concepción, was generally thought to have been the central organizer. The event, which took place in the university's theater, began with representatives of major parties giving speeches, and thus seemed to be a typical leftist staged rally, but then the microphones were opened to the floor and the event transformed. Participants from over a hundred social movements and local political organizations—unions, peasant groups, students, shantytown residents, and others—spoke up and took over the event, demonstrating the extent and development of participatory organizations. "This transformation from a typical political event into an open assembly," Schlotterbeck maintains, "marked a point of inflection for Chile's revolutionary process." The scales had shifted from the representative version of popular power of the government and the major parties to the practices of participatory democracy at the core of the popular power developed by the movements (Schlotterbeck 2018, 112, 92, 106).

Social Property and the Common

These popular power practices and institutions of direct participation also played a central role in the transformation of property ownership. The Allende government's economic program, as I mentioned, called for the creation of a mixed economy, composed of public and private property. A "private property area" was allowed to remain and was accompanied by a "social property area," created primarily by nationalizing selected sectors and industries. The mixed nature of this economic project, of course, was not particularly original: the mixture of forms of property, in various proportions, characterized the economies of both socialist and capitalist states. What was really new was the way that participatory democratic practices threw into question the accepted notion that "social property" must be controlled by the state.

The paradigmatic practice of the participatory popular power movements was the *toma*, which referred to the seizure or occupation of not only factories, as in the case of Yarur, but also land for housing and farms. As an example of land seizure, in May 1970, a few months before Allende's election, at the encouragement of the MIR, between two and three thousand *pobladores* (which in this context refers to the urban poor) occupied land in the city of Concepción to create Campamento Lenin, an enormous set-tlement. Once the settlement was established, the occupiers created their own social institutions, including a health clinic, elementary school, and childcare services. Like the workers of the Yarur factory a year later, the residents of the camp created a participatory governance scheme. "Similar to the assembly-based tradition of Concepción student politics," Schlotterbeck explains, "Campamento Lenin pobladores organized themselves collectively into a general assembly of several hundred pobladores that functioned as the highest community authority" (2018, 74, 70). Such assemblies and other institutions of participatory democracy established self-management and self-governance as guiding principles of the new social arrangement.

What type of property, then, is created by a *toma*? To a certain extent, of course, it is inevitable that some aspects of the old property relations per-sist. In part—but only in part—the occupied factory comes to be managed by the state as "social property," and the housing settlement of the poor bears characteristics of private property, with each person or family claiming its own space. To the extent that the factory *toma* transfers private property to public control (that is, state control) and the land *toma* distributes private property to the poor, the two forms of property, private and public, remain unchanged. Those property relations are radically transformed, however, by participatory democratic institutions of collective self-management. When the use of land, resources, and means of production is guided by institutions of participatory democracy, such as the assemblies of workers or *pobladores*, then what was previously property becomes something altogether dif-ferent. One might say that the government's concept of "social property" is given new meaning, in which "social" refers not to state control but rather to self-governance. This is a corollary to the earlier point regarding the two meanings of popular power, the one resting on representation and the other on participation. But really, calling this social *property* (even in this sense of "social") is imprecise because democratic self-management transforms property into the common. An introductory definition of "common," then, which contrasts it to both public and private property, highlights the partici-patory democratic structures that decide access and use.[9]

The results of the various *tomas*, then, were a mixture between property and the common, but this mixed situation established a tendency toward—or, rather, nourished a desire for—further change. The mixture in the case of the Yarur factory configured a relationship of co-management between the workers and the state. After the *toma*, for instance, in addition to worker assemblies, there was created a new board of directors (with half the members directly elected by the workers) and a coordinating committee, formed with delegates from each production committee, other worker representatives, and union officers, in order to mediate the relationship between work sections and management (Winn 1986, 210). Such partial arrangements of worker control, however, Franck Gaudichaud claims, created a thirst for more: "The fact of putting forward the standard of worker participation, favoring certain forms of control over the process of production, and nationalizing many large businesses released among the workers a participative energy. The workers thus began to give ever more concrete content to notions of 'worker participation' and 'social property' advanced by Allende."[10] Once property was seized collectively in these various social contexts, then, a tendency was set in motion from property toward the common.

The Sorcerer Loses Control

According to one standard account I cited earlier, the difference between the Allende government and the Far Left parties along with the social movements was primarily a question of speed. All were oriented in the same direction, aimed at constructing socialism, but whereas the government strove to implement moderate changes at a measured pace, its allies to the left pushed to move more quickly—leading to a revolutionary pace that Allende could no longer control. If we focus instead on the forms of popular power organized through mechanisms of democratic participation, however, then the question becomes not merely a matter of speed, because the two sides were not aimed at the same destination. They did not even understand the name of the goal in the same way. One side aspired (at least in the short term) toward state control of economic and political decision-making, such that popular power would mean representing the people and social property would mean state ownership. The other side, in contrast, which employed the *toma* of property as a central tactic, sought democratic decision-making in economic and political affairs, casting popular power as participation and configuring social property as a tendency toward the common.

It is thus not simply a question of gradual versus rapid change, moderates versus radicals. Allende's election and the actions of his government inspired political forces of a qualitatively different type, characterized not by centralized control but by democratic participation. Allende was something like the sorcerer who can no longer control the forces of a netherworld, a revolution from below, which he has summoned with his spells. Once let loose, those forces cannot easily be shut back up. This is not to say that popular power, participatory democracy, and the common were fully developed in the Chilean Revolution. They certainly were not. But the political forces aimed at these goals were essential components—the most innovative ones—of the revolutionary process.

6

Commission Democracy

Without asking the state which path to take.

—José Afonso

The 1974 Portuguese Revolution was initiated by an event that defied standard political assumptions: the Armed Forces Movement (MFA), composed of left-leaning colonels and other midlevel military officers, engineered a coup d'état, in which almost no shots were fired, to oust the Estado Novo government, the longest-lasting fascist regime in the world. With respect to other military coups in the 1970s, the Portuguese "Carnation Revolution," as it was called, was anomalous not only for the lack of violence but also for its progressive political direction. Less than a year earlier, the military coup in Chile had overthrown a democratically elected socialist government and installed a brutal right-wing dictatorship; nearly two years later a coup in Argentina brought a military junta to power; and in Turkey the military conducted coups in both 1971 and 1980 with the pretext of combating leftists. Military coups of the seventies, in short, generally served to combat leftists and established right-wing or fascist regimes. The coup in Portugal moved in the opposite political direction. The MFA aimed to end not only fascism at home but also colonialism abroad, terminating the brutal wars that had maintained Portuguese control over Angola, Mozambique, and Guinea-Bissau, and eventually ceding independence to the colonies. Within Portugal, the MFA favored a generally progressive agenda: its economic policies opposed the control of corporate monopolies and, to some extent, questioned the rule of capital, and its political positions were, in general, critical of the role of established political parties, favoring instead mass democratic participation.[1]

Due to its anomalous role and the power it wielded in the revolutionary period, the MFA—and especially its charismatic leader Otelo Saraiva de Carvalho, known simply as Otelo—was the focus of attention within the country and among the many journalists and political observers from abroad.[2] And yet the most exciting innovations of the revolution arose from below, from the movements characterized as promoting "popular power," a term employed earlier in both Chile's revolutionary period (Chapter 5) and the liberation struggles of Portugal's African colonies (Chapter 2).[3] The most distinctive aspect of popular power movements in Portugal is the way they were able to invent novel institutional forms—various types of commissions—that implemented the goals of revolutionary democracy and anticapitalism. But, really, rather than talking about democracy and anticapitalism in the abstract, it is more accurate to focus on the ways the movements confronted the immediate problems facing them in very practical terms (and, for better or for worse, with little theoretical elaboration): first, their experimentations with participatory governance and decision-making; second, their efforts to distribute and use social wealth outside of the regime of private property.[4]

Portugal may seem like an unlikely site for such experiments given its social and political conditions in the mid-1970s. Not only was it the poorest country in Western Europe, but also, as I said, had suffered for decades under a fascist regime. And yet, immediately following the coup, there was an explosion of creative, democratic action that aimed not at a "democratic transition" to join the liberal, capitalist norms of the dominant European countries but rather to go well beyond that. Portugal's popular power movements managed to distill the aspirations for democracy and access to the common that were expressed by a range of movements throughout the world in this period—and, to a certain degree, realize those aspirations in new institutions.

To orient those unfamiliar with the events, it is useful, simplifying greatly the historical developments, to divide the revolutionary process into two great phases defined by successful and failed coups, the dates of which were constantly repeated during the period like mantras. (The constant threat of coups, real and imagined, is, indeed, another reason for the prominence of the military in analyses of the period.)

April 24, 1974: the successful coup led by the MFA that toppled the fascist Estado Novo regime. Revolutionary advances in the first period, from April 24, 1974, to March 11, 1975, were relatively moderate: some of the most brutal institutions of the fascist regime, such as the secret police, were dismantled; the colonial armies were decommissioned and steps taken toward colonial independence; and the popular power movements made widespread local advances in factories, land occupations, and housing occupations, though without much coordination among them.

March 11, 1975: the failed right-wing counterrevolutionary coup led by General Antonio de Spinola. The second period, from March 11 to November 25, was much more radical than the first: the MFA formed a Revolutionary Council with executive powers to nationalize banks, insurance companies, and some key industries, and the popular power movements became more militant and better organized, accelerating the occupations. By the summer and fall of 1975, the commissions, sometimes in alliance with the MFA, had created conditions approaching a situation of dual power, acting especially in local contexts as a parallel governance structures.

November 25, 1975: an unsuccessful coup attempt by paratroopers linked to the Communist Party. This was followed immediately by a successful right-wing coup that effectively put an end to the revolutionary process.

Commission Democracy

The basic organizational unit of the popular power movement was the commission, an institutional structure designed for democratic deliberation and decision-making that was key to the grassroots, participatory character of the movement.[5] After the overthrow of the fascist regime "a vast ocean of representative commissions emerged that were elected in assembly processes, with very varied forms and norms, but that addressed the legitimacy of direct action and the need for responsible and agile structures of direction and representation" (Pérez Suárez 2020, 207). Commissions structured each of the three primary streams of the popular power movement: workers' commissions, which occupied factories and initiated worker self-management; residents' or neighborhood commissions (comissãoes de moradores), which occupied empty houses and improved neighborhood infrastructures; and rural commissions, which conducted land occupations and organized worker-run farms.[6]

The commissions functioned by simple democratic principles. Residents' commissions were typically born, for instance, when a general assembly of the neighborhood was called to confront local issues, most notably housing problems, but also the need for child- and eldercare, lack of infrastructure, or abusive city regulations. During an initial assembly a list of demands would be formulated and a commission elected (Downs 1983, 155–156; Pérez, cited in Varela 2019, 130). The commission then met each week or every other week, and within the commission were established working groups on specific issues. The same basic structure animated the workers' commissions and the rural commissions. These commissions also had a spiraling effect of increased politicization, so that as more people participated, more commissions were formed. It is estimated that between May and October 1974 four thousand workers' commissions were established, "one in virtually every workplace" (Robinson 2011, 264). The key was the direct participation of all in decision-making and, when power had to be delegated, the constant responsibility of representatives to the represented.

The nature of and relation among commissions evolved over the course of the revolutionary period. In general terms, as the revolution developed, commissions began to link together in networks to create coordinating institutions and thus more extensive bases of power. These larger institutions operated across two axes. First, they were able to expand by bringing together committees focused on the same social problem or field in different parts of the city or country. The Revolutionary Council of Porto Residents, for example, which formed in June 1975, included delegates from most of the residents' commissions in the city and, in that way, posed an institutional means of scaling up. The Revolutionary Council was able to act on the demands of the residents' commissions and contest decisions made by the city government. Second, commissions expanded their range by organizing together with other types of commissions: residents' commissions, for instance, with workers' commissions and soldiers' commissions. A coordinating institution created in September 1975 in Setúbal, an industrial center near Lisbon, brought together commissions along both axes. The secretariat of the struggle committee (*comité de luta*) in Setúbal was composed of six delegates from workers' commissions, four from residents' commissions, and five from soldiers' commissions. The *comité de luta* operated sometimes in collaboration with city government and sometimes autonomously (Downs 1983, 171–173; 1989, 58–62; Varela 2019, 231–233).[7]

Some observers of these democratic experiments in Portugal were convinced that the popular power movements were merely spontaneous, that they refused organization and institution, and that this lack was a central factor in the failure of the revolution. Paul Thibaud, for example, writing from France, blamed "the absence of formal structures" in the popular power movement: "This testifies to a persistent lack of institutional reflection and practice, failing which liberatory movements are doomed either to 'succeed' in a totalitarian, that is to say perverse, manner, or else to fade away" (1976, 334). Thibaud was mistaken, however, to think the popular power movement was structureless or lacking in institutional practices. It is true that the movement had no recognizable leaders, at least ones that were known beyond the local scale.[8] It is also true that the movement did not begin with institutional structures already in place, nor did it borrow ready-made institutional forms from elsewhere. Instead, popular power was an institutionalizing movement, which is to say that it invented structures as it went along. The formation and development of commissions was clearly an institutional project—an experimentation with novel organizational forms beginning at the local level and working progressively toward larger scales to create organizations that were more democratic and more open to participation than the existing ones.

Closer to the mark are those who questioned whether the commissions, even coordinated together in citywide structures, could achieve a scale large and powerful enough to sustain the revolutionary process and defend against reactionary forces. "If the dream was to become reality," Phil Mailer asserts, "self-mobilisation on an enormous scale would have to be undertaken and certain new institutions created. Throughout the whole of the Portuguese revolution this was to remain the biggest problem of all. And it was to remain unsolved" (1977, 298). Perhaps with more time coordinating committees, like the Setúbal *comité de luta*, could have achieved a larger, national scale. But the time of the revolutionary process was brief.

The end of the revolutionary process did not entirely put an end to the democratizing political role of commissions. In March 1976, for example, four months after the revolution had drawn to a close, a *comissão de moradores* in Ferrel, north of Lisbon, initiated a protest against the construction of a nuclear power plant near the town and set up a special *comissão de apoio à luta contra a ameaça nuclear* (commission to support the fight against the nuclear threat). The protest at Ferrel corresponded with a wave of movements in the mid-seventies in Europe and North America to block construction of nuclear power plants, including those at Wyhl, Germany, Malville, France, and Seabrook, New Hampshire. Stefania Barca and Ana Delicado claim that the "most important driver [in this Portuguese antinuclear protest] was the struggle over the democratization of public decision-making," which drew on the experiences of the revolutionary period (2016, 520). We will see in Chapter 14 that the other antinuclear movements were also focused on democratization and participatory decision-making, although the Portuguese movements rested on a particularly solid foundation after the development of commissions in the revolutionary period.

Making Private Property Common

The actions of all three streams of commissions—workers' commissions, neighborhood commissions, and rural commissions—challenged the rule of private property in a fundamental way: factories, houses, and land were occupied and in many cases managed collectively. These actions were largely autonomous, independent of outside forces. The political parties, including the Communist Party, had little part in the occupations, and most parties opposed them. Correspondingly, as in the construction of the democratic framework of the commissions, the appropriation of private property was advanced with few theoretical pronouncements or references to historical models. Instead of general calls for the abolition of private property, for instance, private property was simply recognized in each local instance as an obstacle to social well-being and an injustice to be overcome. Only when one takes a step back to see the whole set of actions across the country and in the different social domains does a pattern emerge of a coherent project to transform private property into shared and collectively managed common wealth.

The decision to occupy factories, for instance, appeared to workers' commissions as an immediate necessity, most often when confronting a business closure. Remember that the Portuguese revolution took place in the midst of a global economic recession and just a year after OPEC initiated its oil embargo. Furthermore, immediately following the fall of the fascist regime, there was an extraordinary wave of strikes, which built on a trend of labor militancy that had been growing during the last years of the dictatorship.[9] Such conditions led numerous businesses in Portugal, many of them foreign-owned, to close. Instead of accepting the closures and thus unemployment, however, workers decided to occupy factories and manage production themselves.

One highly publicized occupation took place at a factory in Montijo, near Lisbon, owned by Sogantal, a French sportswear manufacturer, at which forty-eight women were employed to sew precut pieces of jogging suits. After the company refused worker demands for a wage increase, a one-month paid vacation, and a thirteenth-month bonus, the workers conducted a slowdown strike. When Sogantal responded by closing the factory in April 1974, the workers refused to leave and continued production in the self-managed plant with the existing stores of materials (Hammond 1988, 82–83; de Sousa and Palla 1975). Similar circumstances were repeated throughout the country in businesses large and small. By 1975 there were 975 businesses in Portugal that had been occupied and were self-managed by workers (Varela 2019, 215).[10]

The residents' commissions and their housing occupations were, like the factory occupations, direct, pragmatic responses to immediate needs, and of all the organizations on the Far Left, according to Hammond, the residents' commissions had the most clearly expressed ideological vision (1985, 212). In 1974 almost 30 percent of Portuguese families lacked minimally decent housing (Downs 1983, 153). Widespread slogans at the time declared, quite sensibly, that no one should remain unhoused as long as there are empty houses. At first, the occupations targeted vacant dwellings in public housing projects that were either unfinished or held empty because of corrupt systems of distribution, but later empty private housing was also occupied. Actions of the residents' commissions also extended beyond occupations of existing structures. Some of their achievements included construction of new public housing, reduction of rent, prevention of evictions, and provision of childcare. Furthermore, many commissions took a more radical path in the second phase of the revolutionary period, after the failed right-wing coup: "The movement split after March 11 [1975]," writes Boaventura de Sousa Santos, "into those residents' commissions that chose the path of democratic legality . . . and the revolutionary residents' commissions" (1982, 277). Eventually, the most radical and best-organized residents' commissions took on the role of both coordinating occupations and distributing the houses to those most in need. As I said earlier, by summer and fall 1975, revolutionary residents' commissions were creating coordinated institutions, constituting councils, and committees at the city level.

In rural areas, especially Alentejo, in the south of Portugal, where the latifundia system maintained landholdings in large estates, commissions of landless workers occupied the land and self-organized agricultural production. The occupations were begun by day laborers but eventually involved a wide range of agricultural workers. In rural Portugal, where poverty and unemployment were endemic, the problem of "surplus population" was exacerbated in this period in part by the end of the colonial regimes, due to the return from Africa of demobilized soldiers and colonists, and also by the global economic recession, which forced the return home of large numbers of Portuguese workers who had migrated to both Portuguese cities and other European countries (Bermeo 1986, 62–63). Although the government debated land reform and eventually implemented a limited form of it, the commissions took direct action immediately, occupying and cultivating land, as well as occupying vacant housing, in some cases the houses of wealthy absentee landowners.

The rural commissions appropriated property to meet the needs of the poor, as did the worker commissions and the residents' commissions. In the countryside, too, there was little theorizing of these actions, but rather direct, pragmatic action by the poor themselves. The film director Thomas Harlan, whose 1975 documentary *Torre Bela* followed the course of one rural occupation, recounts how hesitant the occupiers were when they first took control of a landowner's villa: "In the beginning they looked like birds that had inadvertently entered into a house. First, they walked close to the walls and it was only later that they ventured toward the center of the rooms." What is striking about Harlan's poetic description is that although the poor are so unused to the luxury of such a dwelling, they soon find ways together to make use of it.

It is easy to see, especially when looking at the actions of the three streams of commissions together, that they all attacked or undermined the bases of private property, even when this was not part of their rhetoric. They took property—a factory, a field, or a dwelling—and put it to use, regardless of the wishes of its owner. "None of these measures, taken individually, challenged the capitalist foundations of society or the class nature of state power," maintains Santos, referring to the broad set of developments after March 1975 of which the occupations were a central part. "However, all these measures taken together . . . did indeed bring about a revolutionary crisis" (1982, 264). The effect of the commissions should be considered like a swarm. Although each occupation was so particular and local that it did not raise the broader issue of the rule of private property, the entire set of them, like a swarm of termites, was effectively eating away its foundations.

The popular power movement, as I said, was more pragmatic than theoretical. Indeed, no renowned intellectual, Portuguese or foreign, was put forward by the movement. Alfredo Margarido, the Portuguese poet and essayist, observing the revolution from Paris, lamented that the popular power movement was doomed by the fact that it "never put forward the necessary theorists" and never produced adequate theoretical work (1980, 181). In my view, one should focus instead on the strong theoretical propositions that were already inherent or incarnated in the actions of the commissions. Contra the rule of private property, they asserted a theory of needs, equality, and common use. In response to the fact that people were landless and un-housed, poor and deprived, social wealth was made common. Resources were appropriated and put in the hands of those in need. The occupations thus set in motion a kind of leveling of the most extreme social inequalities, distributing resources more equitably, in response to people's needs. And all of this was organized through democratic participation and managed autonomously.

Popular Power Movements Between the Military and the Parties

The role and importance of the popular power movement has often been ignored or misconstrued—especially by observers outside the country—because of assumptions that either the political parties or the military was in some way guiding the revolutionary process. Henry Kissinger, for instance, then US secretary of state, and those like him who could only see the revolution through a cold war lens, was obsessed with the Portuguese Communist Party (PCP). Because Kissinger considered the PCP to be the only effective organized political force in the country, the party was for him the primary threat (Del Pero 2011, 631). In fact, Kissinger seemed able to understand the Portuguese situation only as a repetition of the Bolshevik Revolution: when Mário Soares, then leader of the Socialist Party, suggested to Kissinger that he was overestimating the power of the PCP, Kissinger responded, rather comically, "I believe you are naive . . . you are a Kerensky," as if Soares were unwittingly paving the way for a Bolshevik takeover (Del Pero 2011, 630).

The PCP did have great prestige at the time of the revolution, especially among the lower classes, in part because of its courageous decades-long op-position to the fascist regime, but the party did not favor the popular power movements, both because of the participatory democratic structures of the commissions and because of their illegal actions against the rule of private property. The PCP warned that occupations would simply provoke right-wing forces and provide an excuse for a fascist reaction. More generally, the PCP maintained that the time was not ripe for anticapitalist revolutionary agitation since Portugal was in a phase of "democratic national revolution," prior to the construction of socialism (Pérez Suárez 2020, 207). During the course of the revolutionary process, the PCP was undoubtedly close to some currents of the popular power movement, especially workers' commissions, but this relation was often ambiguous and at times merely an effort to achieve hegemony over them. "It was a contradiction of the PCP's practice in 1974 and 1975," Hammond maintained, "that it strove to contain initiatives of popular struggle when those initiatives were essential for every decisive advance of the revolutionary process" (1980, 159). Most important, however, is the fact that the land, housing, and factory occupations along with the self-management arrangements—all the different facets of the popular power movement—were autonomous, without direction from any outside forces.[11]

The relation between popular power movements and the military is more complex. Throughout the revolutionary process, the MFA, or a significant segment of it, served as a key ally for the commissions and the other progressive forces that demanded popular power. This was an odd couple for obvious reasons, most notably the fact that military organizations generally maintain centralized authority and hierarchy whereas the commissions sought to extend equal democratic participation as far as possible. This contrast may not be as extreme as it first seems, since elements of the MFA during revolutionary process attempted to put in question established military hierarchy: the initial coup was made, after all, by midlevel officers (notably captains) against the generals who were loyal to fascism; and during the revolutionary process some soldiers organized commissions to bring democratic elements to the barracks. There remained a gulf, nonetheless, between the popular power movements and the military, which certainly contributed a constant tension to their alliance.

There is no need to question the progressive nature of the political views of the MFA and Otelo, its most powerful leader, or to doubt the sincerity of their alliance with the popular power movements.[12] It is important, nonetheless, to keep in mind that the alignment of the objectives of the MFA and the popular movements was only partial. The MFA proclaimed its intention, for instance, to destroy "fascist state power," and, indeed, many of the most overtly fascist aspects of the state, such as the special police, political prisons, and paramilitary militias, were dismantled, but the "state apparatus was otherwise kept intact, with its fifty-year heritage of authoritarian ideology, recruitment, training, and practice" (Santos 1982, 264). The schemes of participatory governance established by the commissions obviously pushed toward a much more extensive transformation. Similarly, the MFA's challenge to the power of monopolies was not, in general, anticapitalist, whereas the occupations directly challenged the rule of private property. One might say that the MFA and the movements were most securely aligned with respect to their enemies. Most notably, of course, they were united in their opposition to the forces seeking a return to fascism (among the military, the political class, and the capitalist class at home and abroad), but they were often also allied in efforts to achieve local political goals by sidelining the primary political parties as well as the municipal and national bureaucracies (d'Arthuys and Gros 1976, 39; Ramos Pinto 2008, 1034). A tactical alliance held them together.

The popular power movement, then, must be recognized as a political actor in its own right. Not only did it arise autonomously—not the product of the PCP or the MFA—but also, even when acting in alliance with those groups, it maintained its own specific political character. Moreover, even though the popular power movement may not have been the most powerful in the balance of political forces, it was the source of the most significant political innovations, whereas the political parties generally followed standard political scripts.

Specter of a Lisbon Commune

When evaluating the Portuguese Revolution and especially the role in it of popular power, therefore, it is important to identify the political innovations that, although in some respects specific to the Portuguese experience, resonate with the desires and actions of other revolutionary movements of the period. First, one should not judge the popular movement with respect to winning state power in standard terms. Paul Sweezy, for example, after having visited Portugal in 1975, viewed the political agenda in a way that discounted the achievements of the commissions and the popular power movement. "The all-important problem now," he claimed, "is the location and wielding of political power, and unless or until this is resolved nothing much else is likely to be decided" (1975, 2). From such a traditional conception of the contest for power, including the internal dynamics of state politics, the popular power movement appeared insignificant. It did not field candidates in elections and certainly did not develop the means to take state power by force. It did not even promote any recognizable leaders to speak for it.

The revolutionary potential of the popular power movement as a whole— including the various commissions, the occupations, and the projects of self-managed production—is best recognized as a process constructing the prerequisites for a situation of dual power. This is a matter not of creating a rival, second power homologous to the state but rather of developing an alternative mode of social organization and governance. The revolutionary potential of the popular power movement, then, was not to win the battle for political power and take control of the state apparatus as it currently exists, but to transform radically the apparatuses of the governance of social life through the creation of new institutional forms.

The commissions experimented with alternative democratic institutions in a wide range of aspects of social life, at small scales initially but progressively at larger ones. Some participatory commissions, as I said, decided how to organize production in factories, some managed who could live in a house, others determined who would work the land and how, and yet others decided how to organize childcare and eldercare in the neighborhood. Resident commissions even established popular judicial systems to adjudicate rent and property disputes (Santos 1982, 261–262). And the principle of each commission was that those who are directly involved—the workers in the factory, the residents in the neighborhood, the cultivators on the land—should make decisions and manage wealth democratically. Each occupation and each commission might be thought of as a micro-counterpower, standing separate from and in opposition to the state and capital. When different types of commissions started coordinating together throughout a city, however, as in the Setúbal *comité de luta*, they began to suggest the possibility of a situation of dual power.

Reasoning along these lines, Santos laments that the various components of the popular power movement "could aim no further than the creation of pockets of dual power." Furthermore, since the state, too, was unable to control political developments, Santos concludes, "This was less a situation of dual power than a situation of dual powerlessness" (1982, 265–266; see also Santos 1979, 156–160). Santos is undoubtedly right that a situation of dual power was not achieved, but it is worth noting that there circulated in the final months of the revolution something like the specter of it. In November 1975, right-wing forces spread rumors of the formation of a "Lisbon Commune," which would have been, presumably, an institutionalized coordination of the commissions into something like the Paris Commune, capable of casting out the bourgeoisie and its state. It is unclear whether the right-wing propagandists believed this was an imminent threat or merely used it as a scare tactic, but the simple fact that it was a plausible fear is testament to how advanced were the developments toward a dual power situation (Mailer 1977, 331). In any case, if one is to evaluate the extent to which the weakness or failures of the popular power movement led to their defeat, their ability to construct the prerequisites of dual power should be the measure.

The Revolution's Achievements

The revolutionary process can also be evaluated, not according to whether it was in the end victorious but on the power of its primary innovations, which can be summarized by its having forged an alternative path of revolution in two respects, with respect to democracy and property, both of which countered the established tenets of existing state socialism.[13] First, whereas the dominant notion of socialist transition and the vision of socialist society mandated centralized decision-making in the party and taking control of the state apparatus, the popular power movement presented in practice a revolutionary process of power distributed in the participatory structures of the commissions that, once coordinated together at a sufficiently large scale, posed the potential of a form of governance alternative to the existing state apparatus. The geometry and topography of the two paths are clearly distinguished: organization from above versus from below, and power emanating from the center versus power articulating from the local. Moreover, the second path, which the popular power movement forged, offers a concept and practice of democracy that is radically different from that offered not only by the socialist states but also by the liberal capitalist order.

Second, whereas the dominant model of state socialism aims at the abolition of private property in order to concentrate property in the hands of the state, the popular power movement took resources such as land, housing, and factories out of the realm of property and made them common. Standard property conceptions recognize only two possibilities, either private property or public property. Through the popular power occupations, schemes of self-management, and democratic decision-making structures in Portugal, however, like in the *tomas* in the Chilean Revolution, social wealth was made into something different from property, neither public nor private. Decisions were to be made democratically by those who used the resources: housing plans should be made by residents' commissions; factory production should be organized by workers' commissions; land use should be determined and cultivation decisions should be made by rural commissions; and so forth. This second divergence from state socialist models overlaps substantially with the first, of course, since public property (along with private property, too) requires centralized decision-making structures, whereas construction of the common relies on democratic governance and self-management of wealth.

What most stands out in the Portuguese experience is the development of new institutions that facilitate greater participation in decision-making. Popular power was not spontaneous or structureless. On the contrary, Portugal's commissions not only constituted effective means for participation in specific local sites, for factory and agricultural workers and for urban and rural residents, but also posed the basis for scaling up to the municipal and national levels. These processes of innovation were cut short after a year and a half, without realizing their aspirations, but they opened a new path toward revolutionary democracy for others to follow.

7

Promise of Another Democracy

> On the fifth day of the uprising the joy of triumph and liberation
> spread across the whole city like a sunrise. . . . For the first time since
> the peasant rebellion of 1894, the people had seized a region and
> were ready to forge a new order on their own.
>
> —Lee Jai-eui

Numerous protest movements emerged in South Korea in the 1970s despite the country's brutal authoritarian regime. The movements were significant, according to the standard narrative, insofar as they inspired and
laid the groundwork for later democratization movements, culminating
in the 1987 June Democratic Struggle that instituted practices of liberal
democracy approximating those of the dominant countries in Europe and
North America.

Although the 1980 uprising in Kwangju, a midsized city near the southern
tip of the peninsula, may at first sight seem to fit neatly as a stepping-stone
in this historical development from dictatorship to democracy, on closer
inspection it does not because the forms of participatory democracy it
instituted, however briefly, have little to do with the kind of democratization that took place at the end of the 1980s. The Kwangju uprising remains a
touchstone in national memory and a powerful point of reference for subsequent movements, in fact, because the autonomous organization of participatory governance during the five days when the people controlled the city
alluded to a new political form well beyond the standard liberal models. The
uprising continues to serve as a beacon, in other words, insofar as it held out
the promise that another democracy is possible.

The South Korean political situation of the 1970s, dominated by President
Park Chung-hee's authoritarian regime, provided few openings for democratization of any sort. In 1969, while serving his second term as president, Park
pushed through a constitutional amendment to remove term limits, allowing
him to run for a third term. Then, in fall 1972, facing growing protests and

troubled by a narrow electoral victory the previous year, Park consolidated power by dissolving the National Assembly and drafting a new constitution. The Yushin (revitalization) system, which this constitution put in place, formalized the authoritarian regime that lasted throughout the decade. By 1979, however, the Park government was in grave crisis on economic, political, and social fronts. In a bizarre series of events, on October 26 of that year, during an argument over dinner, the chief of the Korean Central Intelligence Agency shot and killed President Park, briefly elevating the prime minister, Choi Kyu-ha, to the presidency; Choi was then deposed on December 12 by a military coup led by General Chun Doo-hwan. The downfall of Park, then, did not lead to a more democratic political system, as many had hoped. Instead, the country passed quickly from civil authoritarian regime to military dictatorship, all with the sometimes tacit, sometimes explicit approval of the US government under Jimmy Carter.[1]

Protests against the newly formed military dictatorship built on the antiauthoritarian struggles that had developed throughout the 1970s.[2] Students took the lead: on May 15, 1980, 150,000 students demonstrated in the streets of Seoul, but activism quieted in the following days throughout the country, except in Kwangju.

Citizens Battle the Military

The first stage of the uprising was initiated on May 18 when Kwangju students gathered outside the main gate of the university, which, like all universities in the country, had been closed under martial law. An elite force of paratroopers was deployed, and it battled the students for two days. The brutality of repression shocked Kwangju residents and inspired others to join the fight, transforming the social composition of the uprising. A second stage began when "the torch of the uprising was passed from the students to the ordinary working people of Kwangju" (Lee 1999, 56). Street demonstrations on May 20 brought out an extraordinarily large percentage of the city's population: 200,000 demonstrators in a city of just 700,000 inhabitants (Katsiaficas 2006b, 5). The Kwangju residents armed themselves, raiding police stations and commandeering vehicles, in order to form a popular militia. Miraculously, they managed to drive out the military forces. Thus followed a third stage in which for five days, relatively free of the military dictatorship and its martial law, the inhabitants ruled the city autonomously, even though they had continually to fight skirmishes at the city outskirts and guard against government spies and provocateurs. The peace, however, did not last long. On May 27, just twelve days after the uprising began, the military returned with tanks and heavy weaponry for a massacre, leaving hundreds dead and thousands injured.[3]

The story of the uprising is thus a heroic tale of normal residents willing to stand up to an unjust, repressive regime and, in pursuit of a noble cause, risk their lives against extraordinary odds. But the valiant exploits to counter the military and the dictatorship, which occupy center stage, are really only the shell. The real kernel of the Kwangju uprising is not military and antiauthoritarian but political and democratic, and thus contained entirely in the third phase, when Kwangju residents experimented with self-rule. There lies the most innovative aspect of the uprising.

Competing Forms of Democracy

In the first days after the military retreated from the city, the dominant ruling body was the Citizen Settlement Committee, composed of local elites—religious leaders, professors, lawyers, and the like—selected by the vice governor. This committee attempted to negotiate with the national government, making modest demands. It proposed, for instance, that residents would put down their arms if the government would promise no reprisals and admit that the military used excessive force (Lee 1999, 104). But this committee of city elites was politically out of step with the population. A Student Settlement Committee, which had closer ties to the population, was formed, and subsequently the two settlement committees merged, but the combined committee was stymied by internal debates and still had little support among the population (Lee 1999, 107–116). With respect to these committees, then, to say that Kwangju, free of the ruling dictatorship, was democratic would mean conceiving democracy as a system of representation that maintains centralized control, specifically regarding the appointed leaders and elites that composed the committees. And this democracy proved to be ineffective at engaging and mobilizing the population.

But there was another democracy at work in Kwangju. As the role of settlement committees declined, there rose, in inverse relation, open and participatory democratic structures. Many accounts emphasize how the residents themselves quickly organized local committees to ensure functioning of city services and infrastructures, including transportation, health services, and the like. The residents shared food and water, and collectively tended to the wounded and the dead (Katsiaficas 2006b, 7; Shorrock 2015; Shin 2003, xvii). These collective efforts to maintain social reproduction were supported by newly formed political structures. On May 22, for example, people converged around the fountain in front of Province Hall and conducted something like a general assembly. "All walks and classes of people spoke," recounts Lee Jae-eui, one of the participants, "women street vendors, elementary school teachers, followers of different religions, housewives, college students, high school students, and farmers" (Lee 1999, 105). As the rallies and assemblies continued each day, the participants together made their own decisions, often condemning the settlement committees, and affirmed their desire to fight on. This tendency toward democratic participation, however, was obviously only in its infancy when the army began the massacre.

One should be cautious about drawing conclusions from such a brief period of autonomy in which the enemy's overwhelming military force was an imminent threat. It does appear, nonetheless, that two competing notions of democracy were in play in liberated Kwangju, a representative form that concentrated decision-making in ruling committees and a participatory form that through assemblies and rallies opened the decision-making process to a larger portion of the population. It also appears that during the five days of self-governance there emerged a tendency to move from representative to participatory structures. Given the relations of force at the time, of course, neither form of democracy (or any other political structure) could have saved Kwangju residents from the superior might of the military. The alternative and the tendency toward participation are important, nonetheless, as indications of the political desires of Kwangju residents at the time and those of subsequent generations of Koreans that celebrate the event.

The Kwangju Commune

Given the extreme brevity of the uprising, and even more so the period of self-governance, it is surprising it plays such a significant role in national memory. Honoring the dead and celebrating the heroic struggle against the military and the dictatorship are certainly important, but the new political forms created in the struggle are also a focus of commemoration. Jung-woon

Choi sees in the five-day occupation, for example, the creation of a new form of community. When the city was freed from the dictatorship, he claims, the residents formed "not a traditional community but rather an absolute community. This community was not formed because some leader seized a microphone and began to incite the masses. . . . Instead, the absolute community was formed by citizens who autonomously overcame their fears, risked their lives in struggle, and came together freely to reaffirm and celebrate their humanity, their true citizenship" (2003, 6). If one sets aside the mystical overtones of Choi's language, the new community he refers to is best exemplified, it seems to me, by the participatory assemblies, along with the autonomous collective organization of urban transport and infrastructure.

George Katsiaficas, too, claims that the uprising created a new form of community, but he presents the argument in more directly political terms, comparing the Kwangju Uprising to the Paris Commune of 1871. The two events, he maintains, demonstrated "the spontaneous ability of hundreds of thousands of ordinary people to govern themselves." "In both cities," he continues, "an unarmed citizenry, in opposition to their own governments, effectively gained control of urban space despite the presence of well-armed military forces seeking to reestablish 'law and order'; hundreds of thousands of people created popular organs of political power that effectively and efficiently replaced traditional forms of government; crime rates plummeted during the period of liberation; and people felt previously unexperienced forms of kinship with each other" (2006a, 184). The comparison with the Paris Commune is not out of place, he claims, because many Kwangju participants reported they had been part of study groups that read about the commune in the period prior to the uprising. In fact, Tim Shorrock (2015) reports that today many Koreans, especially Kwangju residents, take for granted the connection between the two events. "The idea of the 'Gwangju Commune' is so popular," he maintains, "that the city also gave an honorary citizenship to George Katsiaficas" in recognition of his writing on the uprising." The most important aspect of these comparisons to Paris, it seems to me, is the desire it reveals among Koreans for a democracy defined by participatory structures.

The significance of the Kwangju uprising becomes clearer, I think, when it is situated not beside nineteenth-century examples but among other democratic experiments of the 1970s. In Chile and Portugal, too, as I argued in previous chapters, the movements sought to create participatory democratic forms, although they had the relative luxury of time to develop. The revolutionary process lasted three years in Chile and eighteen months in Portugal. That time allowed the popular power movements to construct effective new institutional forms of political participation in workplaces, in urban neighborhoods, and in rural neighborhoods. Even with years to develop, however, those democratic political experiments were cut short when the revolutions were defeated. The Kwangju experience also resonates with the Fatsa Commune, a democratic experiment in Turkey from October 1979 to July 1980 (see Chapter 17). Like in Kwangju, Fatsa's attempt to institute new democratic forms took place in a situation of constant threat from the national military (along with fascist groups). Perhaps Kwangju, if given time, would have come to resemble revolutionary Santiago or Lisbon, with a wealth of participatory political institutions. What the Kwangju uprising most shares with these other examples, then, is the expression of a mass desire for a new democracy grounded in participatory mechanisms, a desire that circulated across national boundaries throughout the seventies.

PART III
REVOLUTION INSIDE AND OUTSIDE THE FACTORIES

8

Ungovernable Factories

> It is this new and changing working class that was the basis for the
> new level of wildcat strikes, for a doubled rate of absenteeism, for an
> increased amount of violence in plants where guns are often openly
> carried. It is a new working class that no conceivable contract settle-
> ment can control or immobilize.
>
> —Martin Glaberman

In the 1970s, according to the standard narrative, the US working class and
its unions suffered a devastating tragedy. In the course of that decade, amid
economic crises and stagflation, US business and political elites transformed
the economy, traded factories for finance and services, initiated an exodus
of manufacturing jobs to other parts of the world, and thereby sent into
steep decline the power and membership numbers of trade unions. The US
working class—and the US Left more generally—is still today mourning, the
story goes, the loss of factory jobs and the waning of the industrial unions.
The experiences of radical workers in the seventies, however, complicate any
rosy view of a past with good factory jobs and strong union leadership, because the early seventies was a season of extraordinarily intense rank-and-
file insurgency directed precisely against factory jobs and union leadership.
These workers often saw the dominant unions as acting in concert with ownership and thus as an antagonist, not an ally. They were not against labor
organizing, of course, but instead advocated more democratic worker organizations and sought more control of the industrial production process.

Karl-Heinz Roth, writing on radical German workers in this period, defined the "other" workers' movement (*die "andere" Arbeiterbewegung*), which
flourished in many countries in the 1970s, in terms of worker militancy that
refuses the dictates of not only management but also traditional unions
(1974). Whereas the official workers' movement primarily makes economic
demands for wages and benefits, the other workers' movement makes political demands to transform power relations within the factory and, at times,
in society as a whole. Although the official movement, then, served as a

stable, reliable partner with business management and ownership, the other was subversive and unruly.

Seen in this light, radical US industrial workers in the 1970s, the other workers' movement, succeeded in forcing the capitalist regime to retreat. While asserting their independence from the official unions, they were able to threaten the structures of factory discipline and control so deeply that they jeopardized the governability of the entire factory system, forcing economic and political leaders to embark on a profound restructuring of the capitalist system in order to undermine the power of organized industrial workers. This accomplishment, however, did not allow them to realize their goals of greater democracy and control both inside and outside the factory. In general, in fact, the radical US industrial workers were unprepared to further their project on the new terrain resulting from capitalist restructuring. They were unable to discover a new orientation for class struggle in which industrial workers were no longer the central protagonist or to find the means to articulate effectively with other liberation movements, which confronted structures of domination on the basis of race, gender, and sexuality. In subsequent chapters, I will analyze how such strategies of articulation were pursued more effectively in the context of other liberation movements. This 1970s cycle of industrial worker struggles in the United States was defeated, then, but it was not a failure. Rather, it was a project well begun that has yet to be completed.

How Industrial Crisis Became Political Crisis

In the early 1970s, the US industrial working class was the most prominent segment of the national labor force, and internationally it enjoyed a preeminent position, with labor movements in other countries looking to it for guidance and inspiration. The number of industrial strikes and the intensity of industrial conflict in the first years of the decade were among the highest of any period in US history. "In 1970 alone," Jefferson Cowie reports, "there were over 2.4 million workers engaged in large-scale work stoppages, thirty-four massive stoppages of ten thousand workers or more, and a raft of wildcats, slowdowns, and aggressive stands in contract negotiations" (2010, 2). More important than the number of strikes, moreover, was the nature of their demands. "More and more workers," Martin Glaberman claimed in

1972, with respect to the Detroit auto industry, "are refusing to accept factory discipline" (1972, 88). Young workers, in particular, who had not become habituated to the way the dominant unions accommodated management demands, were increasingly unwilling to accept the petty despotisms of the workplace and obey the dictates of foremen and supervisors.

A 1972 strike at the Lordstown General Motors (GM) assembly plant in rural Ohio, fifteen miles from Youngstown, which was closely watched nationally and internationally, highlighted the changing composition of the industrial working class and the ways it had incorporated aspects of the powerful social movements of the times. At Lordstown, GM boasted the fastest and most efficient assembly line in the world, which allowed the company to reduce the workforce and lay off workers. Management celebrated the innovation as a solution to the industry's problems with low productivity and profits. Workers at Lordstown, however, who were younger than at most plants—the average age was just twenty-five—did not accept these developments passively. In part because of their youth, the Lordstown workers were relatively inexperienced in union politics, which management may have thought to be an advantage, but they also represented a cultural shift from the previous generation of workers: many of them were Vietnam veterans, and a large number called themselves "hippies," had long hair, took drugs on and off the job, and had a general antiauthoritarian attitude. Management soon discovered that these young workers were unwilling to accept the brutal conditions of the plant. They filed grievances through their union against the layoffs, the speed of the line, and more generally the strict discipline in the plant, but they also expressed their opposition directly through a variety of autonomous tactics, including small-scale sabotage of the automobiles on the assembly line. Management responded by doubling down and intensifying the same disciplinary regime the workers had protested in the first place, leading the workers to vote to strike in March 1972. In contrast to their elders, these young workers, many observers remarked, were not afraid of management, and thus management efforts to impose discipline lost much of its bite. After three weeks on strike, the workers won a modest victory: GM agreed to return the line to the previous speed, rehire the laid-off workers, and enact other relatively minor reforms. Despite the modesty of the victory, Lordstown had a large effect: it was widely covered in the national and international press, and it served as a signal for management and business leaders—and, certainly, for workers at other plants—that rebellious industrial workers were no longer willing to accept company dictates and factory discipline (Aronowitz 1973, 30; Chamayou 2021, 12–13; Cowie 2010, 7–8, 48).

The workers' central demands in many US industrial conflicts in the early 1970s, like Lordstown, were not primarily about wages but rather about work conditions and, more broadly, power relations in the factory—demands that resonated, as I said, with social movements that aimed to change power relations in society as a whole. The refusal of discipline and authoritarian management was complemented by demands for more democratic participation regarding the size of the workforce, the speed of the line, and the regulation of time regarding breaks and the end of the day—in short, power relations in the factory.

Management's deployment of industrial discipline was accompanied by high levels of violence, which had long been an element of the US industrial landscape. One face of this violence was simply the danger of life and work in the factory: in that period, for instance, the National Institute of Occupational Safety and Health estimated sixty-five on-the-job deaths per day in US auto plants, about half of those from heart attacks, in contrast to an average of seventeen US military deaths per day in Vietnam in 1970 (Georgakas and Surkin 1975, 88; National Archives n.d.). Workers in many other industries, the mines in particular, also suffered extraordinary health problems with numerous fatalities. Beyond such "accidents" was another face of industrial violence that was an integral element of the disciplinary structure: direct and deadly attacks against workers, with armed guards at factory entrances, management-hired thugs together with police deployed against striking workers, and a host of other authority figures, including politicians, judges, and priests, all lending ideological and material support. "Repression," claims Cal Winslow, "both by employers and from the state, played a significant role, and striking workers, in particular in the absence of official union support, were often defenseless in the face of violence" (2021). Workers increasingly armed and defended themselves against management violence and its extensive disciplinary regime. "The submerged guerrilla warfare present in the [auto] plants," asserted Linebaugh and Ramirez, "broke out in the open during the summer of '73" (1975, 75). Workers began to challenge the armed disciplinary apparatus with weapons of their own.

The workers' refusal of factory discipline and violence, their political demands regarding power relations in the plant, and the intensity of their revolts led André Gorz in 1972 to proclaim "a crisis of despotism in the

factory" in both Western Europe and North America—not merely an industrial crisis, but a political crisis, a crisis of governance. How long, Gorz asked
rhetorically in an essay published earlier that same year under his pseudonym, Michel Bosquet, can one govern the factory simply using intimida-
tion and repression (Gorz 1976, 58)? The "other" workers' movement was
becoming ungovernable.

Workers Refuse Union Hierarchy and Control

Before investigating further the crisis of governability and how economic
and political elites responded to it, I should highlight the independence of
these workers from the dominant unions, which they saw to be siding predominantly with management. The conflict is difficult to understand based
on standard assumptions regarding the relation between workers and their
unions: for instance, that trade unions are the primary or even sole organ and
agent of workers' struggle; that unions are the direct and adequate representation of the workers' needs, interests, and desires; and that without union
leadership and representation, the workers' movement—even the working
class itself—would cease to exist.[1] The resurgence of the "other" workers'
movement in the early 1970s runs counter to these assumptions: rank-and-
file worker militancy not only bypassed established union structures but also
often attacked them directly. The major unions predominantly joined with
management in counteroffensives against these militant workers. Roth's analysis of the terms of conflict between workers and unions in West Germany
after a wave of industrial wildcat strikes in August 1973 resonates strongly
with the US situation. "In contrast to 1969, in fact," Roth asserts, "there were
no mechanisms of reformist mediation or rising salaries to counteract worker
rebellion. Every step that the workers took in August to affirm their needs
for more life and less work was this time a punch in the face against four
years of cynical and unscrupulous union and business policies that aimed to
take back from the mass industrial workers most of the modest concessions
made in 1969 and 1970. It was thus easy to foresee that the new symptoms
of a brutal union-management counteroffensive like that attempted in ex-
emplary form in the Spring and Summer of 1973 would be reproduced on
a mass scale" (1974, 17). From the standpoint of the official workers' movement and, moreover, based on the assumption that the workers' movement
is unimaginable without the leadership and representation of the traditional

unions, how could the practices and demands of this other workers' movement be anything but a suicidal death drive?

A first step toward understanding the logic and rationale of workers' autonomy in this period is to recognize how resistant the major unions were to reforms to address corruption, unrepresentativeness, and authoritarianism. An extreme example was provided by Tony Boyle's presidency of the United Mine Workers of America (UMWA) and Jock Yablonski's relatively moderate campaign to unseat him. Yablonski's challenge was one of the most prominent campaigns in a wave of union reform efforts across the United States at the time. Rank-and-file miners supported Yablonski, who accused Boyle of dictatorial leadership practices and being deaf to workers' demands for reform, including increased safety in the mines, improved healthcare (especially to prevent and treat black lung disease), and more democracy in the union. In a December 1969 UMWA leadership vote that was widely recognized to have been rigged, however, Boyle won a landslide victory, allowing him to maintain his position, and the reformers had no recourse to contest it. Falsifying election results with impunity is itself convincing evidence of the corruption and the enormous obstacles facing reform efforts, but soon the situation was made even clearer. Boyle and his leadership group, perhaps still feeling threatened, concluded that Yablonski had to be eliminated and sent three assassins to murder him, his wife, and his daughter in their home on December 31, 1969. The brutality of the murders stunned and enraged union members, giving new impetus to the union reform movement at UMWA and other major unions. But this is not a story in which tragedy finally led to radical change. Although reform movements in subsequent years did achieve some limited successes, they did not fundamentally transform union structures. The extreme audacity of the UMWA election manipulation and the savage brutality of the Yablonski murders were symptoms of the dictatorial power and impunity assumed by leadership, to varying degrees, of the dominant unions.[2] The continuing corruption and authoritarianism of unions and their resistance to reform was a founding condition of the other workers' movement.

Another thwarted reform attempt, a challenge within the United Auto Workers (UAW) initiated by Black autoworkers and the Revolutionary Union Movements (RUMs), highlighted the persistent racial hierarchies in the dominant unions. In 1968, one of the founders of the Dodge Revolutionary Union Movement (DRUM), Ron March, campaigned for the position of trustee in UAW Local 3, the local for the Hamtramck assembly plant (formerly Dodge Main), where DRUM was formed. The subordination of Black workers in both the factory and the union was extreme: roughly 60 percent of the workers in the plant were Black, almost all in low-skilled and semiskilled positions, whereas plant management and supervisory positions were virtually all white, and although 30 percent of workers in the UAW were Black, almost none occupied leadership positions (Tripp 1994, 7; Georgakas and Surkin 1975, 32). The racial challenge posed by the Ron March campaign is all the more significant because of the UAW's reputation for support of the civil rights movement and struggles for racial justice in the past. "Although the UAW claimed to be the champion of justice and racial equality," commented Luke Tripp, who was later a member of the executive committee of the League of Revolutionary Black Workers, "its own almost exclusively White executive structure and racist practices betrayed just the opposite" (Tripp 1994, 4). On the first ballot, Ron March received the most votes, which qualified him for the runoff election. As the runoff approached, however, DRUM supporters and campaigners suffered increasing harassment and repression from factory supervisors, union authorities, and the police. DRUM contended, furthermore, that the runoff election was rigged so that the union's preferred candidate would win (Georgakas and Surkin 1975, 40–41; Bird, Lichtman, and Gessner 1970). The measures the UAW deployed, aided by management and the police, to defeat Ron March were further evidence for the workers in the RUMs of the extreme difficulty if not futility of reforming the unions from the inside.

The most militant workers in all industries and in all parts of the country had little hope that such reform efforts could transform their unions enough, and this is the second step to understanding the "other" workers' movement. "It is possible to remove union leaders and replace them," Stanley Aronowitz lamented, "but it is not possible to transcend the institutional constraints of trade unionism itself" (1973, 219). Fundamentally, workers recognized that the purpose of the established unions was not to carry out the will or represent the interests of the workers. The unions did not even really serve to *mediate*—as an independent or objective force—between workers and management. (See the discussion of the "end of mediation" in Chapter 15.) Instead, although the major unions did consistently help workers, usually in the form of wages, benefits, or job security for those with seniority, their real raison d'être was to provide employers with predictable, stable labor relations and a reliable, disciplined labor force (Aronowitz 1973, 219). High wages and job security in exchange for labor docility, bowing to the norms of industrial discipline, was the bargain that defined the mentality of union leaders and structured the dominant unions. However, for workers aiming not merely at higher wages but rather at more democracy and some form of self-management in the workplace, and thus transforming power relations in the factory—in short, for those aspiring to *political* transformations—the union was most often an obstacle, or even an enemy. That explains why radical workers often organized autonomously, without (and sometimes against) the unions.[3]

The number and intensity of wildcat strikes (that is, strikes undertaken by workers without the authorization of their unions) grew rapidly in the early 1970s. They not only were aimed at changing conditions in the factory and the relations of power there but also served as a protest against the traditional unions. A new working class was emerging, which was led by a generation of young, unruly workers unafraid to refuse the disciplinary regime. And, as Glaberman's words quoted in the epigraph to this chapter indicate, the traditional tools available to the unions, such as the contract settlement, had little effect in this domain. Linebaugh and Ramirez extended this point: "Perhaps the most significant development of this period [1973–1974]," they asserted, "is the weakening position of the Union in its mediation of the struggle" (1975, 82). And in these years, the declining position of the official workers' movement was counterbalanced by the rise of the other workers' movements.

All of these rebellious workers who bypassed union control to challenge factory discipline and who even attacked the unions themselves, I should repeat, were by no means opposed to labor organizing; what they rejected was the hierarchical mode of organization of the traditional unions, and what they aspired toward was a new, more democratic mode of labor organizing. Bill Watson, echoing the hopes of many of the participants and allies of this early 1970s wave of worker militancy, foresaw in the workers' invention of a new repertoire of practices, independent of the unions and against the despotism of the factory, the emergence of "a new social form of working class struggle . . . post-unionism" (1971, 84). Class struggle, they maintained, needed new organizational structures.

Black Workers Take the Lead

The autonomous organizational experiments of Black autoworkers played a central role in developments outside the traditional unions. Indeed, any concept of the "other" workers' movement in the United States has to be strongly inflected by race, recognizing the prominent role played by Black workers. The unrepresentativeness and authoritarianism of unions strongly overlaps with their ingrained racist structures. "The exploitation experienced by all workers," claimed Georgakas and Surkin, "was compounded for black workers by the institutional racism which pervaded every aspect of factory life" (1975, 28). For revolutionary Black autoworkers in the late sixties and early seventies, the overlapping and intersecting projects against capitalist domination and racial subordination had to be carried out against both the factory bosses and the union bosses. DRUM and the RUMs at other auto plants in Detroit were thus not aimed only or primarily at reform within the UAW. They were not simply caucuses within the union, in other words, but instead organized workers directly and sought more radical transformations. A generational divide further reinforced this division: unlike older Black workers who felt loyalty to the union due to past labor struggles, David Lewis-Colman maintained, "many younger workers viewed the UAW and auto companies as indistinguishable [and] tended to view the older black UAW activists . . . as part of the labor establishment" (2008, 93). These young workers, unwilling to accept traditional disciplinary regimes and racial hierarchies in either the factory or the union, invented new institutions for struggle.

In June 1969, in order to unite the local RUMs that had developed in the different plants in Detroit into a single political unit, the League of Revolutionary Black Workers was formed as an umbrella organization. The league was not simply a trade union in parallel to the UAW or other unions. It was instead a political organization aimed at antiracist and anticapitalist social transformation with Black industrial workers at its center. In US revolutionary struggle, they asserted, Blacks are the vanguard, and Black workers are the vanguard of the vanguard (Bird, Lichtman, and Gessner 1970, minute 48). The league, in other words, sought to extend the struggle beyond the factory walls and thus shift the project from worker liberation to social liberation, but always with Black industrial workers solidly in the lead, as the central protagonists, the vanguard of the vanguard.

In order to expand their political project beyond Detroit and create a national organization, some members of the league's executive committee launched in December 1970 an even more ambitious project: the Black Workers Congress (BWC). The BWC combined Black power and workers' power, making worker self-management (that is, "workers' control of their places of work") a primary objective (cited in Georgakas and Surkin 1975, 131). The BWC experiment, however, was short-lived. Intense internal conflicts arose among its central leaders, who were also leaders simultaneously of the league. One line of conflict pitted those who insisted priority should be given to local organizing and who were dedicated to the RUMs in the Detroit plants against those who advocated the primacy of national-level organizing. By the end of 1971 the league was dissolved, and by the following year militants of the BWC had shifted into other projects (Georgakas and Surkin 1975, 131–150). These organizational projects of revolutionary Black workers centered in Detroit—the RUMs, the League of Revolutionary Black Workers, and the BWC—lasted only briefly, but they all testify to the desire for a workers' movement independent of the dominant unions to strive for political transformation both within the factories and in society at large. Keep in mind that even when these movements moved outside the factory and successfully posed the project for liberation on the social terrain, they still maintained the centrality of the industrial worker as primary protagonist, in the vanguard position with respect to other workers and to other social struggles.[4]

US industrial workers were not alone in reaching such a peak of power in the 1970s. I will investigate the Italian situation in Chapter 10, but here, to give an idea of the breadth of the phenomenon, I want briefly to sketch the developments of Argentina's industrial workers' movement, which merits a chapter of its own. As in other countries, the labor movement in Argentina was divided between the "official" unions centralized in the Confederación General del Trabajo, which was generally allied with Peronism and the state, and "internal commissions" of workers in each factory, which sought to be independent of union control. The high season of industrial actions, which radically challenged the government, began with paralyzing industrial strikes in the city of Villa Constitución in March 1974 and March 1975, and finally the general strikes of June and July 1975 in greater Buenos Aires and throughout the country. The official unions participated in these strikes, but increasingly the autonomous workers took the lead. Key was the formation of *coordinadoras interfabriles* (inter-factory coordinating organizations) that brought together the internal commissions of many factories and thus posed the power of autonomous workers at a national scale outside the control of the official unions. In this period, the *coordinadoras* constituted, according to some scholars, "an embryonic form of dual power," creating a serious crisis for Peronism and the state (Werner and Aguirre 2007, 14).[5] Perhaps more than anywhere in North America or Europe, in Argentina industrial workers' power in the factories seemed positioned to lead a general social and political transformation. Less than a year after the general strike, however, Argentina's military coup brutally put an end to all forms of workers' power. In the United States and Europe, the counterattack against workers took a different form but eventually was no less effective.

The Twin Crises of Industrial Governability and Social Governability

Radical industrial workers in the early seventies felled a Leviathan: the great US industrial machine. By the middle of the decade, those in charge—from the most powerful business and political elites to factory managers and foremen—identified the upsurge of worker militancy as an existential threat to the entire system of industrial production. The problem, they understood, was not only the quantity and length of strikes or the increasing acts of sabotage, absenteeism, and the like, but also and more importantly the political nature of the workers' demands, in particular their refusal of factory discipline and their efforts to transform industrial power relations. The fact that the established unions could not come to their rescue—that the unions were no longer able to discipline the workers, guarantee industrial peace, and ensure stable productive relations—made their situation even more dire. André Gorz recognized already in 1972 that the overriding fear of owners and managers in the face of worker demands to transform conditions and relations of production was not losing profits but losing control. "In reality," he wrote under his pen name, Michel Bosquet, "the reasons for the owners' hostility are not primarily technical or economic. They are political. . . . [T]his is the end of the despotic authority and power of big and small bosses" (Gorz 1972). The owners and managers understood that since they were facing a crisis of governability, they had to seek a *political* solution.

It is by now commonplace to cast the 1970s as a period of crisis in the United States (and elsewhere), but most often this refers primarily to economic crisis, including two oil crises, a crisis of falling rates of profit, crises of inflation and stagflation, debt crises, and so forth. What gets lost in such accounts is the political crisis, which was more fundamental. Samuel Huntington's famous 1975 Trilateral Commission report, a lucid assessment of the political crisis from the side of those in power, warned of a decline of authority, undermining the rule of elites. Democracy itself and, in particular, the increasing demands of formerly docile segments of society, he declared, were the problem. If this "democratic distemper" was not treated with powerful medicine, he warned, US society as a whole would become ungovernable (Huntington 1975, 102–106). Huntington's argument is symptomatic of the growing panic and dread among the US power elite in these years of the coming ungovernable society. For them, the militant industrial workers, with their insubordination and demands for participation and transformed power relations, were front and center in this terrifying landscape.

The political and economic transformations in the seventies, Grégoire Chamayou argues, were reactions to these threats. When factory managers, business leaders, and management theorists analyzed the worker insurgency and indiscipline that had emerged in the early seventies, Chamayou continues, they recognized with trepidation what Gorz, from the other side, had celebrated as the crisis of factory despotism. Rather than thinking only in economic terms, then, they knew they needed a political project to check and overcome the political initiatives of the workers. Moreover (and this was something Gorz had seen, too), supervisors and managers recognized that, faced with the workers' refusal of factory discipline and authoritarian command, if they were to respond as they habitually did, with more discipline and more repression, they would only throw gasoline on the flames and make the factories even more ungovernable. And in this entire development they foresaw with dread not only ungovernable factories but ungovernable societies.

Seen in broad outline, two primary operations allowed those in power to address the threat successfully. First, since the subversive, rebellious industrial workers could not be placated with union-brokered deals and could not be quelled with added repression, the only solution was to eliminate them—or, rather, depose them from their hegemonic position. The great transformation of the US economy over the course of the 1970s, shifting large portions of industrial production to other parts of the world, implementing intense automation schemes, and reorienting the US economy to other sectors, was an enormous gamble and sacrifice on the part of US business and political leaders. It was their best bet, however, to counter the progressive and revolutionary workers' movements and to defuse the threat of industrial rebellions. Standard historical accounts generally designate other forces as the drivers of postindustrial restructuring. Some theorists identify impending economic crises of various sorts (accumulation crises, crises of the rate of profit, oil crises, inflation crises, and so forth) as the primary force behind transformation. Others high-light the fact that business and political leaders (visionary to some, dastardly to others) foresaw that they could manufacture more cheaply in subordinate countries and, furthermore, that they could make greater profits in the United States with immaterial production, primarily service labor and finance, and so these leaders created the political and economic conditions, through revised tax codes and the like, to enact the transition. This is all true, but the process is cast in a different—and clearer—light when one recognizes that workers' re-bellion in the United States and many other countries was the prime mover of capitalist restructuring. If workers cannot be disciplined and factories are not governable, then the only solution is to transform the composition of the working class at the heart of the problem. From this perspective, the great US postindustrial transformation in the seventies—the closure of factories, increased automation, the shift of industrial labor to subordinated parts of the world, the economic reorientation toward finance and services, and so forth—was required to quell the threat of worker insubordination, put an end to the economic and political centrality of industrial workers, and thereby, the elites hoped, ensure the governability of society.[6]

Chamayou gives the example of management theorists who countered worker calls for workplace democracy in the 1970s not only in order to pre-serve the authority of the private government of the firm but also to develop more broadly a practical, strategic conception of governance, no longer aimed solely within the individual business but instead oriented outward in concentric waves, such that strategic management could govern also the so-cial world outside of the firm, ruling over workers, shareholders, consumers, and other social forces. Once the ruling classes raised the alarm of a coming ungovernability, Chamayou maintains, they could justify the implementa-tion of increasingly authoritarian governance structures over society as a whole (2021, 196). Given his analysis, then, Chamayou judges that too much attention has been dedicated in recent years to the *economic* project of ne-oliberalism beginning in the 1970s, and not enough to the *political* project of strategic management. In this case as well, the significance of this shift in perspective is to reveal the real menace against which these changes were directed. Simplifying a great deal, one might say that whereas neoliberals, fo-cused on economic policy, were united against Keynesians and proponents of government intervention in the economy, the proponents of strategic man-agement in the seventies were united against the social and political threats of worker rebellions and other liberation movements. (See Chapter 15 for further analysis of the transformation of economic and political structures of power in the 1970s.)

The Limitations of Radical US Industrial Worker Militancy

Recognizing that both of these operations—dismantling the apparatus of industrial production to undermine the power of the industrial working class and constructing a new regime of authoritarian governance—were responses to intensifying worker militancy allows us to evaluate the workers' movement of these years in a new light. Some historians maintain that radical worker militancy simply burned itself out and had no lasting significance. "By 1974–1975," Cowie writes, for instance, "the various insurgencies, despite their energy and creativity, rarely found a place in the national discourse, achieved little lasting institutional presence in the labor movement, left almost no legacy in American politics, and, most significantly, failed to become an enduring part of the class awareness of the nation's workers" (2010, 70). They left no legacy, Cowie implies, *because* they were so radical. I maintain, in contrast, that the subversive content of industrial worker insurgency is what made them such a powerful force at the time and what lives on most strongly. These workers—refusing to accept their subordination in the factories, rejecting the disciplinary regime of industrial production, and contesting the structural racial hierarchies in the factory and the union—succeeded, through strikes, sabotage, and myriad other tactics, in making the system of industrial governance untenable. At the same time, by contesting the hierarchical structures and business-friendly practices of the traditional unions, they posed the demand for the transformation and democratization of labor organizing.

Some of the limitations of the radical US industrial workers' initiatives during these years, which impeded them from carrying their political projects further, are highlighted in comparison to the accomplishments of other movements during these years. One of the achievements of the Autonomia movement in Italy in the mid-seventies, as I will argue in Chapter 10, was the way it was able to move out of the factory and into society, recognizing that the end of the centrality of the industrial worker did not mean the end of class struggle but, instead, called for its transformation and renewal. The need for such a reorientation of class struggle had long been present, but it became particularly urgent when, in the course of the seventies, the processes of deindustrialization, automation, and outsourcing of manufacturing eroded the position of the industrial working class. The Autonomia movement's attempts to recast working-class struggle by taking account of multiple figures of labor (including waged and unwaged work, the precariously employed and the unemployed, reproductive labor, service work, and so forth) and by seeking to organize them in new, more democratic network forms were a significant advance, even if in Italy, too, their efforts were only partially successful.[7]

A second and more significant limitation is the fact that industrial worker movements, even the most radical ones, were among those least willing or able to articulate with other liberation movements on equal terms. Lane Windham argues that the 1970s, far from being the end of the US working class, was the era when women and people of color, gaining access to better-paid and more secure jobs, began to transform unions and experiment with other forms of worker organization (2017, 3). Such important analyses make clear that unions and the workers' movement became increasingly fertile ground for articulations with other movements. A prerequisite, however, for the articulation of struggles along lines of class, race, gender, and sexuality, according to feminist analyses I will investigate in Chapter 11, is that the different structures of domination in society must be recognized without priority among them. Too often, however, labor movements, even with the changing composition of the working class, continue to pose capital as the master narrative and regard other structures of domination as subordinated to it. Perhaps the extraordinary power of radical workers within the factory in the early seventies made it difficult for them to get outside—that is, to transform a project of worker liberation into one of social liberation, not with industrial workers in the lead but guided by multiple movements articulated together, all on equal footing.[8]

These two reorientations—regarding the multiplicities of labor and class struggle, on the one hand, and articulations with other struggles, on the other—would have been necessary for an adequate response to the capitalist restructuring of the 1970s. After capital has emphasized the social nature of production in the wake of processes of deindustrialization, multiple forms of struggle organized on the social terrain are the only way to renew a project of liberation. That is a problem inherited from the 1970s that we are still yet fully to resolve today.

9

Self-Management in the Watch Factory

Who on the Left is not in favor of self-management?

—Pierre Rosanvallon

Worker self-management would surely be a sad affair if it merely meant that workers take over the jobs of the managers and administrators and continue just as before: factory discipline replaced by self-discipline and exploitation by self-exploitation, even if the owners' profits are eliminated. For self-management to have liberatory potential it needs to fulfill at least two criteria: it must transform work conditions and power relations within the factory, and it must expand its horizon outside the factory to change social relations. Industrial self-management, in other words, must be oriented toward social self-governance. The brief experiment in the mid-1970s of worker control at the Lip watch factory in Besançon, France, which galvanized the French Left with echoes of 1968, serves as a test case that illuminates the possibilities and pitfalls of the strategy of worker self-management in the current stage of capitalist relations.[1]

A Productive Strike

When the Lip workers heard rumors in June 1973 that the company was seeking foreign buyers and might close all or part of the plant, they were well prepared.[2] The previous month they had reconstituted their action committee (*comité d'action*), which had originally been formed during the May 1968 strike, and they had secured the backing of two major French union confederations, the General Confederation of Labor (CGT) and the French Democratic Confederation of Labor (CFDT). On June 10, workers occupied the factory in order, they said, to protect the equipment and maintain their own salaries, preventing layoffs and effectively blocking any possibility that the plant would be closed in full or in part. In addition, the workers took hold of a stock of twenty-five thousand already completed watches and other materials.

Two days after workers occupied the plant, management, hoping to negotiate a rapid settlement, called a special meeting of the business committee (*comité d'entreprise*)—a committee set up by the company that included workers in a merely consultative role. In that meeting, management threatened that if workers did not accept their decisions for the good of the company, they could be forced to file for bankruptcy and eventually lay off workers. Some workers, however, took advantage of the meeting to steal documents from the briefcase of one of the administrators, and those documents showed that, contrary to what management said, the company had already made the decision to lay off 480 workers and close several sections of the plant. The workers decided to hold hostage overnight in the plant a group of administrators, interrogating them and searching their offices to learn further details of the plans for restructuring, layoffs, and sale.[3]

Less than a week later, on June 18, a general assembly of workers and unions arrived at the decision to restart production at the occupied plant under worker control using the existing stock of materials. They began what they called a "productive strike"—a seeming oxymoron, a strike that does not stop production but instead continues it. Workers produced watches, sold them, and ensured that everyone in the occupied plant received at least a minimum salary. They managed the factory for almost two months, until mid-August, when the government ordered riot police (*gardes mobiles*) to evict the workers and occupy the factory themselves. An accord between workers and management, which was not reached until January 1974, was at best a modest (and temporary) victory: all workers were rehired and, in exchange, the workers returned the stolen documents and the proceeds from the watches sold during the occupation. Watchmaking subsequently limped forward for a few more years under different management with ever fewer workers until final closure of the plant.

More Democratic Participation and More Humane Work

The "Lip affair," as it was known in France, played a significant role in the political imagination of the French Left and was heralded as a realized example of self-management. People throughout the country bought watches as a solidarity gesture. Workers opened the factory to visitors, and intellectuals, workers, and militants belonging to various leftist parties made the pilgrimage to Besançon to learn about the occupation and participate in demonstrations. In subsequent years, workers at several other factories in France, dubbed *les enfants de Lip*, attempted "productive strikes" on the same model (Vigna 2015, 107–111).

One of the accomplishments of the worker occupation was to transform decision-making structures within the plant and introduce mechanisms for greater democratic participation. Specifically, the workers shifted the power relations among three organizations that differed with regard to the way and degree to which workers were involved in decision-making processes. At the top, with the narrowest measure for worker participation, was the business committee (*comité d'entreprise*), at which administrators announced their plans after the initial occupation and attempted to negotiate with the workers' representatives. The structure of the *comité d'entreprise* assumed the passive collaboration of the workers, whom management would inform regarding its plans. Second, with a broader measure of worker participation, the General Assembly afforded some direct input from workers, but ultimately union leaders determined the agenda and had the final say. A visiting leftist observing the General Assembly at Lip, for instance, characterized it as merely an occasion to applaud good news and to legitimate decisions taken by others (cited in Reid 2018, 110). Finally, the broadest measure of worker participation was found in the commissions and subcommissions that workers established in the factory. The first commissions were created the day of the decision to restart production, and eventually there were thirty-five commissions and numerous subcommissions dedicated to all practical aspects of the production of watches and the management of factory life: upkeep of the plant, managing stock, organizing the canteen, welcoming visitors, planning cultural activities, and the like (Reid 2018, 111). The important point is that workers exerted downward pressure toward the base of this triangle during the months of the occupation, shifting power away first from the *comité d'entreprise* and then from the General Assembly toward the commissions, demanding for all workers ever greater participation in decision-making.

This pyramid of decision-making organizations shows, first of all, that Lip workers' political demands for greater democratic participation in decision-making, in line with worker experiences in many other countries in the early 1970s, required some degree of autonomy from union and party control. Xavier Vigna, analyzing worker insubordination at Lip and other French factories in this period, maintains that recognizing the political capacity of workers forces us, in effect, "to suspend and to interrogate the traditional equation whereby workers = unions (and left-wing parties)" (2015, 14). Workers needed to achieve autonomy from the unions and parties in order to exercise their democratic political capacities. Even though the conflicts between Lip workers and the two union confederations that sought to direct the struggle, the CGT and the CFDT, were not as violent as some of the clashes in other countries, and even though the workers did not seek to exclude union leaders, the Lip workers increasingly objected to union decisions being imposed on them, especially as negotiations proceeded toward a settlement in October and November 1973. "Lip will not be Grenelle," the Lip workers chanted, referring to the union accords that ended the May 1968 strikes against the wishes of many workers (Reid 2018, 156). Through the commissions, in particular, Lip workers developed a culture of autonomy and democracy on the shop floor.[4]

In addition to democratic participation, the Lip workers attempted to transform the conditions of work. They objected, for example, to the extremely routinized tasks and strict division of labor on the assembly line. "On the watch assembly line," explained Charles Piaget, a CFDT representative at the plant, "one worker sets the hour hand, then at the next station another sets the minute hand, then a third the second hand" (Piaget 2018, 17). To counter the deadening effects of repetitive tasks and rapid movements, the workers created a system whereby they rotated work stations and responsibilities while also slowing down the line. They used the greater power they had won to make life in the factory less mechanical and more human.

The Lip experience thus provided a test case for understanding the meaning and potential of worker self-management (*autogestion*). The Lip workers, during the short period of occupation, successfully took control of and managed the various phases of the production and distribution processes and thus, one might say, demonstrated that the roles of managers, bosses, owners, and the like were superfluous, that the workers could do it all themselves. But, as I said at the outset, workers running the factory the same way as it was run previously would be a poor conception of self-management. The Lip workers did, in fact, go beyond that and transform work relations and power relations in the factory. They altered the assignment of tasks and the rhythms of work, and, more importantly, they shifted power away from the existing centralized structures and toward the organs most open to democratic participation of all workers, such as the commissions and subcommissions. This was thus not only an economic reorganization but also a political project to transform factory life.

From Self-Managed Factories to Self-Governed Societies

Pierre Rosanvallon, writing in the mid-seventies, provided both a synthesis of many varied conceptions of self-management circulating in France at the time and his own view regarding what the term should mean. In a previous era, self-management discourses and actions, Rosanvallon claimed, focused on negative demands or, rather, a set of rejections. The call for self-management refused, on the one hand, models promoted by both sides of the cold war divide—specifically, capitalist social democracy and state socialism; here the nonaligned legacy of the Yugoslav experiences of self-management was clearly evident. On the other hand, Rosanvallon continued, self-management rejected various forms of authority, technocracy, and bureaucracy; here the continuing ethos of 1968 was prominent (1979, 99). However, the self-management movements of the seventies, with Lip as an example, made a great advance by complementing these refusals with positive proposals of new arrangements of work and life, demonstrating "a capacity to live and organize differently" (Rosanvallon 1976, 101). The reorganizations of productive activities in the Lip plant and the tendency toward more participatory structures correspond well with Rosanvallon's claim.

Rosanvallon added a second requirement for self-management movements of the seventies, however, against which the Lip experience measured up less well: that the democratic project extends outside the factory walls. "Self-management should not . . . be reduced to industrial democracy because it is not limited to the work site [*l'entreprise*]" (Rosanvallon 1976, 15). Projects of self-management must reconfigure the relationship between economic activity and other forms of social activity, he continued, in such a way that workplace democracy can be a basis for creating a democratic political society (Rosanvallon 1976, 17). Self-management inside the factory must generate new forms of self-governance outside, with new forms of social life and mechanisms for democratic participation. Some of those engaged in the Lip strike were certainly oriented in this direction. Workers in the action committee Lip en Lutte, for example, declared that the achievements of reorganized work tasks and greater democratic participation inside the factory had the potential for significant change outside: "This struggle demonstrates," proclaimed a leaflet they distributed during the occupation, "that another society is possible, an egalitarian society where workers take charge of their own affairs" (Berger 1973, 560).

The Lip workers, however, despite such desires and despite the significant changes within the factory, did not during the brief period of the strike reach beyond the factory walls and embark on a process of social transformation. Perhaps this is why, although many activists and intellectuals celebrated the Lip strike as a realized example of self-management, "the Lip workers did not speak of self-management" (Reid 2018, 11). The workers maintained instead that self-management "would be impossible in a capitalist regime" (Berger 1973, 563). Since the political and economic conditions for a lasting arrangement of worker control at a single factory did not exist in France (or any other capitalist regime), it was inevitable that the Lip occupation could only last a few months. Moreover, the conditions were lacking for expanding the political effects of the factory to the social terrain outside. Like the struggles of US radical workers I analyzed in Chapter 8, French industrial workers (even during the Lip occupation) were not able to move effectively outside of the factory to participate with other movements in a process of social revolution.

The lack of adequate conditions is clear when the situation of the Lip occupation is contrasted with that of similar factory occupations and self-managed production in Chile and Portugal (see Chapters 5 and 6). The worker takeover of the Yurar cotton factory in Santiago, Chile, in April 1971, for instance, took place against the background of numerous land occupations and government nationalization campaigns. Similarly, not long after the workers at the Sogantal sportswear manufacturer near Lisbon occupied the factory and organized production themselves in April 1974, there were hundreds of other worker-occupied factories across Portugal, in addition to a vast wave of housing and land occupations collectively managed by participatory committees. Such examples of worker self-management in Chile and Portugal were able to last longer, not only because they were supported or tolerated by relatively sympathetic governments but also because they were part of a vast web of other transformative, participatory social projects.

The Chilean and Portuguese revolutionary experiences highlight the potential and limitations of industrial self-management for fulfilling Rosanvallon's mandate regarding social transformation. The occupied, self-managed factories in Chile and Portugal were not the origin or van-guard of the processes of social transformation. The industrial workers did not stand apart at the helm. Instead, the self-managed factories participated relatively equally in a vast web of components of struggle, including land occupations, neighborhood commissions, and more. Crucial, as I said earlier, are the feminist analyses I will interpret in Chapter 11 regarding the interwoven structures of power and need to create the conditions for articu-lation among struggles.

I would thus extend Rosanvallon's claims regarding the social and political potential of worker self-management. In addition to realizing the important changes that self-management can accomplish within the factory, industrial workers must find the means to play a role in a larger social process, without any illusions of their centrality or their leadership role, and, ultimately, to articulate with struggles oriented against other structures of domination. These are some of the necessary conditions revealed by the Lip affair for the passage from worker self-management to social self-governance.

10

Laboratory Italy

Those were the years of the first and only attempt at communist revolution in the heart of mature capitalism.

—Paolo Virno

Italian revolutionary movements in the 1970s were remarkable for being able to theorize how capitalist relations of production were being transformed and new mechanisms of control deployed, grasping changes in real time, as they occurred. Think of them as canaries in the coal mine that registered early what others too would suffer—but, really, that image is too passive. Better to consider them as so many eccentric scientists in a new laboratory, experimenting with mixtures of previously unknown substances, which sometimes blow up in their faces but also occasionally conjure up mysterious alchemies. What matters most is that they were able not only to understand how the structures of domination were changing but also to invent concepts and forms of political organization able to engage with and contest that new world.[1]

This is a drama in three acts. In the first, between the late sixties and early seventies, Italian industrial workers became the primary protagonists of revolutionary struggle. As in North America, Latin America, and other countries of Western Europe, the revolutionary force was not the "official" workers' movement, with its established parties and unions. In these years, although the Italian Communist Party (PCI) consistently gained votes and developed a project for entry into the governing coalition, the most innovative and combative worker activity took place in movements outside the PCI and its affiliated unions, to their left, and often in explicit conflict with them. As I argued with respect to the United States in Chapter 8, in Italy, too, the "other" workers' movement, in which workers organized autonomously to attack factory discipline and capitalist domination, arrived at the point of making industrial and social relations virtually ungovernable.

The second act, situated around 1973, was the pivot. Economic and political elites in the dominant capitalist countries, frightened by workers'
insurgencies and various orders of crisis, set in motion various processes that
reduced the role of industrial labor and commodity manufacturing, such
as automation and transferring factories to subordinated countries, which
eventually together served to reorient the domestic economies toward the
production of immaterial goods, services, and finance. The Italian anomaly
begins to appear in this act since many on the Italian radical Left were able
to theorize more swiftly and more clearly than others the nature and political
consequences of this process. They understood that revolutionary struggle
could no longer center on industrial workers and their interests and needs,
and they recognized that this did not mean the end of class struggle but
rather entry into a new phase of it.[2]

In the third act, then, the most important one, Italian activists, on the basis
of their theorizations of the new terrain of political conflict, began to imagine
and construct new revolutionary constellations that included but were no
longer centered on industrial workers. They experimented with the means
to link together a multiplicity of struggles, including those of feminists,
students, industrial and public sector workers, unemployed and precariously employed workers, gay liberation activists, and others, each of which
strove for liberation on its own terms, in ways that sometimes conflicted with
others. To realize this linkage would require devising adequate organizational structures that could articulate diverse movements without reducing
the relative autonomy of any of them.

Focusing on the transformation in Italy among these three acts helps illustrate one of my overall arguments in this book: whereas the power
structures, political formations, and paradigms of struggle of the 1960s,
which constituted a culmination of a long process across the mid-twentieth
century, belong to an earlier phase, those of the 1970s challenge and explore
the fundamental conditions that still define our political reality today. Even
though adequate analyses of the new structures of power and new organizational forms were not fully elaborated in Italy in the seventies, the movements
did identify and confront key political problems that we face today—in particular, those posed for revolutionary movements by the changing nature of
capitalist relations and the problem of multiplicity within the movements
themselves. The Italian movements of the seventies were not able to solve
these problems adequately. An articulated, organized constellation of multiple movements appeared on the horizon as a goal in this period, but it was

only partly realized before the extreme repression of the late seventies swept away the movements' gains. Nonetheless, their theoretical and practical experiments chart paths that remain open to us today.

To highlight and investigate this transformation will require not only reconstructing the general course of events and the primary actors but also following the development of concepts that served as guideposts for movement practices and theorizations. This conceptual approach is particularly appropriate for the Italian case not only because discussions among activists in the revolutionary movements of the seventies were conducted in intellectually rich, technical vocabularies but also because the movements gave rise to an extraordinary set of political thinkers who have since been widely recognized internationally. In each act, then, I emphasize concepts that give special insight into the political projects; in addition, I devote special attention to how the meanings of key terms shifted over the course of these developments, in line with the overall movement of this drama.

Act 1: Organizing Workers' Autonomy

Between the late sixties and early seventies, Italian revolutionary movements, centered on industrial workers, achieved an extraordinarily high level of intensity that threatened both the capitalist class and the national political order. By the time of Italy's "hot autumn" of 1969, worker rebellions had reached maturity, and together they demonstrated the potential for several new conditions of struggle: the emergence of mass industrial workers as primary protagonists of revolutionary struggle; the autonomy of a large segment of workers from the unions and the traditional parties; and the capacity of this autonomous workers' struggle to spill out of the factory into the city and, thus, to serve as a base and focal point for a general social rebellion.

One conflict at Fiat's enormous Mirafiori auto plant in Turin in July 1969, which initiated the "hot autumn," was read by militants throughout the country as a signal that a new phase of political struggle had arrived. In the early months of 1969, Fiat workers had gone out on strike several times and, moreover, continually demonstrated their autonomy from the unions, even if only in very small ways. In May, for instance, Fiat workers participated in a union-led strike but then extended it by an hour and added their own demands to the unions' list. In response, the unions, recognizing they were losing control of worker activism, called a general strike for July 3 demanding a resolution to workers' housing problems, a theme they thought would gain back support from the workers. The union strategy, however, did not work. The self-organized "student-worker assembly" at Fiat decided to take advantage of the union-led strike inside the factory to launch their own demonstration outside, in the streets. As soon as their march moved outside the factory gates, with over three thousand workers plus many people from the neighborhood, the police attacked, preventing them from going to the city center and forcing them onto Corso Traiano, a wide avenue near the entrance to the plant. Police wielded billy clubs and rifle butts and shot tear gas. Demonstrators built barricades and threw rocks. The battle continued for hours, and by the end of the night hundreds had been injured or arrested. The battle on Corso Traiano highlighted all three new conditions of the new workers' struggle I cited above: the workers acted autonomously from the unions and parties that claimed to represent their interests; they attacked factory discipline and ownership; and their struggle came out of the factory and into the city, suggesting it could play the central role in a general social rebellion (Giachetti and Scavino 1999).[3]

Two revolutionary parties created in the late 1960s, Potere Operaio (Workers' Power) and Lotta Continua (Continuous Struggle or The Struggle Goes On), aimed to organize worker insurgency in this new phase of struggle. Both were present to varying degrees in the major cities and the major factories throughout the country; both had leadership structures composed primarily of intellectuals; and both published newspapers that, in addition to reporting on events, created a political line and a common vocabulary. Significant differences separated them and they often competed with each other, but most important for my argument is that they were equally dedicated to the central position of the industrial working class in revolutionary struggle. High school students, university students, and professors, along with a wide range of other activists, played important roles in these parties, but they did so by "going to the factories" in such a way that industrial workers remained the focal point. Indeed, the political program of industrial workers dominated the political imaginary of the entire radical Left in these years, and these parties were a result and expression of that centrality.

I should emphasize that even though the factory remained the center of gravity, the belief that industrial workers could also come out of the factory and lead a social rebellion was essential to the politics of these two parties and the radical Left in general in this period. That is why the image of workers together with people from the neighborhood battling police in Corso Traiano quickly became iconic. Lotta Continua launched the slogan "Let's take the city" (*prendiamoci la città*), which served as the guiding idea for militants inside and outside the party for the next several years. The primary idea was to extend attention from the factory to society, and from a limited conception of the working class to a broader notion of the proletariat, conceived as all those who are oppressed by capital, and thus focusing on housing, transportation, schools, and so forth. "Struggle on the social terrain," explains Luigi Bobbio, a member of Lotta Continua, "was seen as an element that gave more power to the factory struggle insofar as it permitted workers' autonomy to invest at once all aspects of capitalist domination" (1988, 81). In the early seventies, then, even such expansive conceptions of social struggle were still anchored in "worker centrality" as an axiom of political organization.[4]

I want to pause at this point for a first theoretical investigation. Two concepts that characterized the political developments of this first act and that served as guiding principles among radical workers and Far Left political groups from the early sixties onward were "the refusal of work" (*il rifiuto del lavoro*) and "workers' autonomy" (*autonomia operaia*). Like many other concepts that emerge in the context of political struggle, these were not ascribed to any one thinker but developed collectively and were thus given a range of meanings that evolved over time. In fact, we will see shortly that the shifting meanings of these concepts corresponded to the changing political needs of the movements over the course of the three acts.

At base—or, rather, as background to the concept—the refusal of work names the primary weapon that workers wield against capital. The strike is the ultimate refusal, but there is also a wide variety of microrefusals, including slowdowns, workplace sabotage, absenteeism, and the like. When they refuse work, workers are not refusing productivity or creativity per se; rather, they are refusing the command, discipline, and work conditions imposed on them by capital. The refusal of work should also be understood against the background of the state socialist orthodoxy that celebrates workers and work. Whereas that orthodoxy glorified work and preached a "liberation *of* work," these workers proposed instead a "liberation *from* work."[5]

Workers' autonomy is in many respects a concept allied to the refusal of work. It can be situated, first, in relation to the Italian trade union movement's claims in these same years to independence from the political parties, and thus their assertion that the unions were free to bargain with management and declare strikes of their own accord (Balestrini and Moroni 2021, 445). Workers' autonomy, then, takes one further step, independent not only of the political parties but also of the official unions. Some of the political consequences of workers' autonomy are immediately evident: workers themselves, not their appointed union or party representatives, must have the power to make political decisions and take action of their own accord. The self-organization of struggles, which was key to worker autonomy, was manifest in the increasing use of the wildcat strike, a paradigmatic instrument of workers' independence, and in the propensity of workers to turn against unions when they brokered deals that conceded to management demands. The script of striking workers battling not only management and the police but also the unions was repeated continually in Italy and other countries throughout this period.[6]

Calls for workers' autonomy were often addressed by creating institutions of democratic self-governance. "At Fiat, for example," maintained André Gorz in 1972, "the workers' struggle against the capitalist work organization has produced *autonomous* workers' demands and organizational forms (assembly line and shop committees revocable by the base, self-limitation of work pace, and so on). In such situations owners have not only made no 'democratic' concessions but have done everything possible to smash workers' autonomy and resistance, and to prohibit organs of direct democracy in the factory (assemblies, committees, councils) and re-establish the power of trade-union regimentation based on indirect representation" (Gorz 1976, 59). Gorz formulates an equation that puts all the elements together: the refusal of work ("the workers' struggle against the capitalist work organization") plus workers' autonomy (no longer being subject to trade union claims "based on indirect representation") equals a democratic political project of a new type embodied in participatory assemblies, committees, and councils.

Act 2: End of the Centrality of the Industrial Worker

It might seem ironic that just after Italian industrial workers had so fiercely demonstrated their power in the late sixties and early seventies, just as they had reached the point of threatening the national capitalist order, the rug was pulled out from under them. Workers' struggles had made the country's productive system so ungovernable that the ruling political and economic powers were forced to dismantle the existing productive and social relations in order to undermine the workers' power. (Chapter 8 focuses on the corresponding experiences of the US industrial working class.) Factory labor was progressively displaced from the privileged position in national capitalist production, principally through automation and outsourcing, and, correspondingly, the factory worker tended to be ousted from a hegemonic position in class struggle.[7]

Another conflict at Fiat's Mirafiori plant, this one in March 1973, illustrates how the political terrain had changed. Fiat management, citing the economic recession, had begun a process of restructuring to include layoffs and automation. Workers responded with an eight-hour strike, an "internal demonstration" in which ten thousand workers marched through the various workshops of the plant, blocking all entrances and exits and effectively stopping all production. The next day, when workers at Mirafiori decided to occupy the plant and then held it with arms for three days, all the other sections of Fiat in Turin followed suit. The strike ended in victory in the sense that management granted extra vacation and equal pay raises for all workers. But in the following months and years the restructuring continued and intensified, and what may have seemed like a victory began to look more like defeat.

One might think that with such a massive show of force, occupying several plants for three days, the workers were more powerful than ever, but this event was interpreted by many in the revolutionary movement instead as a symptom of weakness. Antonio Negri, for instance, just after the strike, criticized the Fiat workers for having adopted a merely defensive program, concentrating exclusively on resisting capitalist restructuring (2021b, 446). Moreover, he lamented, they had isolated themselves. "Why didn't the Fiat workers," he asked, "go out of the occupied factory?" (2007, 83). The hope generated in 1969 that worker struggle could lead a wider social rebellion, when Fiat workers battled police in the streets together with others from the neighborhood, now evaporated, with the workers closed up in the plant. They had become merely "the party of Mirafiori," representing only themselves. The 1973 Fiat strike thus signaled the end of the centrality of the industrial worker and, specifically, the end of the promise that workers' struggle could lead a broad social insurrection.

This brings us to another theoretical interlude: the end of the centrality of industrial workers was interpreted by a conceptual shift from "the factory society" to "the social factory." (I should note that although I attribute relatively fixed meanings to these two concepts, their usage among different authors was by no means uniform.) In the early 1960s, Mario Tronti designated the factory society as the entire proletarian world that surrounds and emanates from the factory: "At the highest level of capitalist development, this social relation becomes a moment of the relation of production, the whole of society becomes an articulation of production, the whole society lives in function of the factory and the factory extends its exclusive dominion over the whole society" (Tronti 2019, 26). The term "factory society," on the one hand, registers that capital requires various forms of social cooperation and reproduction ("the whole of society becomes an articulation of production") and, on the other, maintains the factory's centrality to and "exclusive dominion over" all social production. The factory society is thus a concept that belongs to Act 1, illustrated, for example, by the Fiat workers spilling out of the factory in 1969 to lead a wider social struggle, but one that always stems from and finds its rationality back in the factory and the leadership of the industrial workers.

The social factory, in contrast, is a concept that moves between Acts 2 and 3. It no longer posits the centrality of industry in capitalist production and the industrial worker in proletarian organization; instead, it casts society as a whole as a kind of factory—that is, as the site of not only capitalist production but also, as feminist theorists highlight, social reproduction. Mariarosa Dalla Costa and Selma James, for instance, conceive of "the social factory as organization of the reproduction of labor power," thinking specifically of women's unpaid work in the home (1972, 22). This feminist analysis of the social factory demonstrates, as Kathi Weeks explains, that "the time of production continues well beyond the formal working day, the space of production reaches beyond the discrete workplace, and the relations of production extend beyond the specific employment relation" (2011, 142). Whereas the factory society maintains the centrality of the factory as site of production and the industrial worker as protagonist of struggle, the social factory decentralizes these figures, opening to a wide multiplicity of forms of social production and reproduction, and thus also necessarily an equally wide plurality of protagonists of struggle.[8]

This conceptual development corresponds to organizational tensions (and eventually crises) within the two parties I mentioned earlier, Potere Operaio and Lotta Continua. One should keep in mind that despite these tensions, the opportunity for activists, especially young people, to participate in the workers' struggle through these parties was extraordinarily productive and, in many cases, life-changing. Membership in the party offered an intense training in political militancy, which many activists subsequently translated into other social struggles. These two parties, in particular, functioned as incubators for a generation of intellectuals and activists on the left. That said, however, internal challenges emerged increasingly forcefully in the early seventies.

Strongly contested in particular, especially by feminists, was the assumption (shared by both parties, to some extent) that the industrial worker, almost exclusively male, occupied the central position as the protagonist of struggle and subject to be liberated. One emblematic example: Mariarosa Dalla Costa, a member of Potere Operaio, was dissatisfied with its male-centered politics and left the party in June 1971 to help found a feminist organization (The Door), and the following year she published *Potere femminile e sovversion sociale* (*Women and the Subversion of Community*)—signaling, with the title's shift from workers' power to women's power, a different protagonist of revolutionary struggle. Dalla Costa provides only one example of a variety of feminist currents that contested the orientation of the parties (see also Fortunati 2013). Tensions created by gender politics led to crises in both Potere Operaio and Lotta Continua; indeed, the dissolution of Lotta Continua after its October 1976 party conference at Rimini was explicitly due to the rebellion of the "women's section" (Bobbio 1988, 176). And feminists were only one of many currents that contested the axiom of industrial worker centrality.

The vanguard function of the parties and, more generally, their formal and informal hierarchies was another source of tension, one closely related to the first insofar as the leadership of the parties was primarily male and oriented toward industrial workers' struggles. Both Lotta Continua and Potere Operaio prided themselves on being born from and remaining close to the movements, but in the course of the seventies this vanguard function was increasingly out of step with the movements. Balestrini and Moroni interpret the March 1973 Fiat strike as a symptom of this fact. "The Mirafiori occupation," they claim, "determined the collapse of the role played by the revolutionary groups, eliminating their vanguardist function" (2021, 444). Indeed, the "vanguardist function" was one of the central issues that resulted in the dissolution of Potere Operaio after its June 1973 convention.[9]

The great capitalist crisis and restructuring of the seventies, I should emphasize again, along with the end of centrality of the industrial worker, were not interpreted by these groups as the end of class struggle or of the workers' movement but rather as a transition of revolutionary working-class politics, dictated in part by the new composition of the class itself. As Sandro Mezzadra explains, these theorists and activists "understood perfectly the meaning of the end of the centrality of the factory and they tried . . . to invest the force accumulated by the workers' struggle in the social terrain on which production was being organized" (2021, 326). The legacies of revolutionary class struggle and their powers were to be redirected in line with the new class composition, but the shift had to go further than that: the movement had to not only theorize the transformations of capital and the working class but also recognize other structures of domination and articulates with different protagonists of struggle, including feminists, unemployed youth, precarious workers, gay and lesbian activists, and others. It would take time, however, for this challenge to be fully registered, let alone successfully addressed.

Act 3: Constellations of Autonomia

For the third act it is convenient to lead with theoretical reflection and then proceed to the practical and organizational developments. In particular, the ways in which the concepts of autonomy and the refusal of work changed with respect to when we first encountered them allow us to measure the effects of the end of the centrality of the factory and to glimpse the contours of a new political agenda.

Regarding the concept of workers' autonomy, the demand for the independence of workers from the dictation of the parties and the unions as well as the affirmation of worker self-organization did not decline, but, in line with the notion of the social factory, analogous demands were added regarding new subjects and new social spaces. No longer was autonomy limited to direct interactions with management, the decision to strike, or even life in the factory as a whole: in the mid-seventies, Balestrini and Moroni maintain, "the expression 'workers' autonomy' . . . came to mean that workers' very existence, a community of proletarian solidarity, could organize the social conditions of exchange, production, and cohabitation independently from bourgeois legality. Autonomy from the law of exchange, from the law of selling one's time, from the law of private property" (2021, 445–446). This expansion of the concept clearly strains against the "worker" designation; indeed, in this period the term "workers' autonomy" was increasingly trimmed to simply "autonomy." The journal *Rosso*, for instance, deemed in 1973 that a new way of doing politics would have to be based on different "autonomies," including "autonomous movements of young people, women, marginalized social strata, repressed and exploited by capital." The editors of *Rosso* thus proposed a coordinated revolt of all those who are able to support "the growth of workers' autonomy without renouncing their own autonomy and their own practices regarding their own specific needs" (Gruppo Gramsci 1980, 96). The project thus became not only to make all aspects of proletarian life, including the varied forms of social production and reproduction, independent of capitalist control, but also to organize a constellation of different autonomies as a coherent political project (Berardi 2007).

Like workers' autonomy, the concept of the refusal of work was revised and expanded in the mid-seventies in light of the shift away from the centrality of the factory. One step in this process was the expansion of the terrain and objects of refusal beyond the workplace to include the varied relations of the capitalist social order. "The theme of the refusal of work was . . . and still remains a terrific lever," Antonio Negri claimed, "because it brings with it a wide set of demands, from the reduction of work time to the theme of a social or political wage, up to the entire restructuring of the social working day and the politics of public spending" (2021a, 634). The refusal of work, then, became a tactic not only for wage workers but also for everyone faced with the structures of capitalist domination (see also Pizzolato 2017).

The feminist deployment of the concept accomplished a second step, by emphasizing that the refusal of work can also be deployed as a tactic against patriarchal domination. Mariarosa Dalla Costa revised and reoriented the traditional concept, insisting that women, even women engaged in unpaid domestic labor in the home, "must refuse the myth of liberation through work," exemplified in "the rejection by millions of women of women's traditional place" (2017, 49). The refusal of work thus took on a more directly social character, and varied social practices of refusal became second nature to young activists in the seventies. "The concept of the refusal of work which had cut across the 1960s and the first half of the 1970s," Balestrini and Moroni write, "now finally found its most effective generation, one that made this concept the central element of their cultural, social and political identity" (2021, 539). Just as workers' autonomy was transformed into a set of "autonomies," so too the workers' tactic of the refusal of work multiplied and gave rise to practices of refusal against multiple structures of domination.

These theoretical and practical political innovations, of course, required a new form of political organization. Soon after the dissolution of Potere Operaio in 1973, many of the former activists formed a new organization, Autonomia (Autonomy), composed of a broad network of local committees and collectives throughout the country, both in metropolitan centers and in provincial towns. Patrick Cuninghame is right to emphasize that, in contrast to Potere Operaio or Lotta Continua, "*Autonomia* was not a political organisation or party, but a broad, heterogeneous social movement, made up of differing and sometimes mutually antagonistic internal tendencies . . . with marked local and regional differences" (2002, 202). The negative mandate for the organizational form of Autonomia was clear: it had to break from both the tradition of the centralized vanguard party and the axiom of the centrality of the industrial worker. The positive mandate was equally clear, albeit abstract: Autonomia needed to create a plural form of political organization that afforded autonomy to a wide multiplicity of participating groups and collectives while providing them the means to articulate their struggles together effectively. "Only a diffuse network of powers," declared Antonio Negri in 1977, "can organize revolutionary democracy" (Negri 2005, 279). This aspiration to democracy in the organizational experiments of Autonomia highlighted not only the independence from capitalist command and discipline but also the (at least relative) autonomy of the various elements or sectors of the movement in the network.

The key feature of Autonomia (and the prime organizational challenge it faced) was thus its internal multiplicity. The "area" of Autonomia, as it was often called to emphasize its heterogeneity, designated a constellation of collectives and groups loosely held together. The multiplicity of this constellation operated along at least two axes. First were the heterogeneous forms of labor. Once the figure of the industrial worker was no longer deemed central, diverse figures of labor (most of which have long existed) came into full view: service workers, care workers, unpaid domestic laborers, precarious and informal workers, those engaged in legal and illegal forms of work, and so forth—together, of course, with workers in small and large industrial settings. "Every regional collective that was part of Autonomy," explain Castellano and coauthors, "traced the concrete particularity of class composition in that area, without experiencing this as a limitation, but rather its reason for being" (Castellano et al. 1996, 231). Second are the diverse structures of domination along with the distinct struggles for liberation: those of the new proletarian strata, youth and students, the unemployed, feminists, gay liberation activists, and more.[10] "Autonomy constituted a vast area like a galaxy," maintains Negri, "in which one can recognize some constellations, some smaller formations of diverse political histories, different cultural forms, different imaginations, each also with its own newspapers, communications networks, and meeting places" (2021b, 444–445). The internal multiplicity of the constellation of elements in Autonomia corresponded to its fluid external boundaries. The designation of Autonomia as an "area" also indicated that its influence, especially its theoretical developments, extended far beyond its organized boundaries. The "portability" of the theoretical proposals and frameworks that emerged from Autonomia both increased the range of its influence and blurred the boundaries between what was inside its area and what was outside.[11]

One widespread practice that constituted the area of Autonomia in this period was the construction of proletarian youth centers, which consisted of autonomous, self-managed social spaces that often included free radio stations, canteens, headquarters for different political groups, and concert spaces. Young people, many without the possibility of finding housing outside their parents' home, created centers, often by occupying vacant public or private buildings illegally, with some similarities to squatters' movements in other European countries. Nanni Balestrini provides, in his signature style of fluid prose without punctuation, an excellent depiction of the construction of a cultural center: "Within just a few days there was a great convergence of people all the dispersed people of the movement began to pour in all kinds turned up workers students unemployed people women drop-outs old people comrades from the extra-parliamentary groups anarchists it was a different place from the usual sort of centre the groups had it was a movement centre and since it was big there was plenty of room there for all these differences."[12] These autonomous social centers also served as bases of political education and provided first experiences with collective self-governance.[13] Autonomy at this point clearly referred not just to labor politics but also to experimentation with new ways of living separate from or in the interstices of the dominant society.[14]

Also characteristic of the area of Autonomia along with other groups on the Far Left were various practices of mass illegality. One such practice, "self-reduction" (*autoriduzione*), aimed at protesting and rectifying the excessive cost of living. Activists organized the payment of a collectively determined "political price" for rent, food, electric bills, and transportation (Cherki and Wieviorka 1980). For example, after the cost of transport tickets in Turin was raised by 30 percent in August 1974, militants set up tables to sell alternative tickets at the old price; similarly, after electricity rates had gone up, "self-reduction committees" issued alternative electric bills at a 50 percent discount (Ramirez 1975, 144–145; Gray 2018, 333–334). A second practice of mass illegality was "proletarian shopping" (*spesa proletaria*). Two representative examples indicate the nature of this practice: on a day in October 1974, a group of workers, unemployed people, students, and other proletarians expropriated two supermarkets in Milan, inviting all the other shoppers to join them in not paying; and in December 1976, sixty families in Rome participated together in a "proletarian shopping" spree at a Standa supermarket (Bianchi and Caminiti 2007, 107, 184). Housing occupations constituted a third practice of mass illegality to address proletarian poverty. In Rome alone in the early 1970s, more than three thousand apartments were illegally occupied (Soresina 2020, 1393). "Appropriation," maintain Castellano and coauthors, "became part of collective practice in all aspects of metropolitan life: free or 'political' shopping, occupation of buildings for open activities, the 'serene habit' of young people not paying for movies and concerts, and the refusal of overtime and the extension of coffee breaks in the factories. Above all, it was the appropriation of free time, liberation from the constraints of factory command, and the search for a new community" (Castellano et al. 1996, 232). These practices were certainly not viewed by activists as theft or looting. They were merely collectively reappropriating some of what had been taken away.

Autonomia Formulates a Problem

To many observers in more traditional political groups, the organizational project of Autonomia was destined to fail for at least two reasons. First, to those for whom the industrial working class remained the ineluctable anchor of progressive politics, the heterogeneous subjectivities mobilized by Autonomia appeared as something like the lumpenproletariat—chaotic, morally suspect, and politically dangerous.[15] Second, to those dedicated to vanguard party structures, these experiments in decentralized and network organization could only appear as hopelessly incoherent. While former Lotta Continua activist Luigi Bobbio, for example, admired how Autonomia attempted in the mid-1970s to follow the direction of the movement—"following the movement" was a practice that Lotta Continua, too, had always taken pride in—he criticized Autonomia for having failed to complement this with a unifying organizational structure: "Relying on the movement without attempting to interpret and govern it (as the 'area of Autonomia' does . . .), means abandoning oneself to the thousand rivulets that compose it" (Bobbio 1988, 179).[16]

It is certainly true that Autonomia did not successfully articulate its diverse components into a coherent movement or develop a powerful and lasting organizational structure. Although activists in Autonomia frequently cited the need for connections among the struggles of industrial workers, feminists, gay and lesbian activists, students, and many others, the organizational mechanisms and structures remained at best informal or implicit. The relative poverty of these links is highlighted by a comparison with organizational projects of articulation that create strategic multiplicities, some of which I analyze in Chapters 11 and 12. Crucial in those cases, I argue, and necessary for articulation, is a theoretical reasoning that recognizes the interwoven and mutually constitutive nature of various structures of power with no priority among them and, correspondingly, arrives at the political decision to refuse to grant priority to any liberation struggle over the others, allowing for the constitution of strategic multiplicities as a new form of struggle. The widespread recognition among activists in Autonomia of the end of the centrality of the industrial worker as the protagonist of struggle, beginning in the mid-seventies, prepared the terrain for such a political operation of articulation, even though it was not accomplished.

The failure of Autonomia to organize its vision of political multiplicity was certainly due in part to its own weaknesses and uneven internal development. On the one hand, many components within Autonomia did provide space for different groups. "The storm that the feminist movement provoked in male-female relations and the subsequent explosion of homosexual collectives," writes Franco Berardi with respect to Autonomia, "thus found a territory in which to consolidate, in which to transform the customs of living, sleeping, eating, smoking" (1980, 162). On the other, many male activists, even those who expressed support for feminist movements and their role in the area of Autonomia, were unable or unwilling at the time to abandon their antagonism or simply their indifference to the demands of feminist and gay activists. What was needed was a process of political education to overcome these obstacles, but that was cut short by external factors, notably the waves of state repression, on one side, and the political threats posed by clandestine armed groups such as the Red Brigades, on the other. In Chapter 17 I will analyze the attempt by a segment of Autonomia to deploy a dual strategy and construct a double organization in order to allow for the development of democratic social and political projects while being able to defend against increasingly militarized state repression. Even such attempts, however, could not ultimately resist the repressive onslaught.

Having been defeated, however, is not the only or most significant criterion for evaluation, as I argued repeatedly. It is worth repeating Robin D. G. Kelley's claim, which I cited in the Introduction: rather than success or failure, we should evaluate movements based on the power of their vision. In my view, and this might amount to the same thing, the important criterion is whether a movement is able to discern an essential political problem. In the case of Autonomia, one such problem was how to articulate together a constellation of movements and thus organize a lasting and politically effective multiplicity.

In order to understand how Autonomia discerned that problem and managed to gather together some of the prerequisites necessary for solving it, it is helpful to look back at the progression among the three acts described earlier. One significant accomplishment was to recognize, after the end of Act 1, the inadequacy of a political and theoretical perspective centered on the industrial working class. Moreover, this shift was interpreted within Autonomia not as the sign of a final exhaustion of class struggle or a farewell to the working class but rather as a mandate to investigate the nature of the new class composition, defined by its internal heterogeneity. Another key accomplishment was to grasp a second axis of heterogeneity: not only is the proletariat internally diverse, but also it is joined by other struggles against different structures of domination, such as heteropatriarchy. Earlier I tried to explain how these first two elements were expressed and consolidated by the revised meanings of autonomy and the refusal of work. Finally, a third achievement was, after having rejected the centralized structures of traditional and vanguard parties, to imagine and set in motion (albeit incompletely) a new organizational structure. The task of this new structure—alluded to with terms such as "area," "network," "galaxy," and "constellation"—was to articulate together these heterogeneous subjectivities and struggles, including a range of workers (waged, unwaged, precarious, and unemployed), feminists, gay liberation activists, students, and others.

All of this allowed Autonomia to formulate the problem of political multiplicity, or what Sandro Mezzadra calls the "puzzle of the relationship between the heterogeneity of subjects in struggle . . . and the necessary unity of action" (2021, 327). A fully realized multiplicity would have to establish, on the one hand, the relative autonomy and equal participation of each of these components; on the other, it would have to articulate these components together so as to form a lasting structure capable of contesting successfully the ruling order. Autonomia never arrived at that goal, but individuating the problem clearly is itself one of the most significant treasures that the movements of the seventies bequeathed to us.

Figure 1. Congress of the African Party for the Independence of Guinea and Cape Verde (PAIGC) in Guinea-Bissau, 1973. The liberation movements in Guinea-Bissau, Angola, and Mozambique, while combating Portuguese colonial rule, sought to construct a revolutionary democracy based on local committees in the liberated zones.

Photo: Arquivo Amílcar Cabral, Fundação Mário Soares

Figure 2. Gay rights demonstration in Trafalgar Square, London, including members of the Gay Liberation Front, circa 1972. In addition to a sexual revolution, gay liberation movements in the seventies generated a subversive mode of life.

Photo: London School of Economics Library via Wikimedia Commons

Figure 3. A painting by Julia Chavarría, a member of the base Christian community in Solentiname, Nicaragua, of a massacre by Nicaraguan soldiers, illustrating the Gospel passage in which Herod orders the slaughter of the infants (Matthew 2:16). Peasants in the community read the Gospels to interpret their own experiences, which led many of them to join the Sandinista insurrection.

Photo: Estate of Ernesto Cardenal

Figure 4. The 1972 trial of members of the People's Mujahedin Organization of Iran in Tehran. Many militants and organizations mixed Muslim and Marxist elements as part of the revolutionary movement.

Photo: Institute for Iranian Contemporary Historical Studies

Figure 5. Members of the Movimiento de Izquierda Revolucionaria. During the Chilean Revolution, the slogan "popular power" was interpreted differently by the major parties and by the popular movements.

Photo credit: Patricio Guzman, *The Battle of Chile*

Figure 6. Workers during the occupation of the Sogantal factory in April 1974. During the Portuguese Revolution, hundreds of factories were occupied and self-managed by workers. Workers' commissions, rural commissions, and neighborhood commissions were formed in order to pursue the revolutionary process from below.

Photo: Antónia de Sousa and Maria Antónia Palla, *O caso Sogantal*

Figure 7. Mural celebrating the 1980 uprising against the dictatorship in Kwangju, South Korea. For five days, the citizens held off the military and attempted to construct participatory democratic structures, later known as the "Kwangju Commune."

Photo: May 18 Memorial Foundation

Figure 8. After workers in Besançon, France, took over the Lip factory in 1973 and self-managed production, it became an act of solidarity throughout the country to buy watches from the self-managed factory.

Photo: Bernard Faille/Bibliothèque municipale de Besançon, Photographies de l'Est Républicain

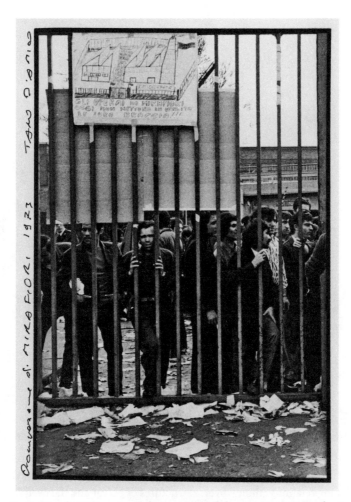

Figure 9. In March 1973, autoworkers occupied the enormous Mirafiori plant in Turin, Italy, but stayed inside the gates. They did not come out of the factory to join other social struggles and battle police, as they had four years earlier. The strike was interpreted as both a high point of worker power and a symptom that industrial workers were no longer able to lead a broader revolutionary movement.

Photo credit: Tano D'Amico

Figure 10. Members of the Combahee River Collective marching to protest violence against women in Boston, 1979. The collective theorized both the interlocking relations among diverse structures of power and the need for articulation among struggles for liberation.

Photo: Estate of Ellen Shub

Figure 11. Members of the Third World Liberation Front at San Francisco State College in 1968. The front created a strategic multiplicity composed of students from different ethnic and racial groups on campus.

Photo: Terry Schmitt

Figure 12. The Third World Women's Alliance at the August 1970 Women's March for Equality in New York City. Feminist organizations were able to extend multiracial organizing to confront capitalist, imperialist, and heterosexist structures of power.

Photo: Eugene Gordon/New-York Historical Society

Figure 13. Over twenty thousand mourners gathered in King William's Town, South Africa, in September 1977 for the funeral of Steve Biko, leader of the Black Consciousness Movement, who had died in police custody. Biko explained how "Black" functioned as a political concept in the movement and allowed for the inclusion of militants from many racial groups.
Photo: UWC Robben Island Mayibuye Archive and South African History Archive

Figure 14. In 1971 Japanese peasants and militants built wooden fortresses and dug tunnels to protect their encampment against a police siege. Fierce battles to prevent the construction of Narita Airport, near Tokyo, lasted over a decade.
Photo: Shinsuke Ogawa, *Sanrizuka: Peasants of the Second Fortress*

Figure 15. Occupation in Millau, France, in August 1974. Activists from throughout the country came to the Larzac plateau in central France to create an encampment to prevent the expansion of a military base.

Photo: Aveyron/Getty Images

Figure 16. In February 1975, local residents, most of whom had not participated in politics previously, occupied the nuclear reactor construction site near Wyhl, Germany, and created an encampment, which blocked construction for almost nine months and ultimately led to cancellation of the plant.

Photo: Photograph by Leo Horlacher. © 1975 Leo Horlacher. Courtesy of Archiv Soziale Bewegungen]

Figure 17. Activists of the Clamshell Alliance formed affinity groups and
established consensus decision-making as part of their struggle to stop
construction of the nuclear power plant in Seabrook, New Hampshire.
Photo: Estate of Ellen Shub

Figure 18. Bernardine Dohrn, future member of the Weather Underground, speaking at the 1969 SDS national convention in Chicago. Like some other armed organizations, the Weather Underground conducted symbolic actions to reveal injustices committed by the government.

Photo: David Fenton/Getty Images

Figure 19. The Conference Against Repression at the sports stadium in Bologna, 1977. In Italy and other countries, as state repression became more intense, some organizations developed a dual strategy whereby they could defend the movement while developing democratic social projects.
Photo: Tano D'Amico

Figure 20. Fikri Sönmez, who was elected mayor of Fatsa, Turkey, in 1979, initiating the Against the Mud campaign. Together with the revolutionary movement Devrimci Yol, which helped hold off fascist violence, Sönmez created a democratic local government that prosecutors later denounced as the "Fatsa Commune." Sönmez was arrested and tortured in 1980 and died in prison five years later.

Photo: *Demokrat* newspaper

Figure 21. In protest against repression against leftist movements, demonstrators in Naples, Italy, in 1982 carry a banner proclaiming "We are all subversives."

Photo: Luciano Ferrara

PART IV
STRATEGIC MULTIPLICITIES

11

Feminist Articulations

A Theory of Intersectionality *Avant la Lettre*

There is no such thing as a single-issue struggle because we do not
live single-issue lives.

—Audre Lorde

The theoretical projects in the 1970s that most successfully explored the
interwoven nature of racist, capitalist, and patriarchal structures of power
had to navigate between two potential dangers that their analyses posed for
political organizing. On one side were notions that registered the importance of different structures of power but maintained, nonetheless, a hierarchy among them. The most prevalent examples recognized that capitalist
social relations are related to racial and gender structures of power but that,
in the end, capital provides the master narrative. If this were the case, then
at the level of organizing, anticapitalist struggle would have to take priority,
perhaps led by a socialist or communist party, with sections to address the
"race question" and the "woman question" as secondary issues. The same
logic holds for conceptions that pose racial structures or patriarchy to be
primary, with similar consequences for political organizing.

On the other side, a second threat, which often arose in reaction to the
first, was formed by analytical frameworks that hold each structure of domination to be completely autonomous, operating according to its own laws,
without subordination to any other. Since this perspective does not recognize the ways in which the structures of power are mutually constitutive,
it necessitates that struggles be organized separately: a feminist struggle
against patriarchy, an antiracist struggle against white supremacy, a socialist or communist struggle against capital, and so forth. External alliances
among struggles can be forged within this framework, but there is no basis
for internal organizational relations.

Some theoretical projects of the 1970s, however, were able to navigate between these two dangers by developing a double concept of articulation, theorizing one articulation among the structures of power and another among the struggles for liberation. Before turning to the texts, it is worth noting that these theories regarding the interlocking structures of power and the potential articulation among struggles were advanced most significantly on feminist terrain (more than among socialist and antiracist groups that were not feminist). We will see similarly, in Chapter 12, how organizational strategies of racial multiplicity were often developed among feminist groups. What is it about feminist theory that provides a context more receptive to and more capable of addressing these issues of articulation and multiplicity?

Capitalist Patriarchy and Equal Significance Without Measure

The development of the concept of capitalist patriarchy by socialist feminists in the late 1970s provides a prime illustration of the successful navigation between these dangers.[1] Here is a simplified account of their theoretical developments that highlights the conditions of articulation, even when that term is not featured in these texts. The prerequisite or point of departure for a concept of capitalist patriarchy is the notion, theorized by radical feminists earlier in the seventies, that patriarchy is an autonomous structure of power, a structure that reproduces the social superiority of men and the subordination of women. The crucial move was to designate the system of patriarchal relations as distinct and independent from capitalist relations of production and command. Feminists were struggling against entrenched positions on the Left, as I said, that assumed capitalist domination, with its class and imperialist hierarchies, to be the master category of power, such that patriarchy, when recognized at all, was subsumed as an effect or subcategory of its structures. Establishing the autonomy of patriarchy in this way effectively led to a conception of two parallel power structures that run throughout society: a relatively gender-blind structure of capitalist domination and a relatively class-blind structure of patriarchal power.

The notion of capitalist patriarchy, of course, takes shape only by bringing these two structures into relation. That concept, as Zillah Eisenstein asserts, requires a synthesis of radical feminist theories of patriarchy and Marxist analyses of capital so as to understand both systems of power together (1979b, 6). In contemporary society, Heidi Hartmann maintains, a "strong partnership exists between patriarchy and capital" (1981, 19). It is not sufficient, however, merely to add together analyses of two autonomous structures. The concept of capitalist patriarchy is based on the premise that capital and patriarchy are not, in fact, entirely independent but instead intimately interrelated and mutually dependent (Eisenstein 1979b, 6, 22). Mutual dependence here means not only that capital benefits from patriarchal hierarchies but also that it adapts to the needs of patriarchy; symmetrically, patriarchy benefits from and adapts to capital. This does not negate the theoretical proposition of patriarchy's autonomy but rather qualifies it. Both capital and patriarchy are relatively autonomous structures that are, nonetheless, mutually constitutive. The claim is not that capital could not exist without patriarchy or patriarchy without capital in all historical and social contexts, but rather that in the modern world the two structures of power have become completely intertwined. Capitalist patriarchy, then, names the process of articulation between them.

There is, however, an additional and crucial condition for this process of articulation, which remains implicit in many arguments: there is no priority between the structures. The concept of capitalist patriarchy would collapse if either was considered to be primary with respect to the other. It would become merely a theory of capitalism with patriarchal characteristics (or patriarchy with capitalist ones)—that is, a primary structure of power accompanied by its junior partner. Capital and patriarchy, then, in addition to the fact that neither is determined by the other—the claim of relative autonomy establishes that fact—must be recognized as, in some sense, equal.[2]

Iris Young, perhaps the theorist who most strongly emphasizes this point, repeatedly insists that a theory of capitalist patriarchy must grant capital and patriarchy "equal importance" and "equal weight" (1981, 44, 46). By what *measure* can two structures of power be said to be equal? Arguments that propose units or schemas of measure, in fact, generally aim at establishing inequality, and these are exactly the arguments that Young explicitly rejects. For example, a radical feminist tradition points to the fact that patriarchy long existed prior to capitalist society, a quantitative temporal difference that can be construed to indicate its priority. Some Marxists, in contrast, claim the priority of capital insofar as it determines the totality of social relations, whereas gender relations, in their view, determine only a portion. All such arguments of quantitative priority are red herrings, however, because in reality there is no common measure between patriarchy and capital that is adequate for establishing the priority of one or the other. (This is a consequence of the relative autonomy of the two structures.) Perhaps, then, we should translate Young's proposition that they be given equal importance to say instead, with an awkward double negative formulation, that they are not unequal, because the powers of capital and patriarchy are incommensurable.

Another way to address this same point is to say that there is no analogy between patriarchy and capital or, indeed, among any structures of domination, because analogy rests on some index of commensurability. Frank Wilderson, in a very different context, places great emphasis on the fact that there can be no analogy between Black suffering and the suffering of other subordinated social groups. "Analogy mystifies Black people's relationship to other people of color"—and, he continues, to colonized peoples, women, proletarians, and all other subordinated groups (2020, 41). I agree with Wilderson that there is no analogy, but I draw from that fact exactly the opposite conclusion. Whereas for him the lack of analogy to Black suffering confirms that it is incomparably greater and more severe than others and thus must be accorded political and theoretical priority, theorists of capitalist patriarchy like Young suggest, in effect, that all structures of power have no analogy with others. Each is singular, and precisely for that reason there can be no priority among them, which is to say, once again, in more colloquial terms, they are not unequal.

To come back to Young, then, we should not read her insistence that we treat capital and patriarchy with equal importance and equal weight to mean that we have tallied up all of the figures on some abacus of domination or suffering and they have come out even. Nor does it mean that we know they are really unequal but we should set aside that fact because doing so is politically or theoretically expedient. Instead, extrapolating from Young and the other theorists of capitalist patriarchy, to refuse any priority accorded to one structure of power over others follows from the fact that there is no such scale or possibility for comparison or measure that would establish such a relation. This is one way to interpret Audre Lorde's famous admonition that "there can be no hierarchies of oppression" (2000, 89). The singularity of each is exactly what allows us to put them all on equal (or, really, not unequal) footing. This philosophical proposition on the part of Young, Lorde, and others is also strategic, which is to say it is taken with an eye toward the consequences for practice, which I will develop further below.

Capitalist patriarchy is, at base, then, a theory of articulation between two structures of power without hierarchy between them. And the prerequisite for revealing such articulation is that claims to measure the priority of one structure over others have been found inadequate: the two are set on equal footing without recourse to measure.

Racial Capitalism and the Complexities of Articulation

The notion of racial capitalism was developed in roughly the same years as that of capitalist patriarchy and shares its general conceptual structure. To speak of racial capitalism means that the modes of domination of capitalist society are completely enmeshed with those of white supremacy, and that the two axes of power are not only relatively autonomous and equally significant but also intertwined and mutually constitutive. Cedric Robinson, whose 1983 *Black Marxism* is widely recognized as the origin of the concept, puts great weight on the origins of capitalist society and the fact that racial hierarchy was constitutive of capitalist relations from the beginning.[3] Specifically, he challenges and supplements Marx's account of primitive accumulation, revealing that racialism "ran deep in the bowels of Western culture" and, at the time of capital's origins, was already constitutive of European consciousness and power structures (Robinson 2021, 66). "The development, organization, and expansion of capitalist society," Robinson writes, "pursued essentially racial directions" (2021, 2). The question of origins (and primitive accumulation) is important for Robinson because it indicates the co-presence of racial domination throughout the life of capitalist society.

More useful for my argument, however, is Stuart Hall's development of a notion of racial capitalism in the same years, although he does not use that term, because he highlights the mode of articulation among structures of power. Hall begins his 1980 essay "Race, Articulation, and Societies Structured in Dominance" by engaging the work of South African scholars who study the structures of race and class.[4] The majority of them, he says, fall into two tendencies, one economic and the other sociological. Partisans of the economic tendency "take economic relations and structures to have an overwhelmingly determining effect" on social formations such that racial and ethnic divisions and hierarchies "can be attributed or explained principally with reference to economic structures and processes." The social formation is, in short, unified under capital. Capital is not the only structure of power, but it is primary and all others (including racial and, we can assume, gendered ones) depend on it. Partisans of the sociological tendency, in contrast, according to Hall, reject the theory that the social formation is unified under the hegemony of capital and insist instead on its separation into two (or, really, multiple) structures. Social research, they maintain, must thus be based on "the autonomy, the non-reductiveness, of race and ethnicity as social features." "Social formations," according to the sociological tendency, he continues, "are complex ensembles composed of several different structures, none of which is reducible to the other" (Hall 2019, 173–174).

Up to this point, Hall's investigation of the relation between capital and racial hierarchy travels a theoretical path parallel to that of socialist feminist analyses of capital and patriarchy. Like them, he organizes the existing literature into two positions that stand at opposing poles: unity under capitalist dominance versus the separation and autonomy of different structures of power. His next move, still parallel to their path, is to simultaneously appreciate the critical force of each position and yet reject them both. The capitalist economic tendency, he asserts, "is surely correct when it insists that racial structure cannot be understood adequately outside [read: independent of] the framework of quite specific sets of economic relations" (Hall 2019, 175). Conversely, the sociological tendency "is surely correct to draw attention to the specificity of those social formations which exhibit distinctive racial or ethnic characteristics," which is to say that they cannot be entirely explained by or subsumed under the logic of capital (Hall 2019, 199).

The basic groundwork for the argument is now established: the two opposing poles have been recognized and rejected—neither unity under capital nor autonomy from it. Hall, then, still in line with the socialist feminists, proposes that capitalist and racial structures of power (as well as others) are relatively autonomous, that is, they are distinct and yet interrelated. South Africa is not a fundamentally capitalist society with racialist characteristics, nor is it fundamentally a racialist society with capitalist characteristics. The two structures of power are mutually constitutive. This is the point at which Hall introduces the concept of articulation, derived from his reading of Louis Althusser, to explore the nature of this relation between structures, and I will return to some of its complexities below.

Theorizing the articulation between structures of power requires, although Hall does not say this explicitly, that the different structures are granted equal importance, as Young claims, or at least that there is in principle no priority between them. It is helpful at this point to read Hall through the lens of the socialist feminists. If one structure were given priority, then his argument would slide back into the unity argument it initially rejected. Different structures can only be articulated when they are recognized as both separate and interrelated (that is, relatively autonomous) and on equal footing—or, as I said earlier, singular and incommensurable and thus without priority.

Denise Da Silva rightly warns that the question of unity haunts Hall's and Robinson's conceptions of racial capitalism, and her argument applies equally to the socialist feminist concept of capitalist patriarchy (2022, 178). The problem is not that we must choose between a theory of dual systems and a unified theory of a single system. The real problem instead is to understand how two relatively autonomous structures of power granted equal (or, better, not unequal) importance are thoroughly articulated (although not unified). The distinction may seem subtle, but the implications are significant. Racial capitalism and capitalist patriarchy are not themselves unified systems of power; they are modes of articulation between structures of power that never concede their distinctive natures and never entirely merge together.

A complication introduced in Hall's analysis serves, finally, to reinforce the main point. As he works through Althusser's notion of articulation, he has to confront the enigmatic statement, which Althusser stresses, that articulation designates a "complex unity, structured in dominance" (Hall 2019, 197). Let us leave aside the question of "unity," which Hall works hard in the subsequent pages to resolve, and focus instead on the problem of dominance. As I said, Hall and the socialist feminists agree, in my estimation, that dominance granted to one structure of power over others would be fatal for their theories and throw us back into something like economic determinist arguments. Hall's resolution, however, is finely nuanced. Although in general or in principle there is no priority or dominance among structures of power, at the micro level and in specific historical conjunctures, articulation usually does involve one structure playing a dominant role over others in a contingent fashion. Consider in this light Hall's oft-cited statement toward the end of the essay that race is "the modality in which class in 'lived,' the medium through which class relations are experienced, the form in which it is appropriated and 'fought through' " (2019, 216). Should we read Hall to be saying this as a relation between form and content, as if class were more foundational, substantial? That's not the right question because the contingent relations of dominance in each conjuncture do not undermine the general relation of equal importance.

Examples of such contingent relations of dominance within articulation are more clearly worked out in the writings of socialist feminists. Heidi Hartmann, for example, explained that the construction of the family wage served "as a resolution of the conflict over women's labor power which was occurring between patriarchal and capitalist interests at the time" and, in this instance, allowed for the dominance of capital over patriarchy in the sense that capital benefited a great deal more than patriarchy did. In contrast, she continues, with regard to legal custody over children, patriarchy is dominant: historically, fathers have legal custody when children are productive and mothers are granted custody when they are not. "While the family wage shows that capitalism adjusts to patriarchy, the changing status of children shows that patriarchy adjusts to capital" (Hartmann 1981, 22–23). Clearly, Hartmann's examples are not intended to demonstrate that either capital or patriarchy is the primary structure in any general way. The modes of articulation between structures of power allow for instances in which one of them, in specific conjunctures and contingently, exerts dominance over others, without disturbing the general relation of equal importance.

Taking a step back, then, the primary argument is clear in these parallel arguments regarding capitalist patriarchy and racial capitalism. Different structures of power, although relatively autonomous, are articulated together, and the condition of their articulation is that there is no hierarchy or priority between them. For the socialist feminists explicitly (and undoubtedly for Hall in less explicit fashion), this analysis of power is directly related to the potential for political organizing. On the organizational terrain a parallel articulation must take place among struggles with (once again) no hierarchy between them. Let me turn to some other theoretical experiences to highlight this second articulation.

A Political Education in Multiplicity

The brief 1977 "Combahee River Collective Statement," composed by a group of Black lesbian feminists, constituted a conceptual point of arrival of this theoretical process.[5] Like the theorists of capitalist patriarchy and racial capitalism cited above, the collective assumes that the articulation among interlocking structures of power requires they be understood on equal footing, with no priority between them. One aspect of the collective's theoretical contribution is the new geometry of power it recognizes. To add together capitalist patriarchy and racial capitalism, or even another structural pair, such as racial patriarchy, does not alter the geometry of twos. Instead, the collective proposes that many (in fact, an indefinite number of) structures of power function together. This new geometry of power requires a new theorization, one that reveals a multiplicity of powers linked by plural articulations.

There were, of course, precursors that focused on three instead of two. Erik McDuffie chronicles, for instance, the development of such a concept in the work of Black feminists in the US Communist Party from the 1930s to the 1950s. "Black left feminists' key historical significance," he asserts, "rested in their formulation of a theory of 'triple oppression.' Emphasizing the connection among racial, gender, and class oppression, the theory posits that the eradication of one form of oppression requires the concurrent dismantlement of all types of oppression" (2011, 4). We will also see in Chapter 12, in the context of racial multiplicities, a roughly parallel concept of "triple jeopardy" developed by Frances Beal and the Third World Women's Alliance.

The concept of multiplicity contained in the Combahee River Collective's conception, in contrast, focuses not on two, three, or any specific number of interlocking structures of power but, rather, on an open, indefinite set. Key to this is the collective's own process of political education: "A combined anti-racist and anti-sexist position drew us together initially," they write, "and as we developed politically we addressed ourselves to heterosexism and economic oppression under capitalism" (Combahee River Collective 2017, 18). Although they began by confronting two structures of power articulated together (which, given their interwoven nature, might be named racial patriarchy), their political education together in the collective—"as we developed politically"—allowed them to add to their analyses two more structures, heterosexism and capital, that are also articulated, interlocking with, and mutually constitutive of the first two. As the "Statement" proceeds, the collective asserts the importance of analyzing and opposing imperialist structures, which represent undoubtedly another collective development of their political consciousness. Should we total them up, then, and claim that the collective's analysis is aimed at five (rather than three or two) major systems of oppression? It is more fruitful and more accurate, in my view, to put the accent on their process of political education. There is no reason to doubt that, continuing along the path that the collective opens, one should not be able with further study and political engagement to recognize transphobic, ableist, and other structures of power that are equally interlocking. But, one might object, exasperated, where does it all stop? That is the wrong question.

The number and nature of the structures that, articulated together, we recognize as composing the multiplicity of power reflect the current state of our political education.

It is worth pausing a moment at this point to note that in the same years in which the Combahee River Collective was developing its theoretical perspective, Michel Foucault, too, in his courses and his books, was attempting to understand the multiplicity of power. One of Foucault's starting points is shared with all the theorists I have cited in this chapter: the refusal that capital's economic logic determines or subordinates to itself other structures of power. "Can the analysis of power, or the analysis of powers," he asks rhetorically, "be in one way or another deduced from the economy?" (2003, 13). Neither capital nor any other structure is the center of power from which others are deduced. Instead—and on this point, too, his argument corresponds to those we are considering here—"power must be understood . . . as the multiplicity of force relations" (Foucault 1978, 92). Where they diverge, then, is in regard to the nature of the multiple powers to be addressed. Foucault conceives of them primarily not in terms of capitalist, patriarchal, and racialist structures but instead as *dispositifs* of discipline and biopower, which function in specific institutions and concrete assemblages regarding, for example, public hygiene protocols or prison architecture. There is, of course, much more to say about Foucault's theories of power, but here I want simply to emphasize, on the one hand, that multiplicity is a central focus and, on the other, that the powers he investigated are really of a different order than those engaged by these authors, and thus substantial theoretical translation would be required to yield a productive comparison. The fact that these theoretical projects in the 1970s, despite their very different aims, nonetheless share the goal of understanding the multiplicity of power is indication that this is an attribute of the era, a widely sensed theoretical need.

Intersectionality *Avant la Lettre*

Many note that even though Kimberlé Crenshaw introduced the term "intersectionality" into our political vocabulary a decade later, the Combahee River Collective's analysis effectively presents an intersectional view of power structures—that is, as Keeanga-Yamahtta Taylor puts it, "the idea that multiple oppressions reinforce each other to create new categories of suffering"

(2019, 4). One major difference, however, is that the Combahee River Collective's intersectionality is focused on articulations not only among structures of power but also among struggles for liberation. In fact, the feminist authors discussed above who theorize the articulations between and among structures of power in the late 1970s and early 1980s all do so with an eye to questions of strategy, organization, and practice. For Heidi Hartmann, for example, her analysis of the (relative) autonomy of patriarchy and capital implied the need for an autonomous women's movement that acts in alliance with socialist movements (1981, 32). Iris Young's analysis, in contrast, which shows gender hierarchy is just as essential to capital as class hierarchy is to patriarchy, leads her to reject a strategy of two separate struggles: "I have some trouble conceiving," she writes, with some exasperation, "what struggle against patriarchy as distinct from the struggle against capitalism might mean at a practical level." Instead, she continues, "the actual struggle has been and must be against the integrated and virulent *capitalist* patriarchy we live in" (1981, 63). One consequence of the analysis of the nature of the relation between patriarchy and capital, then, is whether the articulation between feminist and anticapitalist struggle should be external (separate struggles in alliance) or internal (articulated struggles).

The Combahee River Collective extends this same premise such that the analysis of multiple interlocking structures of power leads directly to a multiplicity of struggles. Despite their lucid critiques of sexism, heterosexism, and racism on the Left, they repeatedly avow the need to articulate their struggle with those of Black men, white feminists, and others. The different structures of power (because articulated, interlocking) must be combated by similarly articulated struggles. "We are not convinced," they write, "that a socialist revolution that is not also a feminist and anti-racist revolution will guarantee our liberation" (Combahee River Collective 2017, 20). Barbara Smith, a member of the collective, explains years later that coalition was the concept of multiple collective struggle they had in mind, although the term is not used in the "Statement" (2017, 62–66). In my view, articulation rather than coalition is the more adequate concept for grasping the organizational form of multiple struggles. In any case, it should be clear that in the context of the 1970s and specifically in the analysis of the Combahee River Collective, the intersectionality of power implies and requires what Angela Davis calls "an intersectionality of struggles" (2016, 19).

Finally, it should be clear that the multiplicities that all of these theorists analyze and propose are fundamentally strategic. This is not to say that they are somehow distorting their analyses of power in order to fit with political objectives, but rather simply that when doing theory, as we saw above, they are constantly alive to the needs of organization and struggle.

Born in Flames

Two theoretical claims or axioms regarding the potential for revolution today form necessary prerequisites for the political and theoretical developments in Lizzie Borden's *Born in Flames*, a film released in 1983, although production began in 1978.[6] The first regards the location of the film's action, New York City. Mario Tronti argued in the early 1960s that the revolution will take place not where the forces of domination are most vulnerable (the weakest link in the chain of power) but instead where there is the highest level of political development of forces of liberation (the strongest link in the chain of revolution). Tronti, who was able only to think about capital and workers, expressed this vision as bringing Lenin to England. Whereas in 1917 it was necessary to bring Marx (that is, the study of capitalist development) to Saint Petersburg, today the countermovement is necessary: to bring Lenin (and revolutionary organizing) to the high point of capital because that is where the most powerful revolutionary organizations exist (or can be created) (Tronti 2019, 72). For *Born in Flames* that means New York City, capital of the twentieth century, the locus of global power, which is embodied in the final scene of the film by the twin towers of the World Trade Center. New York of the 1970s, in all its intensity, diversity, and squalor, is not only the center of power but also—and more importantly, in line with Tronti's thinking—where revolutionary forces are strongest.

The second prerequisite for the film's development maintains that any successful revolution today must combat simultaneously multiple structures of domination. One of the sentences from the Combahee River Collective I cited earlier—"We are not convinced that a socialist revolution that is not also a feminist and anti-racist revolution will guarantee our liberation"— could easily serve as an epigraph for the film.[7] Indeed, Lizzie Borden, as well as many of the actors in the film, were very knowledgeable about the developments in feminist theory in the 1970s, and they were undoubtedly familiar with the "Combahee River Collective Statement" or texts like it. The film also forces us to return to a recognition I posed at the beginning of this chapter (which might serve as a corollary to this second axiom): that

feminist theory and practice constitute a privileged terrain for engaging political multiplicities, both for analyzing multiple structures of power and for
organizing multiple struggles of liberation.

These axioms together, then, set the scene for the film's action: a near-
future New York City on the tenth anniversary of a war of liberation that
put in place a social democratic government, which claims to be the most
advanced in the world. Borden explains that "the reason for setting it *after* a
social democratic revolution is that so many people think the Left will solve
the problems of women and 'minorities'" (quoted in Sussler 1983, 27). The
opening scenes of the film enumerate all the ways in which gender, class, and
race hierarchies persist, despite the government's glowing enumeration of its
successes. Violence against women continues in a variety of contexts, and
gender and racial divisions of labor, in both waged and unwaged work, seem
unchanged. One should not assume, however, that this is an illustration of
the fact that an anticapitalist revolution will not answer the needs of other
structures of power. No, the revolutionary social democratic government in
power is by no means anticapitalist—to anyone familiar with the tradition of
social democracy this should come as no surprise—and capitalist hierarchies
remain firmly in place.[8]

The primary action of the film follows the organization and actions of the
Women's Army against the supposedly revolutionary social democratic government. A voice-over of FBI agents tracking the group gives us basic information filtered through their counterinsurgency mentality: the army consists
of about a thousand members, and it "seems to be dominated by Blacks and
homosexuals." The FBI is particularly focused on Adelaide Norris, a laid-
off construction worker, who is, in fact, Black and lesbian, confirming the
FBI agents' anxieties. After Adelaide learns of the possibility of acquiring
weapons for the army from female Algerian revolutionaries in the Western
Sahara, she travels to Africa to negotiate the purchase of arms, but on her return to New York she is apprehended by the FBI. We see images of her being
tortured and then lying dead in a prison cell. The government announces
that she committed suicide, but Women's Army members are convinced she
was murdered (reminiscent of activist reactions to the German government's
assertion that Ulrike Meinhof and other Red Army Faction members committed suicide in Stammheim Prison in 1976 and 1977). After Adelaide's
death, the Women's Army, pursued by government forces and increasingly
joined by new members, primarily conducts a communications war against
the government, interrupting a presidential broadcast with a message about

Adelaide's assassination, for instance, and, in the final scene of the film, setting explosives to blow up the communications towers atop the World Trade Center.

What I find most striking is how clearly the film thinks through the problems of multiplicity and articulation posed in feminist theory and practice in the seventies. First, not only are the multiple structures of power—heteropatriarchy, capital, and white supremacy—discovered to be equally significant and intimately connected, but also the struggles against them must be articulated together. In effect, the ruling party considers one structure of power (capital) to be primary, whereas the army theorizes many, which leads to a unified party line in the former case and an articulated strategy in the latter. Three white female journalists who write for the *Socialist Youth Review*, for instance, who criticize the army early in the film for not following the line dictated by the party and its class politics, begin, after Adelaide's death, to support the army against the government because they now recognize the equal significance of class, gender, and race. Here is a practical demonstration of the "not unequal" criterion developed above in relation to Iris Young, but now on the terrain of struggle. The articulation among the struggles that compose the Women's Army would clearly collapse if any one of those struggles (feminist, antiracist, or anticapitalist) was given priority over the others. In effect, the film proposes a new conception of communism (although it does not use the term), defined by the abolition of not just capitalist but all structures of social hierarchy.

Second, the primary tensions within the Women's Army revolve around the fact that different struggles, although relatively autonomous, compose together a multiplicity. We are repeatedly shown scenes of army recruiters being rejected by dedicated activists who do not want to be a part of the organization. They recognize how the struggles are related but refuse a centralized, unified organization, insisting on the autonomy of their own organizations. Midway through the film, at a Women's Army demonstration, a remarkable number of separate groups participate: gay liberation movements, Latinx formations, and so forth. After the rally, Adelaide seeks out Zella Wiley, the figure of political wisdom in the film (played by well-known activist and author Flo Kennedy). Adelaide is frustrated by the lack of unity, despite all her organizational efforts. Zella Wiley responds that unity is a false problem. What is more threatening to those in power, she asks, one lion or five hundred mice? One should quickly add to Wiley's affirmation of the power of multiplicity the need for political composition and organization. In order to be more fearsome than a lion, those five hundred mice must cooperate and coordinate their actions. A multiplicity, in other words, in order to be politically effective must be articulated strategically.[9]

At the end of the film, the Women's Army has not won nor are its prospects for victory clear. But it has successfully established a line of struggle and deployed an array of forces in the fight. One way to think of this accomplishment is that the Women's Army is not repeating the revolutionary dramas of the past, no longer dressing in borrowed clothes, so to speak, not even the seemingly up-to-date fashions of the sixties. From this point onward, as Marx said, revolutions must take their poetry from the future, which is to say, in this case, discover ways to articulate together multiple feminist, proletarian, anti-imperialist, antiracist, and queer struggles.

Principles of Articulation

Among these diverse theoretical paradigms—oriented toward developing concepts of capitalist patriarchy and racial capitalism, and eventually posing the basis for what later will become known as intersectionality—the key accomplishment is a complex theory of articulation, which, even when the term was not used, constituted a collective problematic and shared preoccupation in this period. For convenience and clarity, let me distill from the different theorizations a set of principles that summarize its conditions and attributes.

The first principle of articulation designates a logic of relation among different structures of power by which each is relatively autonomous and yet they are all interwoven and intimately related. The second, corollary to the first, dictates that no priority be given to one structure of domination over others, that there be no imagined hierarchy of oppression. This is not, as I said, because they are measurably equal in any way; in fact, there is no common measure. They are incommensurable. Each structure of power is relatively autonomous and effective in its own way. Third, articulation implies not just two or three but an open set, a multiplicity of structures of power, each in relation to the others, and our comprehension of the number of these structures is a function of our collective political education.

These same principles of articulation among structures of domination hold, too, for the relations among struggles. Relative autonomy, interrelation, equal footing, multiplicity, and political education define the mechanisms of solidarity and collective projects that can articulate feminist, anticapitalist, antiracist, anti-imperialist, and other liberation struggles.

Organizational projects deployed in the 1970s that seek such a multiplicity of struggles, with varying degrees of success, fill many of the other chapters of this book, including the innovative efforts of Autonomia in Italy, the attempts to form racial multiplicities as a political force, and the coalitional projects of gay liberation movements. A twenty-first-century example of 1970s-style intersectionality can help clarify my point. Ni Una Menos, the Argentine feminist movement, born to combat gender violence, has had to counter the threat, according to Verónica Gago, of being limited to "the confines of gender discourse" and thus either only addressing one structure of power or, when engaging others, maintaining gender domination as the master narrative. However, she continues, the dynamic organizational framework of assemblies "allowed us to go beyond solely self-declared feminist organizations in order to bring in compañeras from unions, social movements, community spaces, organizations of Indigenous peoples or Afro-descendants, student groups, migrant collectives, art groups, and others" (Gago 2020, 39). The assembly functions as a tool of political education, as in the case of the Combahee River Collective, that serves to expand the multiplicity of struggles. Furthermore, thinking strategically about the articulation among these struggles requires that no one component—gender discourse and feminist struggle, in this case—be granted priority over the others. Together they form something like a constellation or mosaic of struggles, the more powerful for being articulated without priority. Looking back from this vantage point helps us see more clearly what the demands of these 1970s theorizations look like in a more fully realized form.

12

Strategic Racial Multiplicities

> This perspective underscores the definition of "race" as an open po-
> litical category, for it is struggle that determines which definition of
> "race" will prevail and the conditions under which they will endure
> or wither away.
>
> —Paul Gilroy

When San Francisco State College students went on strike in November
1968, George Murray, a recently fired English instructor at the college and
the Black Panther Party's minister of education, proudly declared, "This is
the first time in this country that barriers have been dissolved between black,
brown and yellow people" (quoted in Ryan 2010, 83). The strike was led by
the recently formed Third World Liberation Front (TWLF), an organization
that brought together several race- and ethnicity-based student organizations at the college. A few months later, across the country, in New York City,
the Third World Women's Alliance (TWWA) was formed as a multiracial
revolutionary feminist organization. Murray was certainly right to highlight
the significance (whether or not it was an historic first) of how the TWLF,
like the TWWA, established a multiracial activist organization. At roughly
the same time, South Africans in the Black Consciousness Movement developed a similar project of racial multiplicity by redefining Blackness in political terms, and a comparable strategic notion of Blackness was deployed by
theorists and activists in the United Kingdom later in the decade. People of
all races and skin colors (except the ruling white population) were potentially
Black, depending on their political actions and their engagement with the
antiracist struggle. In all these political experiences were formed internally
diverse and politically effective racial multiplicities—or, better, antiracist
multiplicities—that established the potential for constructing multiracial
democracies.

Militant racial multiplicities are subversive by their nature. Not only are
they more effective because of their greater numbers, but also their very
form, strategically constructing a common condition among multiple

component elements, subverts racial hierarchies that depend on identity and separation. Regimes of white supremacy have functioned historically, in colonial, settler colonial, and postcolonial regimes, through divisions among and rankings of subordinated races and ethnicities. Racial multiplicities, in contrast, while recognizing different racializations and diverse historical experiences, are able both to highlight a shared state of racial subordination and to establish the foundation for shared struggle. Multiplicities thus have a complex relation to identities and identity politics: they do not negate identities but rather work with them and set them in relation in order to propose and organize a common (and yet internally differentiated) project of insubordination.

Third World Students Go on Strike

When students at San Francisco State College (later San Francisco State University) formed the TWLF in 1968 they were first in a wave of student organizations at US colleges and universities, notably including Berkeley and City College of New York, that, under the rubric of "third world students," forwarded two primary sets of demands: one regarding curricular changes to create courses and programs (or even separate institutions) dedicated to ethnic studies, and the other to expand admissions for students of subordinated racial and ethnic groups. It was essential, moreover, that the different race-based student associations make these demands together: the Central Committee of the TWLF, its decision-making body, was composed of representatives from five previously existing student groups: Latin American Students Organization, Mexican American Studies Confederation, Philippine American Collegiate Endeavor, Intercollegiate Chinese for Social Action, and Black Students Union (BSU) (Ryan 2010, 50). The TWLF constituted a coherent and effective collective political project by articulating together its component student organizations, which each remained relatively autonomous and stood on equal footing with respect to the others. As I argued in Chapter 11, the articulation of struggles and the formation of such a multiplicity would not be possible if one was given priority over the others.

At first sight, it might be perplexing that "third world" was used by the TWLF (as well as the TWWA) to designate US populations. This usage refers, in part, to the fact that African Americans and other racially subordinated US populations have long suffered an internal colonization analogous to that of third world populations and, in part, to the ancestral connections of many US populations to the third world. "Third world" thus means, as Roberto Hernández maintains, "decolonization in a US context" (2015, 140). In addition to evoking corresponding oppressions and shared experiences of coloniality, the term also denotes militancy and struggle. It might thus be useful to translate "third world" employed in this way to mean something like "tricontinentalism," a revolutionary internationalism that links together Asian, African, and Latin American liberation movements, embodied, for instance, in the 1966 Tricontinental Conference in Havana. In that context, then, "third world" couples the shared oppressions experienced by diverse racially subordinated populations with a joint revolutionary project. The designation of the student organization as a "liberation front," which can also appear perplexing in retrospect, was probably interpreted by the activists at the time as doubling or reinforcing the weight of revolutionary seriousness already suggested by "third world," with resonance to the Algerian National Liberation Front (FLN) or the National Liberation Front of South Vietnam (Viet Cong), although the TWLF, of course, was not militarized and did not engage in armed struggle of any sort.

The "third world" student strikes were remarkably successful. At San Francisco State the BSU, after unfruitful attempts at negotiating with the college administration, announced a strike to begin on November 6, 1968, the day after Richard Nixon's presidential victory, and published ten demands regarding curriculum and admissions. The TWLF subsequently joined the BSU strike and declared five additional demands (Ryan 2010, 80–81). The strike lasted five months, with various attempts at negotiation and numerous brutal interventions by police. Finally, on March 20, 1969, the TWLF, the BSU, and the college administration reached an agreement: a Black Studies Department was created as well as a School of Ethnic Studies, and larger numbers of nonwhite students were to be admitted. The TWLF at the University of California, Berkeley, which had strong relationships to the organization at San Francisco State, went on strike in January 1969 with similar demands. And in February 1969 a comparable student occupation and strike began at City College of New York. Although the City College strike committee did not use "third world" in its name, it did employ the term "third world" rhetorically in similar ways, here primarily bringing together Black and Puerto Rican student movements (Ryan 2010). All of these struggles and those like them in the following years at other colleges and universities not only achieved important curricular and admissions reforms but also contributed significantly to a movement throughout the US education system to highlight and transform the study of racial histories and hierarchies.

Third World Women

In December 1968, almost simultaneous with the launch of the student strikes, the Black Women's Alliance (BWA), a caucus within the Student Nonviolent Coordinating Committee, dedicated to countering male dominance in the movement, renamed itself the Third World Women's Alliance. The name change, Ashley Farmer explains, indicated the BWA members' decision to open the organization to other women of color and thereby transform the composition of the alliance (2019, 160). By constructing a multiracial and multiethnic feminist organization, the TWWA, in Angela Davis's words, "represents an early feminist impulse toward acknowledging connections, relationalities, and intersectionalities" (2018, 233).

Among activists in the TWWA and other feminist organizations that emerged in the 1970s, "third world" had a dual focus, one side facing inside the United States and the other outside. Within the country, which was the TWWA's primary emphasis, "third world" solidarity was based on recognizing the shared conditions of diverse groups of nonwhite US women. "Although Asian, Black, Chicana, Native American and Puerto Rican sisters have certain differences," affirms an unsigned essay in the TWWA publication *Triple Jeopardy*, "we began to see that we were all affected by the same general oppressions." Specifically, the essay continues, "the third world woman must always be fighting against and exposing her triple exploitation in this society"—that is, her exploitation on the basis of gender, race, and class ("Women in the Struggle" 1971, 8). As in the case of the student strike organizations, "third world" here functions as a collective name for racial multiplicity that designates not only shared forms of subordination but also, potentially, a coordinated project of liberation.

This inward-facing usage of the term "third world" relied conceptually on an outward-facing one, which highlighted the forms of oppression and struggle shared with those in subordinated parts of the world. Several US antiracist organizations in the late sixties and early seventies emphasized the parallel between inside and outside, between the internally colonized and those fighting colonialism and imperialism elsewhere. "Blacks and yellows in the United States," maintains Amy Uyematsu in a 1969 essay celebrating the emergence of the Yellow Power movement, for instance, "identify with their relatives in the Third World. And although the race situation in America is not strictly analogous to white colonialism and imperialism, the blacks and yellows have suffered similar consequences as Third World people at the hands of the America capitalist power" (Uyematsu 1969, 10). For Uyematsu, the parallel between outside and inside is grounded in a logic of diasporic identification, which she expresses with a family metaphor: the nonwhite relatives of the victims of colonialism and imperialism experience corresponding structures of domination. A 1977 editorial statement in *The Black Scholar* echoes this parallelism, adding that corresponding oppressions lead to corresponding struggles: since "the Third World—the world of the oppressed peoples of Africa, Latin America and Asia—exists just as certainly within the United States as it does outside its borders," the editors reason, "[i]t is therefore not illogical that the rise of national liberation movements in the last several decades coincided with the upsurge of black and Third World freedom movements within the U.S." ("The Third World" 1975, 1).

It is worth noting that the primary aim of invoking the "third world" for these US organizations was not so much to create material connections with revolutionary movements outside the United States but rather, through a circular motion, to connect some US organizations to other US organizations via the outside. Bringing together Black, Latinx, Native American, Asian American, and other antiracist activists within the country, in other words, was facilitated via a standpoint outside—that is, the Third World. From that external vantage point, the revolutionary struggles of nonwhite populations could more easily be seen as potentially articulated together, and then this figure could be translated back into the United States. A second aim was, once again, to invoke the militancy and revolutionary prestige of the liberation movements outside the United States. "U.S. third world feminism," Chela Sandoval proposes, "comprises a formulation capable of aligning such movements for social justice with what have been identified as world-wide movements of decolonization" (1991, 1). US movements can thus follow the lead of liberation movements elsewhere, becoming part of the larger revolutionary process.

It is remarkable that this assumed continuity was so widespread and firmly established among progressive and revolutionary organizations in the United States in the 1970s that it could be taken for granted. There were, of course, some direct connections, such as delegations and material collaborations, between "third world" groups in the United States and the liberation struggles in other countries, notably Chile early in the decade and Nicaragua at the end. But in many circumstances the image of liberation struggles in the third world was sufficient and did not require engagement with their reality. Cynthia Young rightly highlights the potentially problematic situation created when US movements appropriate the term "third world" in this way: "It might be the case," she writes, "that conflating people in the First World with those in the Third World borrows the latter's legitimacy while maintaining the spotlight firmly on the First World" (2005, 14). There are also potential pitfalls posed by how some US "third world" movements, such as the TWLF students, in order to indicate their seriousness and dedication, adopt the rhetoric and imagery of armed struggle from anticolonial movements without, in fact, taking up arms (see, for instance, Ryan 2010, 78). These difficulties posed by deploying the image of third world revolutionary movements within the United States are certainly important, but, to my mind, they should not distract us from the valuable effects of invoking the concept, most notably creating racial multiplicities as an organizational model for struggle.

A Racial Multiplicity Can Ground Other Multiplicities

In the course of the 1970s, the term "third world" was gradually replaced by "people of color" among US activists and theorists. Loretta Ross (2011) maintains that the term "women of color" was initiated by Black women at the 1977 National Women's Conference in Houston. By the late 1970s, many authors and organizations had begun to use the designations "third world" and "people of color" interchangeably. Cherríe Moraga, for instance, in the 1981 preface to *This Bridge Called My Back*, writes, "Throughout the text the word 'colored' will be used by the editors in referring to all Third World peoples and people of color unless otherwise specified" (Moraga 2021, xlix n2).

The term "people of color" preserves and, in some respects, clarifies the two key effects achieved by invoking the third world. First, "people of color" similarly designates a racial multiplicity. This fact can be seen clearly from the other side, so to speak, with reference to how difficult it is to make sense of the term by someone who cannot (or refuses to) recognize racial multiplicity as a political possibility. William Safire, the conservative journalist, Nixon speechwriter, and author of a long-standing *New York Times* column, "On Language," grappled with the term "people of color" in a 1988 newspaper column, long after it, to his regret, had become common usage: "The division is arbitrary between white and people of color, and in time may break down into particular colors already representing racial groups—red, yellow, white, black, brown. As we speak, however, the English language seems to lump the colors together and treats white—the noncolor—as a race and a word apart" (Safire 1988, 20). Safire can only see identity or indifference: he thus understands "people of color" as treating all the colors as the same, indifferently, lumping them together, and predicts that in time they will again revert to separate identities. For a multiplicity, however, "Are they the same or are they different?" is not the right question. Gloria Anzaldúa clarifies the multiplicity within the term "women of color" when she writes, "Not all of us have the same oppressions, but we empathize and identify with each other's oppressions" (2021b, 233). Safire cannot grasp that the term is at once coherent and internally differentiated.

The second key aspect of the term "people of color" is its political and strategic nature, both in terms of analysis and organization. Once again Safire highlights this fact, negatively, since he can only understand "people of color" as a descriptive term. Loretta Ross, in contrast, emphasizes that those who invoked "women of color" at the 1977 National Women's Conference "didn't see it as a biological designation." The term, she continues, "is a solidarity definition, a commitment to work in collaboration with other oppressed women of color who have been 'minoritized' . . . a political designation" (Ross 2011). Rather than lumping skin colors together, then, the term emphasizes the analysis of different structures of oppression and different forms of racialization as distinct and yet interwoven with one another. At the same time, it proposes, as a strategic project, the construction of a plural, coordinated form of struggle.

Given the feminist theorizations of articulation investigated in Chapter 11, it should be no surprise that among feminists, the racial multiplicity designated by "women of color" and "third world" also alluded to or provided the basis for other political multiplicities. "We have come to realize," writes Gloria Anzaldúa, "that we are not alone in our struggles nor separate nor autonomous but that we—white black straight queer female male—are connected and interdependent" (2021a, 254). Just as learning one foreign language makes it easier to acquire another, seeing one political multiplicity facilitates recognizing others. "During the 1970s," Chela Sandoval writes, "U.S. feminists of color identified common grounds upon which they made coalitions across profound cultural, racial, class, and gender differences" (1991, 10). Contra an enduring stereotype that the majority of seventies feminists were dedicated solely to the concerns of white, bourgeois, heterosexual women, US feminist activists and theorists of that era, including white feminists, were centrally concerned with multiplicities, in part following the lead of these invocations of racial multiplicity (Beins 2015, 157; Spira 2014, 123). Feminist publications from the period demonstrate, for example, not only that many feminists tried to find ways to engage and understand the plural forms of race, gender, sexuality, and class domination but also that racial multiplicities provided a crucial model. Tamara Lee Spira, analyzing feminist solidarity with the revolution in Chile, proposes, in fact, that "Third World liberation and US racial struggles *created the conditions of possibility* for this historical articulation of US feminisms" (2014, 123, italics in original). One might hypothesize, further, that the notion of racial multiplicity developed through the use of the terms "third world" and "people of color" provided a valuable foundation for feminists to develop additional conceptions of multiplicity regarding gender, sexuality, class, and other structures of domination.

The connection between US feminist activists and revolutionaries in the third world was, as I said earlier, in most cases more imagined or aspirational than actual.[1] Analyzing US feminist activist journals in the early seventies, for instance, Agatha Beins highlights a remarkable repetition of images depicting a Black woman or a Vietnamese woman with a child in one arm and a rifle in the other. She interprets these images as a means to buttress the revolutionary character of US feminist struggle: since third world women and women of color are undeniably revolutionary, then white feminists in alliance with them verify their own revolutionary character. "Because 'revolutionary' refused to stick to 'feminist,' the radical otherness of women of color and Third World struggles for social justice could provide a kind of cultural capital for women's liberation" (Beins 2015, 170). This mode of identification is not dissimilar, of course, from the way that the students at San Francisco State and Berkeley cast themselves as "liberation fronts" and deployed the rhetoric of armed struggle in order to validate their revolutionary seriousness. These feminist organizations, too, were obviously not advocating taking up arms; instead, for them, like for the students, the identification with armed revolutionaries marked their aspiration to translate such revolutionary activity into their own context, where it would, of course, have to be conducted by different means.

More important than the revolutionary credentials, however, was the conception of strategic multiplicity that US feminists drew, in part, from these racial organizations. As I argue in Chapter 11, feminists were among those who carried furthest in the seventies the analyses of the co-constitutive relations among patriarchal, capitalist, racial, and heterosexist forms of domination, and they most successfully developed, too, proposals for articulation in strategic terms among the struggles of liberation.

Pitfalls for Organized Multiplicities

Many conditions can cause political multiplicities to decompose. Component elements and organizations separating and losing relation to one another is an obvious one. The cause of decomposition that proved to be the most significant danger for racial multiplicities of the 1970s, however, was the emergence of hierarchy among the component groups. Among 1970s US organizations that employed the terms "third world" and "people of color," the principal threat emerged when Black oppression and Black struggle held a position of priority with respect to others. Given the exceptional nature of Black social and political history in the United States, of course, and the many manifestations of the afterlives of slavery, there is constant pressure in this regard. Angela Ryan, for instance, remarks on the difficulties posed for the "third world" student strikes at San Francisco State and City College of New York by the lopsided focus on Black students in the organizations and Black studies in the push for ethnic studies (2010, 258). Regarding the TWLF at San Francisco State, as I said earlier, although its formal structure divided decision-making power equally among the constituent student groups, the BSU still exerted greater sway than others, in part because it had previously been the most active in demanding curricular and admissions changes and also because the Black Panther Party held a position of enormous prestige and influence at San Francisco State, Berkeley and other campuses, inevitably tipping the balance toward the Black struggle (Ryan 2010, 62). In some respects, then, the other groups *joined* the Black students in *their* struggle.[2]

Laura Pulido recognizes a similar danger of lopsided internal relations and obstacles to collaboration in what she calls the "third world left" in 1970s Southern California. She notes, for instance, that whereas Black and Chicana/o movements had decades of history of struggle behind them, Asian American movements had relatively little history, and in some respects that "lack of historical baggage" allowed the Asian American groups to collaborate more readily with other movements (2006, 106). In addition, she continues, differential racializations had direct political implications, such that the relative prestige of movements corresponded inversely to severity of historical oppressions: "Those at the bottom of the racial hierarchy, in this case African Americans, enjoyed an elevated status within movement circles," whereas "Asian Americans, who occupied a relatively more privileged place within the racial hierarchy, were the least sought after in terms of coalitions and partnerships" (2006, 153). Pulido notes with regret that, as a consequence, the frequent gestures toward racial solidarity and cooperation made by Asian American activists were rarely reciprocated by the Black and Chicana/o activists, and this was one of the sources of tension that inhibited and undermined the political project of the third world left (2006, 156).

A multiplicity decomposes or disarticulates as soon as one of its component parts sees itself (and is viewed by others) as superior, casting the others as junior partners. As Pulido emphasizes, however, histories of enslavement and subordination as well as current conditions of suffering *are* unequal. In Chapter 11, I emphasized an axiom of the theories of the interwoven nature of the structures of power as well as the potential for articulation among struggles: the structure of power (and, hence, the struggles for liberation) are not unequal; there is no measure to establish the priority of one over others. Here, in the context of political organizing, the same position is reached by a different route. These groups, in full recognition of the dissimilar histories and present social conditions of different populations, make the strategic decision to construct a political project on equal footing. In the United States, feminists, and especially feminists of color, have dedicated the most energy to maintaining these conditions of multiplicity, even though they were not always successful. Once again, Audre Lorde's well-known remark that among those striving for liberation "there can be no hierarchies of oppression" can serve as a guide. Obviously, not everyone's current conditions and history of subordination are the same—but that is not at issue here. Rather, "no hierarchies" means that a collective project of liberation requires creating conditions so that diverse subordinated groups in struggle can cooperate and articulate together without hierarchy among them. "No hierarchies," in other words, is not so much a statement of fact as a political proposition.

The strategic proposition required for these compositions of racial multiplicity leads also, directly, to a renewed democratic project. Obviously, the equality of participation in self-governance and political decision-making required for revolutionary conceptions of democracy does not imply that participants are the same or equal by any common measure. That equality, instead, is underwritten by a strategic decision that declares all should participate equally in political decision-making. The line is direct, then, between these 1970s efforts to compose what I am calling a strategic multiplicity and the project for a revolutionary multiracial democracy.

Biko Black

In the early 1970s, roughly at the same time that "third world" and "people of color" were deployed in the United States as racial multiplicities, the Black Consciousness Movement (BCM) in South Africa developed a political concept of Blackness that similarly functioned as a strategic multiplicity aimed at the construction of a multiracial democracy. Steve Biko, during his testimony in the 1976 trial in Pretoria, a year before his death in police custody, gave the judges and the court a concise lesson in the political thought and practice of the BCM. Black Consciousness, he explained, envisaged "a comprehensive Black organization that involved everybody," and by "everybody" he intended all South Africans except the white population. Creating such an inclusive organization, he continued, required inviting "people from the Indian and Colored communities within the Black world" (Biko 1978, 79). By this act of hospitality, the Black world would be composed by many colors—a racial multiplicity. The BCM explicitly rejected the officially recognized racial categories of the South African apartheid state—White, Black African, Coloured, Indian or Asian, and Other—which, in practice, were often reduced simply to the legal division between white and nonwhite (Epstein 2018, 98–100). Like "third world" and "people of color" in the United States, "Black" functions within the BCM as a *political* concept and the proposition for a collective project. To be Black was thus defined by neither skin color nor social position nor, especially, apartheid law but rather by political action. Black ceased to be a color, one might say, and became a strategic proposal for political multiplicity.

This strategic usage of "Black" was pointedly a refusal of the apartheid government's category "Non-White." Biko explained to the court the reasoning of members of SASO, the Black student organization, in choosing the term: "Students in fact took a decision to the effect that they would no longer use the term Non-Whites, nor allow it to be used as a description of them, because they saw it as negation of their being. They were being stated as 'non something,' which implied that the standard was something and they were not that particular standard. They felt that a positive view of life, which is commensurate with the build up of one's dignity and confidence, should be contained in a description which you accept, and they sought to replace the term Non-White with the term Black" (Biko 1978, 47). "Non-White" thus served not only to exclude, subjugate, and control but also to form the subjectivity of those it named. For Biko, then, Ahmed Veriava maintains, being Black, since it was an act of collective self-naming, involved not only a rejection of the regime's racial interpellation of "Non-White" peoples but a new subjectification (Veriava n.d.).

The hospitality of Blackness that Biko invoked, however—inviting everybody, as he said, into the Black world—has clear political constraints, in addition to excluding the white population. All are welcome only on the condition that they are prepared to join the struggle. "You know," Biko asserted, "anybody who does not identify with the struggle called the Black struggle towards attainment of our total goals as Black people, that is Black, any color, does not qualify to be called Black" (1978, 120). Anyone, in other words, who stands against or even apart from the struggle—not only Indian and Colored people, but also, seemingly paradoxically, Black people—is not Black. "I must state categorically," Biko maintained, "that there is no such thing as a black policeman. Any black man who props the system up actively has lost the right to be considered part of the black world. . . . They are extensions of the enemy on our ranks" (1987, 78). Such exclusions from Blackness only highlight the strategic nature of the concept. "Black" is open and internally multiple along the racial axis, but along the political axis it poses an unyielding division: either you are part of the struggle or you are not.

Notice that Biko did not claim that the Black, Indian, and Colored populations of South Africa are the same or that their experiences or suffering are equal. This is not an ontological claim, nor is measure the issue. The BCM, instead, made a strategic decision to constitute a racial multiplicity. And in this, what matters most is not identity or history but organization and struggle.

Politically Black Britain

In the late seventies and early eighties, "Black" also functioned as a collective name to indicate a joint antiracist project among Britons of Afro-Caribbean, African, and South Asian descent. "The term 'black' was coined," Stuart Hall explains, "as a way of referencing the common experience of racism and marginalization in Britain and came to provide the organizing category of a new politics of resistance, amongst groups and communities with, in fact, very different histories, traditions and ethnic identities. In this moment, politically speaking, 'The Black experience,' as a singular and uniting framework based on the building up of identity across ethnic and cultural difference between the different communities, became 'hegemonic' over other ethnic/racial identities—though the latter did not, of course, disappear" (Hall 1996, 223). Among British antiracist activists and theorists, like in the South African Black Consciousness Movement, the basis of conceiving "Black" as a multiplicity lies in a double condition: although the forms of racialization, the experiences of migration, and other historical factors are undeniably different, the political concept of Blackness highlights their shared experiences of racial subordination and marginalization in contemporary British society. "Despite their differences," Paul Gilroy maintains, "the 'black professional' in a local authority social services department, the Afro-Caribbean ancillary in a hospital and the hip-hopping Asian youth of West London may all discover within that colour a medium through which to articulate their own experiences and make sense of their common exclusion from Britain and Britishness" (1987, 236). I would add that this shared experience among different groups is not an immediate empirical reality but a political construction, which the proposition of Blackness aims to create and maintain. The collective antiracist political project under the single name "Black" is both common and multiple, internally different.

As in the United States, feminist activists were among those most fully to develop such a racial multiplicity in Britain, here through a political conception of Blackness rather than "third world" or "people of color." The Organization of Women of Asian and African Descent (OWAAD), for instance, was formed in February 1978 by African women who had been active in the African Student's Union. OWAAD functioned as an umbrella organization that brought together "black women" who were activists in African, Afro-Caribbean, and Asian women's movements. It organized actions, for example, against the use of virginity tests on Asian women entering the country, against "suspected person" laws that allowed police to stop and frisk, and in aid of women facing deportation (Brixton Black Women's Group 1984, 84–85). "Black" functioned within OWAAD, in line with Hall's and Gilroy's accounts, as a marker of shared subordination and as the proposition of a collective antiracist project.

This strategic usage of "Black" as a multiplicity in Britain, however, lasted relatively briefly. Its demise was, in part, due to the difficulty of avoiding priority among the component elements and the shared basis. "What we were beginning to learn very quickly," wrote some of the founders of OWAAD, "was that the concept 'black', had very different meanings for those of us living in white-dominated societies and regions, compared to those of us from societies which were ostensibly independent" (Brixton Black Women's Group 1984, 86). In the context of activist projects like this, the different experiences of the women—here migrant women and women born in Britain—made it difficult to hold together the shared "Black experience" that Hall indicated. Furthermore, as in the United States, despite the aim to create a framework without priority among constituent elements, perceived hierarchies threated to undermine the political multiplicity. Some British intellectuals of South Asian descent, for example, maintained that all those not of sub-Saharan African origin were effectively relegated to secondary status in this political conception of Blackness (Modood 1994, 863). Such tensions of difference and inequality are present in any political multiplicity and are not necessarily destructive so long as they are constantly attended to and engaged within the common framework—held together, that is, within a shared strategic project.

One should always keep in mind, of course, that the internal conditions of a political multiplicity can be undermined and tensions exacerbated by external political strategies of control. Paul Gilroy maintains that, in fact, the primary factor that destabilized the 1970s political meaning of Blackness and defeated the antiracist projects in the United Kingdom was not internal conflicts but a new strategy of control that transformed the political terrain. The shift "away from political definitions of black based on the possibility of Afro-Asian unity," he asserts, and toward an idea of "absolute cultural difference between ethnic and 'racial' groups . . . dates precisely from the aftermath of the 1981 riots and is intimately bound up with the governmental responses to those protests" (1987, 39). The government response to the April 1981 uprising against police violence in Brixton, a largely Afro-Caribbean area of

South London, relied on and heightened the separation of and antagonisms among ethnic communities. Yasmin Ali, affirming Gilroy's argument, notes that the government strategy against political Blackness had deep roots in the history of the empire. "In India, Africa and the Caribbean," she writes, "the British had assiduously promoted 'ethnic consciousness' as an effective means of social control, and the historic roots of ethnic antagonisms are deep, and still often live" (1991, 201). Against the threat of a politicized antiracist Black politics, the government resorted to well-worn colonial tactics to undermine the conditions of possibility for such a racial multiplicity.

Subversive Multiplicities

Racial multiplicities, which might, as I said earlier, be better understood as antiracist multiplicities, are, like all strategic multiplicities, not found but made. They are rare achievements and can easily appear to be internally contradictory. The fact that the barriers dissolved, as George Murray said during the San Francisco State strike, does not mean either that Black, brown, and yellow merged in an indifferent, gray unity or that the colors remained detached. A strategic multiplicity is not a mere collection of identities. It is at once internally heterogeneous, composed by a range of diverse, singular elements with in principle no priority among them, and a coherent whole, capable of decision-making and effective common action. Some of the basic consequences of constructing a strategic multiplicity can be understood in terms of the traditional political forms that it prohibits. Centralized party structures (of either vanguard or traditional parties) are anathema to multiplicities insofar as they create unity by subordinating constituent parts. Multiplicities are neither unified nor organized hierarchically. And yet a political multiplicity is more than what is normally meant by a coalition, that is, an alliance in which the participating individual organizations remain separate, attached merely by external connections. Strategic multiplicities are held together by common notions that mark the consistency of their heterogeneous elements, their lack of priority, and the *internal* connections that link them.

In many contexts—and this was certainly true in the 1970s for multiracial organizations in the United States, South Africa, and Britain—strategic multiplicities are fragile and difficult to achieve. One has to fight also to create and maintain the social and political conditions that allow a multiplicity to exist and, as the British example above demonstrated, those in power have a wide arsenal at their disposal to undermine them. That should make us appreciate all the more the successes of these experiments with strategic racial multiplicities.

PART V

ENCAMPMENT AND DIRECT ACTION

13

New Alliances Against the State

The encampment at Larzac constitutes a displacement of resistance not a withdrawal; on the contrary, it presupposes the maturity of the struggle.

—Jeannette Colombel

In rural regions of Japan and France fierce opposition movements held large state infrastructure projects at a standstill for almost an entire decade, blocking the construction of Narita Airport in Sanrizuka, Japan, in the greater Tokyo area, and the expansion of a military base in the Larzac region of southern France, energizing the Left in both countries. According to Kristin Ross, in fact, the conflicts in Sanrizuka and Larzac were "the most defining combats" of the entire era (2018, 321). These activists rejected standard models of protest and did not appeal to the state through established political channels or public demonstrations. Instead, they took direct action by creating semipermanent encampments defending the territory by physically obstructing construction. In addition to being defensive structures, however, encampments were cauldrons of innovation, creating new alliances, transforming the repertoires of political practice, and generating novel social forms.

One key dynamic of the struggles at Sanrizuka and Larzac was the composition of sustained alliances, uneasy at times, between rural residents living at or near the site and radical militants from cities, often students. Despite different political commitments and sometimes conflicting modes of political action, these alliances achieved a consistency and lasting power. The different groups were able to learn from each other and adapt to each other's political goals and activist practices, in part because they effectively lived together over the course of many years. The negotiations and transformations among these heterogeneous populations that compose the movements is where one can identify most clearly the potential for innovation.

These movements were also significant for the ways they directly chal-lenged state authority. Local resistances to construction projects are fre-quently discounted by casting them as merely being "not in my backyard" resistances, motivated by individual interests without regard for the collec-tive good. According to this argument, such resistances, even though often dressed in progressive garb, are, in fact, politically conservative or reac-tionary. The state, instead, is custodian of collective interests that must even-tually overcome the self-interest of shortsighted individual residents. The struggles at Narita and in Larzac, however, explicitly refuted such arguments insofar as they directly rejected the state's claim to act in the common interest and to possess superior knowledge. Movements that advocate defense of the environment, contest militarism, and oppose nuclear weapons and energy, like many other land-based defense movements, claim that they, not the state or the corporations allied with it, are the ones that possess superior knowl-edge and are able to act for the collective good—a characteristic we will see again, in even clearer terms, in the antinuclear movements investigated in Chapter 14.

Strategy and Tactics at Narita

When Japanese government officials in 1966 chose the agricultural com-munity of Sanrizuka, about fifty miles from Tokyo, as the location for the new airport, to be called Narita, they expected little opposition. The area was not densely populated and contained large tracts of unpopulated im-perial lands. However, opposition by the Sanrizuka residents' organization, Hantai Dōmei, was immediate and strong. Still, the residents' resistance would likely have been futile and short-lived if radical students from Tokyo had not quickly joined the fight. University students under the umbrella of the student federation Zengakuren first arrived at Sanrizuka in 1967, and by the 1970s there were contingents from a vast array of radical leftist groups. A large number of the students and other militants from outside the area built huts and armored fortresses on the land, establishing quasi-permanent residency in Sanrizuka in preparation for a long fight. The leftist militants were undoubtedly drawn by the grassroots fight against state authority, and they also saw the airport construction as a militarist expansion. "It will be remembered that the Narita incident occurred during the very same years that the Vietnam War was peaking at its most brutal height," Roger Wilson

Bowen claims. "The left-wing students at Narita," he continues, "and many of the farmers to a lesser degree, saw the Narita conflict as an *extension* of the war" (1975, 599). The government itself amplified this connection when it explained that supporting US needs in the Vietnam War was one reason a larger airport was required (Apter and Sawa 1984, 6).

The rural residents and the urban militants certainly made an unlikely couple, but each was transformed by the encounter. Regarding tactics, the residents gradually moved in the direction of the militants. The Sanrizuka residents' association was led by Tomura Issaku, a socialist and devout Christian, inclined toward nonviolence. During the first years of the struggle, in the late 1960s, the residents, many of whom had participated in the farmers' union but did not have extensive activist experience, attempted passive and nonviolent forms of resistance. After being subjected to violent government tactics and vicious police beatings, however—Tomura himself was savagely beaten by police—the residents became more open to the use of force to defend themselves (Andrews 2016, 172.) As the struggle proceeded in the mid-1970s, with respect to activist tactics the residents generally deferred to the students and other militants, who were adept at quasi-militarized operations and had extensive experience with fierce clashes with the forces of order. The residents gradually adopted the students' repertoire of confrontational practices, which became the model for the movement as a whole.

Regarding strategy, in contrast, the radical militants generally deferred to the residents' association. The movement was open to all leftist groups on the condition that they did not try to dominate the residents' association—and as evidence of this fact, the Japan Communist Party was expelled from Sanrizuka precisely for attempting to dictate strategy (Apter and Sawa 1984, 7). Nearly the entire vast universe of the Japanese militant, extraparliamentary left, including the Revolutionary Marxists, the United Revolutionary Vanguard, and the Revolutionary Labor League, among many others, participated in the airport resistance movement—and in confrontations with the authorities the militants wore helmets with the colors and insignias that identified their group, creating a rainbow effect in the clashes (Bowen 1975, 612). These radical leftist groups, however, well known for often violent sectarian conflicts among them, worked together unusually well in Sanrizuka, perhaps in part due to their shared alliance with the residents. William Andrews characterizes the alliance between residents and militants poetically in terms of two separate pillars of support: "one muddy foot in the camp of this kind

of environmentalist grassroots model, and one bloody foot in the more fun-
damentalist, oppositional and anti-establishment camp of broader political
radicalism" (2016, 168). I consider it more important, however, to emphasize not their continued separation but the ways the residents and the outside
militants, in the decade of living and fighting in concert, transformed each
other through a give-and-take regarding tactics and strategy, and established
together a lasting mode of cooperation.

The Narita resistance movement is notable not only for its long duration but also for the brutality of the conflict and the audaciousness of the
militants. Over the years of the struggle, more than eight thousand were injured in clashes between activists and police and about four thousand were
arrested (Andrews 2016, 174). A remarkable battle was captured in Ogawa
Shinsuke's 1971 film *Sanrizuka: Peasants of the Second Fortress*, one of a series
of extraordinary documentaries that chronicled the long struggle (Nornes
2007, 54–127). In early 1971 the Hantai Dōmei and their activist allies built
to defend their encampment five fortresses made with wood and scrap metal
along with a network of tunnels to travel among them. When thirty thousand police arrived to clear the site on February 22, 1971, twenty thousand
activists were there to face them. The battle was fierce. Police brought in
water cannons; students lobbed Molotov cocktails and fought with bamboo
spears. Eventually, of course, the police overwhelmed the fortresses (Nornes
2007, 92–93).

But that was certainly not the end of it. The resistance movement continued seven more years until the official opening of Narita Airport in March
1978. On opening day, in fact, the activists executed an extraordinarily spectacular operation worthy of Odysseus at Troy. With fourteen thousand riot
police protecting the airport, the movement mounted a march of ten thousand demonstrators at nearby fortresses, but this was only a first decoy to
distract the police. After many of the police had been drawn away from the
airport by the demonstration, a burning truck broke through the airport
gates and hundreds of militants poured into the airport grounds. But this, in
fact, was merely a second decoy. In the midst of the chaos of the two decoys,
a small group of militants, who had gained access to the airport the night before through the sewers, entered the control tower and, after a gunfight with
guards, smashed the equipment and hung a banner from the tower (Andrews
2016, 176). Even this daring exploit, however, which garnered international
media attention, only resulted in a temporary delay. The airport definitively
opened in May 1978.

Everyone to Larzac!

Although its actions were less spectacular than those of the Narita resistance movement, the long-lasting struggle against the expansion of a military base in the Larzac region became a point of reference for the French Left throughout the 1970s. French politics is famously Paris-centered, but along with the movement against the construction of a nuclear reactor at Malville (not far from the Swiss border), the Nantes Commune, and the worker occupation of the Lip watch factory in Besançon, the Larzac struggle decentered French radical politics, creating new destinations for radical militants and students. "Tous au Larzac!" (everyone to Larzac), now the title of a documentary film on the struggle (Rouaud 2011), was a slogan that echoed across the Left. Moreover, the Larzac struggle, like that at Narita, generated a model of direct action against state authority animated by alliances among local residents and militants from elsewhere, which was taken up by numerous movements in subsequent decades.

The French government announced in October 1971 that the Camp du Larzac military base would be expanded to five times its size. The Larzac, a rural plateau in southern France known for the production of Roquefort cheese, is predominantly Catholic and politically conservative. It was thus no surprise that when numerous radical groups descended on the region to protest soon after announcement of the military base expansion, few of the residents participated. The rural residents did not initially mount opposition themselves, and the national federation of farmers' unions, judging the base expansion inevitable, did not oppose it. An early turning point in the struggle was provided by Lanza del Vasto, a charismatic Catholic figure and follower of Gandhi who had founded Friends of the Ark (Les Compagnons de l'Arche) not far from Larzac. In March 1972 Lanza del Vasto conducted a two-week hunger strike in protest of the base expansion, and local residents joined him, fasting for portions of that time. The strike galvanized the residents' resistance and determined its initial orientation in terms of Catholic social justice and nonviolent civil disobedience.

But the resistance of the residents alone was clearly insufficient to stop construction. Like the Narita resistance, the Larzac movement would have been short-lived if not for the influx of leftist militants from other parts of the country. By the mid-seventies, numerous activists had moved to Larzac and squatted on land or bought plots, and throughout France a network of support committees had been established. The primary motivations of those who came from elsewhere were not limited to the Larzac region but aimed at larger environmental and anti-militarist goals. "The force of the Larzac movement," maintains Ross, "lay in the diversity of people and disparate ideologies it brought together: anti-military activists and pacifists (conscientious objectors), regional Occitan separatists, supporters of non-violence, revolutionaries aiming to overthrow the bourgeois state, anti-capitalists, anarchists and other *gauchistes*, as well as ecologists" (2018, 331). Like in Sanrizuka, although there were certainly conflicts, there was a process of rapprochement and exchange by which the long-term residents and the militants who moved to the area learned from each other and eventually formed together a coherent movement. "In the end," one activist explains, "I was less a militant of the Gauche ouvrière et paysanne (GOP) [a Maoist off-shoot of the Parti Socialiste Unifié] than a militant of the Larzac committee" (quoted in Reid 2014, 112).

In the functioning of this alliance, as in the Narita movement, one can recognize that some aspects of the movement were more strongly determined by the residents and others by the militants from outside. The overall strategy in this case, too, was strongly aligned with the residents. "The peasants should decide their own fate" was a baseline principle for leftist participation in the struggle, and thus major political parties that were inclined to impose their own strategy were excluded (Colombel 1977, 1972). Accepting the agenda set by the local residents, in particular the 103 families who refused to sell their land, was a requirement for external participants (Reid 2014, 106). In contrast to Narita, though, the tactics in Larzac followed the nonviolent civil disobedience line that the residents established. Whereas Narita activists donned helmets to fight police with firebombs and clubs, in Larzac the actions, although often illegal, were much less violent. In addition to occupying the land and refusing to sell or to move, the movement also employed a repertoire of harassment and sabotage: letting air out of the tires of military vehicles, for instance, or covering the vehicles with graffiti, or blocking convoys (Reid 2014, 102; Gildea and Tomkins 2015, 591). Such practices of illegality, what Jeannette Colombel calls their "subversive nonviolence," might be conceived as a derivation of their initial leftist Catholic and Gandhian civil disobedience tilted slightly in the direction of the practices of the French radical Left.

What those coming from outside Larzac primarily determined, however, was the democratic mode of organization that eventually characterized the movement, which established an array of committees for both participants in Larzac and supporters in other parts of the country. It is possible that the commission structure was initiated after delegate workers from the occupied Lip watch factory visited Larzac in 1973 and was modeled after their organization, but the experiences in and desires for radical democracy that many other militants brought to the struggle were certainly also an important influence (Reid 2014, 106). Regardless of their origin, the Larzac committees successfully structured institutions of democratic participation in the decision-making process, corresponding to those formed in the same years in Guinea-Bissau, Chile, Portugal, and elsewhere.

The Larzac movement ended in victory when François Mitterrand, after his 1981 election as president, terminated plans to expand the military base.

The Power of Encampments

The activists in Larzac and at Sanrizuka, as I said earlier, not only rejected the authority of the state but also refused the standard practices of protest politics. Instead of petitioning established local, regional, or national political bodies, they took action themselves, blocking construction, in part through frontal attacks, sabotage, and the like, but primarily by erecting and inhabiting encampments. Occupying the land thus emerged as a primary tactic of direct action.

The power of encampments, however, lies not only in what they are able to prevent, such as construction of the airport or the military base expansion, but also in what they create inside, among the activists. In both Sanrizuka and Larzac, residing together over a long period provided the opportunity to compose a mixed movement through complex negotiations between local residents and outside militants. I highlighted above how this took place in political terms. One constant was the mandate for those who came from outside to respect the wishes and follow the lead of the long-term residents, which primarily meant that residents should determine the central strategic goals. But even those goals were not immobile. What was really key and most interesting was the process by which all the groups now residing in the same territory, often for several years, learned from and were influenced by each other at all levels of struggle. In some cases, the repertoire of practices of one group was adopted by the others and became more prominent; in others, one group's organizational forms such as assemblies or commissions spread throughout the movement. All of this, however, would not have been possible without the encampment itself and the extended period of cohabitation.

The process of mutual transformation that takes place in encampments extends well beyond the political decisions regarding tactics and strategy, engendering new forms of life. Kristin Ross maintains that the Larzac and Sanrizuka struggles initiated the principle "that defending the conditions for life on the planet had become the new and incontrovertible horizon of meaning of all political struggle" (2018, 321). Such defense should not be conceived simply as preserving previously established ways of life, such as peasant modes of social interaction and forms of agricultural production, as if all those who came from elsewhere must conform to local traditions. Instead, the heterogeneity of the composition of encampments ensures that, through the interaction among many groups, new forms of life, new social practices, and new relations to the earth will be invented. Whereas on the outside the encampment is formed into a weapon for battle, inside it provides a site for radical experimentations.

The legacies of the Larzac and Sanrizuka struggles continue in Japan and France and extend well beyond national boundaries. Some explicit connections can be seen, for instance, when central figures from the 1970s Larzac struggle, such as José Bové, reappeared in the years around 2000 in the alterglobalization movement and the World Social Forum process, promoting political visions against destructive forms of development and modernization. More significant, however, is the proliferation of long-term encampments in the early twenty-first century that obstruct large infrastructure projects, creating mixed compositions and employing direct-action tactics, including resistance to the Keystone XL pipeline construction at Standing Rock, the NO TAV movements against a high-speed rail line in northern Italy's Val di Susa, and the occupation to prevent construction of an airport in Notre-Dame-des-Landes, France. Equally significant examples of this political legacy are contained in the cycle of urban encampments and occupations launched in 2011, from Cairo's Tahrir Square to Istanbul's Taksim Square, passing through Madrid's Puerta del Sol, Athens's Syntagma Square, New York's Zucotti Park, and many others. The defensive character of these urban encampments may be different, but in them the innovative potential of interactions of heterogeneous compositions is perhaps even more powerful.

14

Antinuclear Democratizations

[The Clamshell Alliance's] most striking legacy was in consolidating and promoting what became the dominant model for large-scale direct-action organizing for the next forty years, used to powerful effect time and time again . . . the prefigurative direct-action model.

—L. A. Kauffman

Antinuclear movements were a prominent component of the Left in the 1970s and 1980s, especially in the United States and Europe. Opposition to the deployment and testing of nuclear weapons, which had been active since the end of World War II, continued, but antinuclear activist energies were more focused in this period on blocking the construction of nuclear power plants. They achieved limited concrete victories, such as blocking or delaying the construction of specific nuclear power plants. But, more importantly, the movements—bolstered by the March 1979 partial meltdown at the Three Mile Island reactor and, later, the April 1986 Chernobyl disaster—shifted public opinion against nuclear technologies.

Although in recent decades, with the exception of Japanese demonstrations after the March 2011 Fukushima Daiichi disaster, antinuclear activism has declined precipitously, some of the core innovations of the antinuclear movements continue to have an extraordinarily wide and profound influence. Like the struggles at Sanrizuka and in Larzac that I analyzed in Chapter 13, the antinuclear movements sought to construct encampments, with some success, in order to block government and corporate construction projects. Most novel about the antinuclear movements, however, were their experiments with new democratic forms, both looking outward to democratize government policymaking and scientific expertise and looking inward to democratize the functioning and decision-making structures of the movements themselves.

Wyhl and Greenpeace: Democratizing Science in Order to Democratize Government

The antinuclear encampment at Wyhl, Germany, provides an example of efforts to democratize government decision-making structures, and demonstrates how these efforts require expanding access to scientific knowledges. On February 17, 1975, the West German government announced authorization for the construction of a nuclear power plant in the forest near Wyhl, a small German town near the French border. That very same day workmen arrived with heavy equipment. The court had not yet approved permits, but companies routinely began construction before court approval as a tactical maneuver because once the site had been cleared the court was less likely to rule against them (Hager 1993, 50). The following day, about three hundred protesters, most of them rural women who had not been previously politicized, held a rally outside the fence, and then entered the site and pitched tents in front of the bulldozers, bringing construction to a halt. When police were ordered to clear the site two days later, television and newspaper journalists were on the scene to record the brutal beatings and arrests of the nonviolent activists.

A small number of local activists returned with wire cutters the next week and occupied the site a second time. The encampment then received an enormous boost from a report on a weekly national television program. The broadcast of this segment, titled "Citizens Against the Wyhl Reactor," showed harrowing footage from the first occupation, in which "normal people" were beaten and dragged off by the police (Milder 2017, 110). West German viewers may have been accustomed to images of police violence against students and veteran activists, but not against the rural residents that populated the Wyhl encampment. As in many other cases, images of police brutality against passive protesters drew national attention to the struggle and outrage against the authorities (Karapin 2007, 142–145). Tens of thousands more activists flowed to Wyhl, swelling the encampment manyfold. The second occupation blocked construction for almost nine months, until November 1975.

Activists transformed the encampment into a makeshift town in the Wyhl forest with a "friendship house," lodging for activists, and a kitchen with eating facilities to accommodate the many thousands of occupiers and visitors.[1] The forest community became a center for cultural life in the Upper Rhine Valley and attracted visitors from other parts of Germany and France. The activists created the Wyhl Forest Community College, which, in addition to practical courses such as "French for German-Speakers," eventually hosted scientific lectures on nuclear energy production and similar topics (Milder 2017, 121–122). "Whereas at first they were worried about defending their own economic existence," claimed Joachim Schritt, "eventually many [activists at the Wyhl encampment] wanted to put a stop to the entire nuclear power program" (quoted in Hager 1993, 50n20). Gaining scientific knowledge was a key factor in the shift in the perspective of the activists over the course of the occupation, from local concerns to broader political positions.

The encampment at Wyhl not only highlighted the potential environmental and social destruction of nuclear technologies, then, but also challenged more generally the government's monopoly over decision-making. The government's assertion of authority is really double in cases like this: it claims to represent the social good over individual interests (which are often dismissed as "not in my backyard" positions), and it asserts exclusive access to expert scientific knowledge that justifies its decision-making power. "Informed citizen protest" in cases like the Wyhl encampment, however, claims Carol Hager, "delegitimized the technocratic form of policymaking that had excluded citizens from decisions that affected their lives" (1993, 43). The activists' education in nuclear science at the Wyhl encampment, then, is the foundation in such cases for the demand to democratize political decision-making because it demonstrates their capacity to evaluate the social and environmental consequences of employing the technological system. The chief minister of Baden-Württemberg, the state where Wyhl is located, clearly saw such demands as a threat to government authority: "If this example finds adherents," he asserted with respect to the Wyhl encampment, "then this country will not be governable any more" (quoted in Sarkar 1986, 234). The West German government, facing public opposition largely created by the encampment and publicity surrounding it, withdrew approval for the Wyhl nuclear plant, and the land eventually became a nature reserve.

The role of democratizing science at Wyhl resonates with the strategy of Greenpeace in the early 1970s. Greenpeace, which up until 1975 was essentially "an antinuclear group with an environmental emphasis," shared with the Wyhl encampment a two-pronged strategy for antinuclear activism: direct action and scientific education (Zelko 2013, 8). In many respects, of course, the projects of Greenpeace and the Wyhl encampment were divergent. Although both engaged in antinuclear activism, at stake at Wyhl was nuclear energy production, whereas Greenpeace's projects in the early 1970s sought to end US and French nuclear weapons testing. Moreover, although both emphasized direct action, in contrast to Wyhl's mode, which was mass oc-cupation of the construction site, Greenpeace's direct actions were generally conducted by small, elite teams aboard their ship. In 1971, for example, prior to adopting the name Greenpeace, when the group was still called the Don't Make a Wave Committee, they attempted to deploy their ship to the border of a nuclear test zone in order to bear "witness to an ecological crime" and pressure the US government to halt tests (Zelko 2017, 320). I want to empha-size, however, that to complement such direct actions and the media atten-tion they attracted, Greenpeace, like the Wyhl activists, recognized the need to develop and spread scientific knowledges. They highlighted the role of sci-entific expertise, publishing scholarly scientific reports about the damages caused by nuclear testing, and eventually attracted respected scientists to the group, with the goal both to influence policymakers and to educate the public. This last element may be the most important, especially with regard to nuclear fusion, a technology so sophisticated that its comprehension was considered to be beyond the capacities of the public. Since government authorities legitimated their monopoly over policymaking through their exclusive access to expert knowledges, by democratizing scientific informa-tion, both Greenpeace and the Wyhl activists demonstrated the potential for democratic decision-making, even regarding nuclear technologies.

The efforts of movements like Wyhl and Greenpeace to democratize sci-ence dovetailed with long-standing efforts by scientists to distribute scien-tific knowledge and educate the public, especially regarding nuclear weapons and nuclear power. The nuclear chemist Takagi Jinzaburō, for instance, was part of a team of Japanese scientists who in 1975 founded the Citizens' Nuclear Information Center, which through its scientific publications and public campaigns played a central role in Japan's antinuclear movements. Takagi promoted a vision of "citizen science" through which an informed public with scientific expertise could claim decision-making capacities over important technical policy issues (Avenell 2016, 95–96). Barry Commoner, a cellular biologist who played a similar role in the United States, "was among the earliest proponents of the social obligation of scientists to pro-vide information to the public so that they can meaningfully participate in democratic decision-making processes" (Brulle 2009, 3). Commoner, a pioneer of the science information movement, cofounded in the late 1950s the Committee for Nuclear Information, which publicized the negative health impacts of nuclear testing (McCormick 2009). Takagi and Commoner are just two of the best-known examples of scientists who sought to make scientific knowledge, especially about nuclear technologies, widely available as a basis for democratic decision-making. The collaboration of such scientists was a necessary condition that made possible the creation of democratizing science movements. "Democratizing science activism," writes Sabrina McCormick, uniting a variety of social movements under this category, "manifests itself in a number of ways: contesting expert knowledge, re-framing science, making political claims, mobilizing scientific resources, and democratizing knowledge production" (2007, 611). Movements such as the Wyhl encampment and Greenpeace demonstrated the necessity of widespread public access to scientific knowledges for a project to democratize political decision-making structures.

The Clamshell Alliance and Feminist Organizing

The Wyhl encampment's successful implementation of direct-action tactics was an inspiration for the initial organizers of the Clamshell Alliance, which was founded in 1976 to oppose construction of a nuclear power station in a tidal marsh near Seabrook, New Hampshire.[2] "The concept of democracy was at the heart of the Clamshell's vision," claims Barbara Epstein, as it was for the Wyhl movement (1991, 82). But the orientation or object of democratization was different. Whereas Wyhl activists emphasized democratizing government decision-making, in part through contesting the monopoly of expert scientific knowledge, for the Clamshell Alliance democratization efforts were also (and perhaps primarily) oriented inward, that is, to create and maintain democratic structures within the movement itself, which were thought to prefigure and help bring forth a future democratic society.

In keeping with the Wyhl experience, Clamshell actions consisted of a crescendo of direct actions to block construction of the plant and focus public attention on its dangers. Although the police never allowed Clamshell activists to create an encampment anything like the one in the Wyhl forest, their increasingly large actions nonetheless gained significant attention. In a first action in August 1976, eighteen activists entered the construction site with the intention of planting trees, but they were arrested for trespassing before they could do so; a few weeks later, 180 activists entered the site and were quickly arrested; and in May of the following year, when two thousand activists, organized in hundreds of affinity groups, tried to occupy the site, more than fourteen hundred were arrested. The Clamshell Alliance failed to block construction of the Seabrook plant, but the US antinuclear movement more broadly, significantly aided by the 1979 Three Mile Island disaster, shifted public and government views on nuclear energy: after Seabrook, no nuclear reactor was built in the United States until 2013.

Some of the most significant achievements of the Clamshell Alliance, however, as I said, were internal, the result of experiments to democratize activist organizational structures. Three overlapping practices, which, although not invented by the Clamshell Alliance, were developed and consolidated by them, have continued to resonate in activist circles long afterward: organization in affinity groups, consensus decision-making, and nonviolent direct action. Affinity groups are "small assemblages of roughly five to fifteen people who take part in an action jointly, planning their participation collectively" (Kauffman 2017, 14). The groups provide basic organizational structure during actions in addition to facilitating active participation and allowing for decentralized discussion and decision-making forums. Democratic participation can be best achieved, from this perspective, on a very small scale. Consensus decision-making in the Clamshell Alliance, at least in its first period, was absolute, requiring complete agreement with no objections for an action to be approved. Finally, the dedication to direct action, such as physically blocking the construction, was accompanied by a strict conception of nonviolence that prohibited violence not only against persons but also against property. Some activists within the alliance eventually challenged these stringent conceptions of consensus and nonviolence, favoring an 80 percent or 90 percent threshold for consensus regarding violence against persons and allowing for property damage (specifically, cutting the wire fence surrounding the construction site) regarding the latter (Downey 1986, 363–364). These disagreements, in fact, were central factors in the breakup of the alliance in 1979.

The objective of the Clamshell Alliance, to stop construction of the reactor, was thus accompanied by the mandate to create a just and democratic internal group dynamic. In certain respects, in fact, the movement "privilege[d] participation over efficiency" (Kauffman 2017, 60). One might say that it maintained that the realization of its goals could only be attained through democratic participation. The radical insistence on democracy and nonviolence in the movement, from this perspective, is aimed to prevent repeating within the group itself the social hierarchies and inequalities that it opposes in the society as a whole. The organizing strategy of the Clamshell Alliance, like so many other subsequent organizing experiences, was thus prefigurative insofar as it sought within the movement to act according to principles that could inform and structure a future, better society.

Although some scholars and activists trace these participatory democratic organizing structures, such as the consensus model and affinity group formation, to anarchist traditions, I find stronger the connection to radical feminist groups (B. Epstein 1991, 69, 81). Clamshell Alliance activists identified democratic and consensus-based relations with feminism, claims L. A. Kauffman, "to such a degree that some called it 'feminist process'" (2017, 55). Radical feminists, in groups such as New York Radical Women, Redstockings, and Gainesville Women's Liberation, had indeed pioneered in the late sixties and early seventies participatory democratic organizing in small groups, which sought as much as possible to avoid traditional leadership roles and centralized decision-making structures. Equality and participation were prioritized within the organizations, and were achieved especially through the practices of consciousness-raising. Efforts were made for everyone to speak at meetings and required that consensus be reached before actions are taken. "Decisions . . . in our group," explained the Gainesville collective, "are as democratic as we know how to make them. If we vote on something, those who are in the minority have a chance to reconsider their vote and decide whether nor not to go along with the majority or whether to stop the group from doing what is has voted to do" (Gainesville Women's Liberation 2000, 71). It is difficult to verify lines of influence, and many other movement sectors experimented with practices of participatory democracy in the 1960s, but the feminist vocabulary and repertoire of practices were at least one framework that was adopted, deployed, and renewed by the Clamshell Alliance and other antinuclear movements.

Democratization as a Problem

It is remarkable that, facing the potential for nuclear catastrophe, the Wyhl encampment and the Clamshell Alliance became platforms for demanding new forms of democracy. One could easily imagine that such an existential threat would push activists, in the name of urgency and efficacy, to adopt fewer rather than more participatory practices and democratic structures. Instead, these movements viewed the (seemingly less efficient) route of greater democracy to be the only means for reaching their goals. Although, as I mentioned at the outset, antinuclear activism has waned in recent decades, the aspirations and practices of these democratization projects cultivated in the antinuclear movements of the 1970s have continued, sometimes in subterranean form, to constitute a vital core of a range of contemporary struggles.

The legacy of the antinuclear movements to seek political change through democratizing science is easily recognized in numerous subsequent activist strategies. Contesting claims to scientific expertise, for example, played a significant role in AIDS activism in the 1980s (S. Epstein 1991). Today, the terrain on which the strategy of democratizing science lives on most clearly is climate activism—in a way, however, that poses conflicting mandates. As in the case of nuclear technologies, the spread and democratization of scientific knowledges about the climate constitute an essential means for transforming existing governmental decision-making structures, which have proven so incapable of addressing the problem. And yet climate science, no less than nuclear science, is extraordinarily complex and presents great difficulties for nonspecialists. Furthermore, climate change, too, presents an existential threat to humanity and the planet, making effective action and swift change paramount. If we wait for the transformative effects of democratization, one might conclude, it will be too late.

The legacies of the democratic experiments internal to movement organizing in groups like the Clamshell Alliance are equally conflicting. Affinity groups, consensus decision-making, assembly structures, and other democratic forms like those deployed in the antinuclear movements have become extraordinarily widespread. One need look no further than the horizontalist practices of the alterglobalization movements and, later, the so-called leaderless movements that erupted in the years following 2011, with variations from Tunisia and Egypt to Spain, Greece, the United States, and Turkey, as well as Black Lives Matter. The refusal of centralized leadership and the construction of assembly structures and other participatory forms, often within encampments, served as experiments with new social and political relations with the potential to be generalized. The Spanish activists of the 15M movement demanded "real democracy now" (¡Democracia real ya!) rather than the sham democracy promoted in contemporary societies. And yet critics, as well as activists themselves, lament that these movements have been relatively short-lived and have not generally achieved their goals.

In both these registers, in terms of scientific expertise and movement organization, democratization clearly is not an immediate, unequivocal solution, but instead appears as a conundrum. In this respect, the antinuclear movements of the seventies had the great merit of identifying a real political problem—a problem, that is, that cannot be dismissed but must be addressed, engaged, and worked through politically, a problem that remains today at the top of the political agenda. In previous chapters we have seen how the problem of constituting a revolutionary democracy resonates through struggles from Kwangju, South Korea, to Setúbal, Portugal, and from Guinea-Bissau to Chile. Linking these diverse experiences and recognizing how together they compose a mosaic gives us a rich vision of the problem of revolutionary democracy.

PART VI

THE CONTINUATION OF WAR
BY OTHER MEANS

15

The End of Mediation

A Theory of Neoliberalism *Avant la Lettre*

> The "party system" no longer aims to represent conflicts, nor to me-
> diate or organize them: it delegates them to "economic interests" and
> poses itself as the specific form of the State, separate from and hostile
> to movements in society. The party system no longer "receives" the
> thrusts from the base; it controls and represses them.
>
> —Sergio Bologna

Since my investigations in this book are focused on the progressive and
revolutionary movements, I generally do not analyze the nature and
transformations of the ruling powers, and thus I speak little of presidential
elections, new legislation, court rulings, government economic policies,
and the like. I make exceptions on two conditions: that the explorations
of the structures of power emerge directly from theorizing within the
movements and that they contribute to strategic decisions. The theoretical developments I analyzed in Chapter 11, primarily among feminists,
fulfilled these conditions: investigations of how multiple structures of
domination are intimately intertwined and mutually constitutive directly
informed proposals to construct strategic multiplicities of struggle. In this
chapter, the relation between theory and strategy is somewhat more complex. Whereas there was widespread recognition among movements in different parts of the world of a tendency by which governance mechanisms of
mediation were being withdrawn, views on an adequate political strategy
in response to this development were, as we will see, more divided and
ambivalent.

One of the clearest symptoms of what I am calling the end of mediation
is the dramatic increase of repression in the 1970s, which was almost uni-
versally recognized by activists in a wide range of national contexts. Given
the analyses in previous chapters, this fact should need little verification

or explanation. One could say, in summary fashion, that increased repression acted on at least three terrains. First, police violence against peaceful demonstrations became significantly more severe and deadlier in the 1970s: the four antiwar protesters at Kent State University shot in 1970 by the Ohio National Guard and the hundreds killed by South African police during the 1976 Soweto uprising in South Africa are well-known examples. Second, political leaders and activists were singled out for assassination or died in police custody under mysterious circumstances: the 1969 Chicago police murder of Black Panther leader Fred Hampton in his bed and Steve Biko's 1977 death in a South African prison are representative. Third, right-wing and fascist groups, often with ambiguous relations to the military, the police, and security forces, increased their activity: the fascist paramilitary Grey Wolves in Turkey, for example, increased their attacks on leftist activists and religious minorities, and through Operation Condor US-supported death squads grew throughout Latin America, especially the Southern Cone. Lethal operations against protesters, assassinations of movement leaders, right-wing terrorism, and other forms of repressive violence were not new, of course, but in the 1970s they dramatically increased in number and severity.

Escalating repression, however, as I said, is only a symptom. The core phenomenon to be grasped is the tendency toward a decline of the mechanisms and institutions of political mediation that had served as pillars of governmental and economic power throughout the middle of the twentieth century.

Mediation and the Political A Priori

Before investigating its demise, however, I should provide a brief theoretical sketch of how political mediation had previously been understood and how it had functioned. Political mediation is generally understood as a mode of governance and administration characterized by interaction, response, and adjustment among diverse political forces. Classic institutions of political mediation are often cast, as the etymology suggests, as being in the middle, that is, between conflicting forces, and thus as relatively impartial arbiters. This basic notion is prominent in a wide range of theoretical frameworks, from those affirming the pluralist nature of democratic societies to those that highlight the powers of civil society.[1] Two institutions that have played particularly significant roles in the previous chapters have often been cast in this mediatory role. The official trade union is thought to mediate antagonisms between workers and management, for instance, both in its daily functioning and in moments of crisis, such as when it negotiates the settlement to a strike. Similarly, the state is cast in a mediatory position insofar as it responds to social pressures or protests with reforms. One oft-cited example can suffice: the Johnson administration and the US Congress are often said to have responded to the long season of civil rights activism with the 1964 Civil Rights Act.

Another angle from which to approach this issue of mediation is via the problem of legitimation, because the functioning of these mediatory institutions and mechanisms was integral to the claims of legitimacy of many forms of authority in twentieth-century societies. When Jürgen Habermas, for instance, theorized a legitimation crisis (*Legitimationsprobleme*, "legitimation problems," in the original title [1976]) and warned that confidence in administrative and political authorities at all levels of society was declining, he was still working under the assumption that legitimation was necessary for stable and lasting forms of governance. By the time Habermas's book was published in 1973, however, the legitimation problem was already losing its purchase.

In previous chapters, we have seen that it was clear to activists in a wide variety of progressive and revolutionary movements of the 1970s that neither the official trade union nor the state played a neutral mediatory role when they negotiated agreements and reforms. Those in radical industrial workers' organizations, for instance, as we saw in Chapters 8 and 10, took for granted that the dominant unions were not simply arbiters standing between management and workers (and much less were they faithful representatives of the workers' interests and desires) but rather were dedicated to maintaining harmonious cooperation with the firm and the capitalist social order more generally. Similarly, there was no illusion among radical workers, feminist, and antiracist movements that the state stood as mediator of plural social forces; many movements sought reforms, of course, but they knew the state stood firmly on the side of those in power. The movements recognized, one might say, that legitimation was no longer a preoccupation for those in power, that they were developing structures of authority that did not rely on it.

It is not accurate, however, to characterize the general theoretical position circulating among these movements as simply denouncing claims of political mediation as pure mystification. It is more precise—and will help frame the strategic options when this mediation is recognized to be in decline—to introduce a nuance into this critique of mediation with aid from more recent scholarship in the field of media studies. Please pardon the leap to a different field of study, but following these media scholars helps flesh out the intuition developed by the 1970s movements: that institutions of political mediation are never simply *between* competing or conflicting forces but rather are guided by a political a priori.

Start with Marshall McLuhan's (1964) famous mandate to focus on media as technologies—"the medium is the message"—which puts emphasis on not the content but the structures of mediation themselves. A further step, which is key for understanding political mediation, is summarized by Friedrich Kittler's claim that "media determine our situation." W. J. T. Mitchell and Mark Hansen explain that Kittler's claim poses mediation in an existential, even ontological frame: "Media form the infrastructural basis, the quasi-transcendental condition, for experience and understanding."[2] Two conceptual operations are central here. First, a medium—Kittler is thinking of media like the telegraph and the gramophone—is clearly not a mere conduit that transmits information or signs but an active mechanism that is socially constitutive, something like an environment or, as Mitchell and Hansen say, an infrastructure that supports and conditions a form of life. Rather than considering a medium as a thing or fixed structure, then, it must be understood as a process: hence mediation rather than medium. The second and more significant shift is to understand mediation as a predetermining or quasi-transcendental condition: mediation is no longer *in-between* but now *prior*. This condition is known in media studies as "the technological a priori"; as Anna Tuschling explains, it is "the idea that media in a certain sense precede every form of perception and signification" (2015, 682). This technological a priori clarifies the distance from McLuhan's earlier understanding. "Unlike Marshall McLuhan, who saw technical media as 'extensions of man,'" maintains Eva Horn, "Kittler saw media as the technological a priori of human thought and history—and thus, rather, *man as an extension of media*" (Horn 2012, 477). Mediation, in other words, in addition to being a mechanism of interaction or expression, includes (perhaps primarily) a directive function. It is productive, not only generating subjectivities but also determining or conditioning a social order. Mediation is situated paradoxically, at once in between and prior, both a technology of interaction and an infrastructure that determines the conditions for experience.

To come back to my argument, then, translating these theoretical innovations of media studies gives us a double characterization of political mediation, which is close to the view held by the radical movements of the seventies. Political mediation, they recognized, involves a set of technologies, social structures, and practices that combine a receptive, interactive function that responds to demands and generates reforms, on the one hand, with a guiding function that maintains the overall structures of power, on the other. The welfare institutions of the Keynesian state and the wage mechanisms of Fordist labor regimes, for example, were simultaneously in between and prior; that is, the same mechanisms of mediation that initiate reforms also allow for the exertion of discipline and control. Following media studies scholars, then, we can say that political mediation accomplishes half of its work "in between," by exerting and maintaining power through continuous engagement and management of social antagonisms in a dynamic reformist process, and the other half a priori insofar as it establishes "the infrastructural basis" for social and political experience.

Beyond the Legitimation Crisis: Neoliberalism Theorized from the Movements

This theory of political mediation—which, admittedly, I have presented in the barest terms—is really only a prerequisite for the theoretical hypothesis that most interests me here. Although mediation had been central to the mechanisms of rule and the reformist operations of capitalist and state power at least since the end of World War II, especially in the dominant countries, in the seventies the operations of political mediation precipitously declined: workers' strikes were less likely to be met with wage concessions, protest movements were less likely to be answered with social or legal reforms, and demands regarding social needs were less likely to result in new or increased welfare provisions. A tendency began, in other words, by which the mechanisms of engagement, negotiation, and reform that had previously been important components of the relationship between power and resistance and that had maintained stability, managing the threats posed by antagonistic social forces, were now gradually being withdrawn.

This tendency was clearly on the agenda of right-wing ideologues, who were well aware, as we saw in Chapter 8, that in the 1970s not only the factories but society as a whole was becoming ungovernable, and that, in response, dramatic changes to the ruling political and economic structures were required (Chamayou 2021). They understood that industrial revolt had risen to unsustainable levels and that rebellious workers could no longer be tamed by the leadership and guidance of the established unions. In the realm of state spending, similarly, economists blamed the structures of reform and mediation, asserting, for example, that the Keynesian state was responsible for growing deficits because it responded too much to social demands. Increasingly, such economists preached "fiscal discipline," which meant, in effect, to curb mechanisms of mediation that respond to social demands (see, e.g., Buchanan and Wagner 1977). Samuel Huntington advocated for a corresponding response to the crisis of governability in the political sphere. Structures of political mediation, he proclaimed, by allowing so many previously inactive segments of society to participate politically (he lists "blacks, Indians, Chicanos, white ethnic groups, students and women"), have precipitated a political crisis (1975, 61). In order to guarantee "the effective operation of a democratic political system," he asserted, some social groups must be made marginal and politically passive, and thus excluded from mechanisms of political mediation (1975, 114). Views of developments in all these fields—labor relations, macroeconomics, and political participation— provide just some of the many ways of recognizing the core fact that, for those in power, the reformist aspects of political mediation came to be viewed no longer as stabilizing social technologies but rather as threats to their authority, dangerous mechanisms by which social forces could undermine the established structures of rule. The technologies of mediation, they believed, in effect, had to be curtailed or destroyed.

On the other side, theorists engaged in revolutionary movements, especially the workers' movement, posed "the end of mediation" as a guiding principle for investigating the ways capitalist relations of power were being restructured in the seventies. According to Antonio Negri, the forms of mediation that had for decades been key tools for promoting capitalist development and quelling worker antagonism were now in crisis (2005b, 71). Karl-Heinz Roth provides a concrete example, which I noted in Chapter 8, of how mediation was no longer deployed as a capitalist tactic to address and contain worker rebellion. During the 1973 West German strikes, he highlighted the fact that, in contrast to 1969, the capitalist class now offered "no mechanisms of reformist mediation or rising salaries to counteract worker rebellion" (1974, 17). The decreasing use of mediation in response to labor revolt was not isolated to West Germany, of course, but was becoming a general condition.

Sergio Bologna presented a corresponding hypothesis with respect to political structures: mediation was being withdrawn from governance practices, he maintained, just as it was in industrial relations. The system of state and parties, he claimed, "no longer aims to mediate and represent conflicts in civil society" as it had throughout the long postwar period. Instead of responding to pressures from the base, he continued, the parties and the state seek merely to control and repress them (1980, 36, 38). Antonio Negri reasoned, in line with Bologna, that since it is now unable to exert hegemony through mediation, capitalist power is forced to resort increasingly to a logic of unmediated command. Whereas the discipline and violence exerted by capital and the state had previously been legitimated—at least in part, at least in appearance—via the social infrastructures and processes of mediation, Negri asserted, it now tended to become, deprived of such means of legitimation, "domination in its purest form" (2005a, 246; see also 283). In a different theoretical register and more distant from the movements, Michel Foucault in these same years attempted to interpret the lack of political mediation with a similar proposition: "Civil war," he declared, "is the matrix of all struggles of power."[3] The violent suppression of worker militancy and social protest in the 1970s, then, were just two of the many fields in which these theorists interpreted a tendency within the structures of power from mediation to domination.

Reading the tendency of governance structures in the 1970s simply in terms of "the end of mediation" is not quite right, however, especially given the lessons I drew from media studies scholars above: namely, that mediation must be understood doubly, as both in between and prior, both a technology of interaction and a quasi-transcendental condition of social experience. This double conception of mediation allows us to pose the hypothesis more precisely. What these theorists claim has declined is really only the first component—in this case, the state and capitalist mechanisms of interaction and reform. The second component, the political a priori, remains intact and, perhaps, hardened, since capital and the state continue to "determine our situation" and form the "infrastructural basis" for political life—but now without the cushion or legitimation provided by the various institutions and technologies of reform and responsiveness. What results is a rather paradoxical situation of a medium without mediation: the ruling powers dictate the modes in which political life can develop but exclude the mechanisms of interaction and reform. This is how we should interpret the tendency by which the structures of power are shifting from mediation to command or domination.

This notion of a tendency toward the decline of mediation is significant, in part, because it constitutes a theory of neoliberalism *avant la lettre*, one closely tied to the experiences of the movements. The refusal of management to respond to workers' demands, the state's increasing unwillingness to meet social protest with governmental reforms, and the progressive dismantling of welfare structures—all of this mixed with an increase of repressive force—were some of the ways in which the movements registered a shift. Neoliberalism, from this perspective, is the form of capitalist economic and political rule in which mediations tend to be eliminated or, at least, pushed to the background. In time, these first threads were woven together into the fabric of a fully consolidated neoliberal economic policy, which has been well elaborated and analyzed by theorists such as David Harvey (2007): the decline of government regulation, the privatization of state and common resources, the drastic reduction of state expenditures for social services, and the undermining of trade unions and worker power—all of which concentrated control in the hands of the capitalist and state elites. Neoliberalism is thus, in part, the capitalist response to the situation, which I investigated in Chapters 8 and 10, of increasingly ungovernable factories and the threat of ungovernable societies posed by organized radical industrial workers.

The hypothesis of an end of mediation also anticipated, in part, a second contemporary theoretical stream of neoliberalism studies focused on democratic political rationality more than economic policy, well represented by the work of Wendy Brown (2017, 2019). Insofar as the mediation of plural social forces was considered, as I said earlier, to be essential to liberal conceptions of democratic social and political institutions, the end of mediation undermines the basic conditions of democratic society. Here the two-part nature of mediation is key. For the movements and theorists of the seventies, the decline of the in-betweenness of mediation—and, thus, the decrease in mechanisms of give-and-take between state and society, capital and labor, and so forth—implies also a hardening of the quasi-transcendental condition, the infrastructural basis of political life, which increasingly takes the form of unilateral command. Whereas Brown draws on Foucault's analyses of *homo economicus* and the increasing imposition of market logic over political rationalities, the seventies theorists I am highlighting here are closer to Foucault's invocation of civil war as the base condition of power—but they arrive at roughly the same conclusion, that neoliberalism progressively

THE END OF MEDIATION

destroys the bases that had been held essential to liberal conceptions of democracy and creates in its stead an undemocratic regime of control.

The theorizations of neoliberalism developed over the last decades are in many respects richer than these early anticipations. The advantage of the 1970s theories, however, was their proximity to the movements and thus their constant focus on charting a political strategy adequate to address the new situation. Put simply, if you want to figure out what to do about neoliberalism, then the 1970s theories might provide a good starting point.

Autonomous Projects Toward Dual Power

It should be obvious that the response of revolutionary movements was not to advocate resuscitating the old institutions of political and economic mediation, effectively restoring the postwar capitalist social order they had so long struggled against. Although their strategies were varied, I group them, in rather approximate fashion, into two broad categories, which were in many cases mixed together.

One category includes movements that, when recognizing the declining effectiveness of protests and labor negotiations and the increase of repression, dedicated their energies to autonomous projects. By autonomous I do not mean retreating from society—for example, in isolated rural communes— but rather taking into their own hands the creation of new social forms, without appeal to the ruling authorities. There is no need to elaborate here the actions of such groups because they have filled the previous chapters, albeit in radically different political contexts. In Chapter 3, for instance, I highlighted aspects of the gay liberation movement of the seventies that, independent of the dominant social order, sought to create new social relations as part of a homosexual mode of life. The various encampments discussed in Chapters 13 and 14 similarly provided an adequate context for autonomous social experiments, bringing together heterogeneous populations that transformed one another in a shared struggle. In Chapter 10, autonomy and democracy were explicitly theorized in the Italian experiments to articulate multiple struggles for liberation into a coherent movement. Finally, in Chapters 2, 5, and 6, the various self-managed democratic institutions created in Guinea-Bissau, Chile, and Portugal—including village commissions, neighborhood commissions, and worker commissions in self-managed factories—all pointed toward how the structures of revolutionary democracy, when they achieve a sufficient scale, open the potential for a real alternative to the dominant structures. Ultimately, the strategy of autonomy, in all these varied instances, alludes toward a situation of dual power, in which revolutionary social relations and political structures exist in parallel to and in competition with the ruling power.[4]

Let me add just one more example that, although small in scale, illustrates well the strategy of autonomous organizing without mediation. In the late 1960s and early 1970s, when abortion was still illegal in the United States, a small collective of women in Chicago, all using the pseudonym "Jane," organized an extraordinarily effective project to offer safe, affordable abortions. They did not protest abortion laws or demand that the state or some other authority provide abortions. They simply did it themselves, and before they were finally arrested in 1972 had performed approximately eleven thousand abortions (Lessin and Pildes 2022). In addition to providing a clear illustration of a small-scale autonomous project, this example helps clarify that in this period the political logic of mediation and reform, to different degrees in different contexts, still functioned. The Janes were delighted, of course, when the US Supreme Court's *Roe v. Wade* decision made abortion legal, partially in response to accumulated feminist pressure. The end of mediation, I should be clear, was a tendency, not an absolute fact. But that tendency was widely recognized by activists, leading to the emergent phenomenon of experimentations with autonomous political projects in small groups like the Janes and, elsewhere, at a mass scale.

Fight Fire with Fire

A second strategic response to the end of mediation—instead of turning away from the ruling authorities, so to speak, to create autonomous projects— directly confronted the state and the forces of repression on equal terms. The first clandestine armed groups emerged, according to Zwerman, Steinhoff, and della Porta, "when the state had escalated repression against the broader New Left," including increasing police violence, implementing emergency laws, criminalizing forms of protest, and heightening use of surveillance and infiltration (2000, 89–90). Intensifying repression together with declining responsiveness to protest and other peaceful forms of political expression was interpreted to require a strategy of armed conflict. I will investigate in subsequent chapters the significant differences among organizations that chose this path, but here I want simply to demonstrate how for some groups armed struggle was judged to be the logical and necessary response to the end of mediation.

This assessment of the new political landscape, for example, constituted the backdrop for the formation of the Weather Underground, which grew out of one faction of Students for a Democratic Society (SDS), an organization that at the time counted roughly a hundred thousand members. That faction of SDS, which emerged victorious in the debates at the organization's June 1969 national convention in Chicago, advanced a platform composed primarily of antiracism (in solidarity with Black Power movements) and anti-imperialism (against the US war in Vietnam), but more important than their stated platform may have been their combative stance and their claim that since the conditions for doing politics had changed, new tactics were necessary. By the time of the convention, SDS members, like activists in the United States more generally, were keenly attuned to the increasing repressive violence on the national and international political scene. The Chicago police riot ten months earlier against protesters outside the Democratic National Convention (DNC) was a fresh memory, as were the assassinations of Robert F. Kennedy and Martin Luther King Jr. In the months after the SDS convention, the assassination of Black Panther leader Fred Hampton by the Chicago police and the opening of the Chicago 8 trial against some of the leaders at the DNC protests reinforced the sense of danger, the injustices of the legal system, and the fact that the authorities could act with impunity. Furthermore, the increasing ineffectiveness of protest politics began to be taken for granted. Anyone who had participated in an antiwar protest in those years had to share the frustration and dismay when seeing that, even as antiwar protests grew ever larger, the US military engagement in Vietnam only intensified. Although many activists had previously believed that protests—if large enough, organized well enough, and sustained over time— could stop the war or, at least, limit its escalation, it was now clear that the mediatory levers linking protest and reform had been severed. "The sense was," remembers Bill Ayers, a core member of the Weather Underground, "we had to do whatever we had to to stop the war" (quoted in Green and Seigel 1983). If protest is no longer effective and repression ever more intense, activists reasoned, a new strategy is necessary.

Across the Atlantic, Ulrike Meinhof, at the time a celebrity journalist, echoed the US activists' frustration regarding the ineffectiveness of protest and the impunity of authorities. She proposed in a 1968 column in the magazine *Konkret* that the slogan "From protest to resistance" should be adopted in reaction to the lack of responsiveness on the part of power: you can protest all you want, she maintained, but power will not change. The "boundary between verbal protest and physical resistance" was crossed for the first time in Germany on a mass scale, according to Meinhof, in the rallies in response to the attempted assassination of the leftist leader Rudi Dutschke in April 1968 by an anticommunist with neo-Nazi ties. "The bullets that hit Rudi," she wrote, "have ended the dream of nonviolence" (quoted in Varon 2004, 205). Leftist activists did not merely chant slogans at the subsequent rallies but threw stones and Molotov cocktails, even though, as she noted, such forms of counterviolence were not enough to change power relations (Meinhof 2008, 240). Meinhof turned this criticism on her own vocation as a columnist in her final magazine piece before going underground. She condemned "columnism" and claimed that in the current environment, political journalism, the occupation she had been practicing for the previous decade, could no longer be effective, no matter how progressive, no matter how eloquent (Meinhof 2008, 249–254). The time was past, she believed, when rhetorical persuasion could contribute to reforming the structures of power. Meinhof herself, a short time later, shifted from verbal protest to physical resistance by joining the Red Army Faction.

Just one more example—among innumerable others—of a specific event, a turning point that convinced activists of the need to move from protest to armed conflict: In Derry, Northern Ireland, on the last Sunday in January 1972, the Northern Ireland Civil Rights Association organized a peaceful march to protest the mass arrests and internment without trial of suspected Irish Republican Army members by British authorities. Instead of allowing the nonviolent march to proceed, British soldiers fired live rounds on the demonstrators, leaving fourteen dead and many injured. "For supporters of the Provisional IRA," writes Daniel Finn, "Bloody Sunday sounded the death knell for the tactic of unarmed protest: from now on, force would have to be met with force" (2019, 100). Any remaining hope that protests would lead the occupying British authorities to reform were abandoned. The Provisional IRA began its bombing campaign later that year.[5]

By highlighting the fact that clandestine armed groups were formed in response to increased state and fascist violence and decreased responsiveness to protest in the late 1960s and early 1970s, I do not intend to argue that theirs was the only or the most effective response. On the contrary, as I said earlier, autonomous political strategies were chosen by many organizations.

Furthermore, I will highlight in Chapter 17 how revolutionary and liberation movements that adopted a dual strategy and formed a double organization were more productive politically at the time and are more relevant for our political choices today. And yet, it is essential to grasp the clear-sighted assessment of the political landscape that served as a basis for the formation of many of the clandestine armed groups. I will explore the trajectories of and important differences among some of these organizations in Chapter 16.

16

Theaters of Injustice

What, in my view, should be questioned here is not the *principle* of armed struggle, nor its methods, which are part of every revolutionary movement, but, at the heart of each specific situation, its real influence on *the whole set of anticapitalist struggles*.

—Félix Guattari

The spectacular exploits of clandestine armed urban organizations—bombings, hijackings, robberies, kidnappings, assassinations, shoot-outs with the police, and more—were at the time and remain today some of the most prominent images of the subversive 1970s. These groups at times drew widespread sympathy and admiration from others on the Left and at others were broadly condemned and despised; they commanded the attention (and animated the deepest fears) of the political establishment; and they completely mesmerized the media. This power of fascination is certainly one key to understanding the role and impact of urban armed struggle in the 1970s, and I will return to it below. But one should keep in mind that focusing on the affective intensities and the mystique of the armed groups has led many analysts astray. Journalists and scholars, in fact, have long relied, explicitly or implicitly, on a standard crutch: they assume that such forms of illegal and violent political action are expressions of irrationalism or fanaticism, which some trace ultimately to the psychopathologies of the militants themselves.[1]

In part to counter such assumptions, I begin by investigating the rational basis of the analyses and strategies developed within the urban armed struggle groups, setting aside for the moment political judgments regarding their analyses or actions. From this relatively neutral vantage point, two foundational elements become clear. I briefly explored the first at the end of Chapter 15: these groups reasoned that since police repression, coupled in many countries with fascist or right-wing paramilitary violence, had markedly increased and since the state had become less responsive and less open to reform, making protest tactics less effective, then new means of political expression had to be invented. The second element that becomes clear is that, by and large, these armed groups were driven by outrage at the injustices committed with impunity by those in power. Their actions thus aimed to reveal the injustices that had been hidden or that the public had simply failed to appreciate sufficiently. In some cases, revealing injustice was accompanied by makeshift trials of the accused and even retribution against the perpetrators.

More important than the object of any single target was the pattern revealed by a series of actions, creating something like a cognitive map of power and its abuses. Hence their highly performative and representational character. Political violence, when deployed by these groups, "was *by design* symbolic"; even a bombing campaign, they thought, could compose "a new practice of storytelling" (Varon 2004, 179, emphasis in original; Ayers 2000, 219). Operations were thus intended to have symbolic significance, which, woven together, could generate an extended political narrative. In this respect, the armed groups aimed to erect a kind of political theater, something like what Bertolt Brecht called a *Lehrstück*, a learning-play. Weapons and violence were necessary but secondary to the real strategic aim: a public political pedagogy to reveal and contest the injustices of those in power.

I thus proceed in each subsection that follows by selecting a pair of clandestine organizations whose actions together illustrate different faces of this political strategy. The pairs are presented in roughly chronological order, which corresponds in many ways to the increasing intensity and violence of the conflicts. Organizing my investigation in this way is designed, as I said, to reveal the rational bases of these groups before arriving at political evaluations.

Fiscal Audits and Public Oversight

One of the most direct means to unveil and combat injustices committed with impunity by those in power was simply to obtain inculpating documents and make them public, with the conviction that transparency will have a cleansing effect, that once people have the necessary information and know what those in power are doing, they will act for change. Although these are illegal activities, arms and conflict are not necessary for this tactic (if all goes well), so it should not be included under the category of armed struggle. And yet it constitutes a baseline for practices of propaganda of the deed, which are central to the actions of the armed groups.

In 1969 and 1970, Uruguay's Tupamaros (Movimiento de Liberación Nacional—Tupamaros) orchestrated a series of operations to document crimes committed by elites and state institutions. Although the Tupamaros were armed, the group's internal handbook explicitly rejected any type of terrorist attack "because it is inhuman, hurts innocent lives, and has a negative political effect." Instead, the handbook continued, "careful study of the circumstances" and "special precautions" were required in order "not to impact human lives" (quoted in Blum 2014, 391). The Tupamaros' first major armed propaganda operation, in February 1969, put these principles into action. After having learned from an inside informant that an investment bank maintained a secret double accounting system in order to shield the financial dealings of wealthy clients, the Tupamaros raided the bank, stole the accounting ledgers, and delivered the evidence to the steps of the state prosecutor. No shots were fired and no one was injured. The evidence led to widespread media reports and multiple convictions (Blum 2014, 391).

The Tupamaros continued in the next two years with a rapid series of operations similarly designed to publicize evidence of injustices. Just days after the investment bank break-in, seven Tupamaros militants, led by the group's founder, Raúl Sendic, raided the country's largest casino and ordered the employees to hand over all the cash, coming away with $11 million. This heist was aimed at raising funds, not uncovering injustices, but afterward the Tupamaros pledged to return a portion of the money to the casino employees, claiming that they stole only from the rich oligarchs, earning them the sobriquet "Robin Hood guerrillas" in *Time* magazine. Subsequent actions combined such Robin Hood–esque tactics with the revelation of injustices. In September 1969 the Tupamaros kidnapped a wealthy entrepreneur, Gaetano Pellegrini, and subsequently released him to his family in exchange for donations to popular schools and clinics. The following year, they raided a house belonging to the Mailos family, members of the Uruguayan oligarchy, after having learned details of how they had obtained their wealth through corruption. In the raid, the Tupamaros stole not only gold ingots but also the family's accounting books, which documented illegal activities. They delivered the evidence to the Uruguayan judiciary, which led to tax fraud convictions (Blum 2014, 391–393). It is striking how, in several of its actions, the Tupamaros functioned as a grand auditor, opening the account ledgers of Uruguay's oligarchy to demonstrate the illegal sources of their enormous wealth.

The series of Tupamaro actions successfully completed without a shot between 1969 and 1970 had some direct political effects: in addition to the specific injustices they revealed, their actions inspired mainstream political campaigns against corruption and contributed to a general social sense of outrage against the oligarchy. But the group also captivated widespread public attention, generating a sense of glamor and power: Uruguayan "society—left wing or not—was fascinated," Pablo Blum maintains, "with the MLN's bold operations" (2014, 392). The actions of the Tupamaros not only enjoyed wide public approval in Uruguay but also captured the imagination of the Left throughout the world (Caula and Silva 2009, 53–59).

In the following years, the Tupamaros' tactics changed significantly due, in large part, to the increasingly vicious war against "subversives" conducted by the police and the military, and the assassinations of many Tupamaro militants by the right-wing paramilitary force Escuadrón de la Muerte. This period of Uruguay's history was brutally ended by a coup d'état in June 1973 (three months before the military coup in Chile), which installed a military dictatorship that ruled for the next twelve years.

To emphasize the political rationality of such operations to reveal injustice, I want to consider another daring exploit, which was conducted entirely without weapons. The Citizens' Commission to Investigate the FBI was not a guerrilla organization, but it was dedicated, like the Tupamaros, to illegal direct action in order to publish secret documents, with the ultimate aim of opening a rogue government agency to public oversight.[2] The commission conducted a single action, but it was an extraordinarily spectacular one: the theft of documents from an FBI field office in Media, Pennsylvania, southwest of Philadelphia. William Davidon, an antiwar activist and physics professor at Haverford College, planned the burglary and recruited the seven other members of the team, most of them highly educated, all young and white, and all involved in the Catholic peace and antiwar movements; four of them had young children (Medsger 2014, 38–39). One member of the group learned how to pick door locks. Another visited the FBI office posing as a college student doing a research project, and the FBI staff, believing her story, allowed her to observe the layout, door locks, and so forth. Others

investigated the security measures and learned that the FBI offices were un-
guarded at night, although security officers at the county courthouse across
the street could see the entrance. The burglars chose March 8, 1971, for their
break-in, the night of the much-anticipated Muhammad Ali–Joe Frazier
boxing match, which was being broadcast on TV. They assumed that the
courthouse security officers would be distracted by the televised fight and
thus fail to detect activities across the street. Despite some tense moments
and unexpected complications during the heist, the commission successfully
came away with several large suitcases packed with files.

The records they stole, in fact, proved more significant than they had
imagined, including mention of the FBI's Counter Intelligence Program
(COINTELPRO), which illegally conducted surveillance, harassment, infiltration, false arrest, and misinformation activities with the aim of destroying and discrediting US political organizations, especially Black civil
rights and Black Power organizations. The commission photocopied the
files and distributed them to newspapers and members of Congress, and
portions were eventually published. The documents allowed journalists to
reveal further details of illegal FBI activities, demonstrating a wide range
of unlawful government activities. In effect, many of the claims of secret
government programs that had circulated for years in the movements,
and which had been dismissed as conspiracy theories, some of them quite
fantastical-sounding, were proved to be true. Remarkably, despite an extraordinary hunt involving hundreds of FBI agents, which at times came
very close to discovering their targets, the eight members of the commission were never caught and remained silent about their actions for over
forty years.

The Tupamaros, at the southern tip of the Americas, and the Citizens'
Commission to Investigate the FBI, in the north, shared a tactic to steal and
publicize documents that demonstrate the injustices committed by those in
power. The major difference between them was not that one group was armed
and the other not (the Tupamaros, during this period, as I said, planned operations carefully to avoid violence and successfully completed numerous
actions without shots fired) but the level of publicity of their actions, since
the identities of the protagonists of the Citizens' Commission and the details
of their heist, although worthy of a Hollywood film, were kept secret. The experience of the Citizens' Commission might be considered, in this sense, an
action of pure propaganda of the deed, dedicated solely to content—that is,
to the documentation of injustice.

Conscience of the Nation

A second pair of urban guerrilla groups of the 1970s constructed extended narratives through bombings of symbolic sites, planning carefully to avoid injuries. The East Asian Anti-Japan Armed Front sought to expose the injustices of Japan's twentieth-century military aggressions against other Asian countries; its crimes during World War II against Chinese, Koreans, and other peoples; and its colonization of territories such as Hokkaido. The members of the front were all Japanese, but they declared themselves "anti-Japan" in the sense they sought to critique the dominant narrative of the national past.[3] "Recognizing that Japanese people who thought of themselves as victims are actually aggressors," explained Daitōji Masashi, one of the front members, "that is the basis of 'anti-Japan' " (quoted in Schieder 2019, 36). Japanese society at the time seemed to them to have forgotten Japan's history of violent aggressions and those responsible for them—and even, in many cases, now celebrated the perpetrators.[4]

The East Asian Anti-Japan Armed Front's first action, in December 1971, was to bomb the Kōa Kannon monument, which includes the Tomb of Seven Warriors Who Died for Their Country and the Memorial Stone of the 1,068 Executed Martyrs of the Great Pacific War. The seven warriors honored by the tomb were leaders of Japan's fascist war efforts, including General Hideki Tojo, all of whom were sentenced to death as Class A war criminals by the International Tribunal after the end of World War II. The memorial stone honors Class B and Class C war criminals who either were executed or died while imprisoned. By calling attention to the monument, the front was not really unveiling a secret, since the site was well known in Japan. Instead, their action attacked the quiescence of Japanese society for condoning and accepting such glorification of the imperial regime. Their critique and outrage, in this sense, were not particularly radical. Imagine if there were a monument in Germany to honor Hitler, Himmler, Goebbels, and the other "fallen heroes" of the Nazi regime. The Kōa Kannon monument bombing was merely highlighting an obvious truth that Japanese society seemed to have forgotten.

In the following year, the East Asian Anti-Japan Armed Front carried out similar symbolic bombings at sites that evoke (and celebrate) Japan's imperialist past. In April 1972 the front highlighted the history of Japan's colonial regimes in East Asia by bombing the crypt of the Soji Temple in Yokohama, which houses the bones of five thousand Japanese who died in colonial Korea. In October 1972 they turned attention to internal colonialism with the bombing of a statue depicting Japanese colonists with an Ainu man that commemorates the hundred-year anniversary of the colonization of Hokkaido. The date of the bombing marked the date in 1669 when the Ainu chief Shakushain, who led a rebellion against the Japanese, was killed. "We are descendants of Japanese imperialists," the front wrote in a 1973 pamphlet; the imperialist project, which continued after the defeat in the war, was possible only because the Japanese people were silent and complicit (cited in Knaudt 2020, 418). The wealth of Japanese society, they maintained, was built through military aggression and forms of colonization and exploitation that continue in the present.

With this series of monument bombings, the front was constructing a political narrative of injustices, but it is important to recognize that the nationalist, imperialist narrative came first. Like the innumerable monuments erected in the United States after Reconstruction to honor Confederate soldiers and generals, the Kōa Kannon monument and the others like it express a clear political narrative, affirming the continuing power of the defeated cause. The front's bombings (like the more recent monument-toppling gestures in the United States and elsewhere), then, are intended to disrupt the dominant historical narrative and create something like a counternarrative that forces Japanese people to recognize the continuing history of injustices.

The East Asian Anti-Japan Armed Front subsequently ceased attacking monuments and, in 1974 and 1975, conducted bombings against eleven large corporations. They employed three criteria for selecting corporations for attack: those that profited illegitimately during the formation of the modern Japanese state in the late nineteenth century, those that participated in the twentieth-century wars of invasion and colonization in East Asia, and those that continued neocolonial practices after World War II (Schieder 2019, 39). The first of these bombings was aimed at the Mitsubishi Heavy Industries headquarters in Tokyo in August 1974. During the war, Mitsubishi had, among other crimes, used Chinese forced laborers in the mines. "From the former colonialist era to the present," the front wrote in a declaration after the attack, "Mitsubishi has functioned as the nerve centre of Japanese imperialism" (quoted in Andrews 2016, 185–186). The series of bombings, in effect, drew a map of corporate criminal responsibility.

The Mitsubishi bombing, however, went tragically wrong. The front took precautions so that none of its attacks would cause human injuries, as I said, but in the Mitsubishi bombing their plan failed. The anonymous call to warn of the bombing and to clear the building came too late—only four minutes before the explosion. Eight office employees were killed and hundreds injured. The ten other corporation bombings went off without injuries, but the front was the subject of an increasingly intense police hunt. Less than a year later, by May 1975, the entire membership of the Anti-Japanese Front had been arrested and the organization destroyed.

The methods and aims of the Weather Underground, which developed in roughly the same years, overlapped significantly with those of the East Asian Anti-Japan Armed Front.[5] As with the Japanese organization, the Weather Underground's primary tactic was to bomb symbolic sites, planning its actions so as to avoid human casualties and damage only property. (In fact, the only casualties of Weather Underground bombings were members of the group itself: three were killed in a March 1970 Greenwich Village townhouse when a bomb they were preparing exploded accidentally.) Like the front, the Weather Underground primarily targeted state actors and corporations guilty of injustices, spotlighting for citizens the evils committed by their own country, and thus serving as the conscience of the nation (Varon 2004, 152).

The crimes highlighted by Weather Underground actions primarily involved anti-Black violence in the United States and war atrocities in Southeast Asia.[6] Each target of a bombing was designed to identify and symbolically exact retribution for a specific injustice, some committed against individuals and others victimizing large populations. A partial list of the targets from 1970 to 1972 shows a clear pattern:

October 1970: the Marin County jail, for Jonathan Jackson's death two months earlier while attempting to free prisoners

March 1971: the US Capitol, to protest the US invasion of Laos

August 1971: the California Department of Corrections, in retaliation for the killing of George Jackson

September 1971: the New York State Department of Corrections, in response to the massacre at Attica Prison

May 1972: the Pentagon, to protest the US bombing campaigns in Vietnam

September 1973: the offices of the Latin American division of ITT in New York, in response to the corporation's involvement in the coup d'état in Chile (Jacobs 1997, 129–148; Berger 2006, 164–172)

The East Asian Anti-Japan Armed Front and the Weather Underground thus sought to choreograph symbolic lessons via explosives and property destruction with the hope of waking up the population to the injustices around them and, perhaps, motivating them to act. "It was political theater," maintains Dan Berger, writing about the Weather Underground, "performed amidst a real battle for the hearts and minds of American youth" (2006, 151). I will return below to evaluate the success of this strategy, but before that I want to add one more pair of organizations.

Military Combat with the State

A third pair of clandestine armed groups, including Germany's Red Army Faction (RAF) and Italy's Red Brigades (BR), shared the basic strategic aim of the East Asian Anti-Japan Armed Front and the Weather Underground: to use symbolic actions to highlight injustices committed by those in power as a form of public pedagogy. These groups, however, eventually engaged in direct combat with the state, displaying extraordinary levels of military expertise and proficiency. With increasingly spectacular actions, the mystique surrounding them grew—and, at the same time, due to the rigors of clandestine existence, they become ever more isolated from the dynamics and debates of the movements. What most importantly distinguishes them from the other groups, however, is that they not only designated the perpetrators of injustice symbolically by damaging property but also exacted retribution by targeting and killing humans. One should certainly condemn these actions morally and politically, but, even while doing so, it is useful to follow the rationality that led to their political trajectories.

Before beginning symbolic actions, the RAF conducted several bank robberies. In September 1970, for instance, when the group consisted of about twenty members, the RAF, with typical flair and proficiency, simultaneously robbed three different banks (Steiner and Debray 1987, 31). The accumulated funds served to purchase weapons and build up a clandestine infrastructure of safe houses, identification papers, and the like, following the script outlined in Carlos Marighella's *Manual of the Urban Guerrilla* (1985). The police hunt for the RAF immediately went into high gear, with dragnets, searches, heightened surveillance, and constant reports in the media. The RAF published communiqués to articulate its political positions and goals, and in 1971 significant numbers (roughly 20 percent) of Germans, especially youth, were reported to express some degree of support for the group (Bauer 2008, 68, 75).

The RAF's 1972 "May Offensive" was a prime example of its early symbolic bombing campaigns. In the span of two weeks the group bombed six sites representative of injustice: US military installations in Frankfurt and Heidelberg, police headquarters in Augsburg and Munich, a judge's car outside his house in Karlsruhe, and the Springer publishing offices in Hamburg. In communiqués released to the press, the RAF explained how the bombings constituted acts of counterviolence and retaliation, linking together the guilt of the US military in Vietnam, the responsibility of a police force and a judge for the deaths of leftist militants, and the Springer publications' systematic incitement of violence against leftist activists. Unlike the East Asian Anti-Japan Armed Front and the Weather Underground, however, the RAF did not plan its attacks to avoid all human casualties: the May Offensive left three dead and scores injured.

The Red Brigades shared the strategy to confront and dramatize injustices, and in their early actions they, like the organizations in the previous group, were careful to avoid casualties. One important characteristic of the BR was that, in contrast to most of the urban guerrilla groups considered above, which emerged primarily from student movements, it had a strong connection to radical workers' movements. It is true that some of the founders had been students (notably in the Sociology Department at the University of Trento), but the formation of the BR should be linked more strongly to industrial worker organizations, notably those at the Siemens telecommunications plant and the Pirelli tire factory in Milan.[7] The BR's initial actions, indeed, were cast as part of the workers' movement and as an extension of workers' self-defense. (Industrial workers in many countries, as I mentioned in Chapters 8 and 10, took up arms in the early 1970s in response to the violence of the police and factory security squads.) These were symbolic operations against, for instance, particularly repressive factory managers, and they involved relatively little violence and only minor casualties. The first BR action against a person was the March 1972 kidnapping of Idalgo Macchiarini, director of the Siemens plant. The captors held Macchiarini for fifteen minutes in a "people's court," interrogated him, judged his crimes, and released him. In the photo distributed to the media, a sign around Macchiarini's neck proclaimed, "Nothing will go unpunished." Similar actions were aimed at other factory leaders: in early 1974, for instance, they set fire to the cars of managers of the Siemens and Breda factories and beat a manager of the Pirelli factory. In April 1974, the BR expanded their actions, kidnapping Mario Sossi, a judge known for his right-wing actions, holding him for thirty-five days, and releasing him in exchange for the promise to release eight political prisoners, a promise on which the government later reneged (Saccoman 2013, 70–71, 94–95). Such mini-dramas were designed, like the actions of many of the other armed groups, to denounce those in power who were committing injustices with impunity and to (at least symbolically) hold them to account.

In the next phase, the levels of violence of both the RAF and the BR rose as they entered into increasingly direct combat with the state. By June 1972, only a month after the May Offensive, a massive police hunt resulted in arrests of the original core group of the RAF, including Ulrike Meinhof, Andreas Baader, and Gudrun Ensslin. In 1974 they were transferred to Stammheim Prison, which had been renovated with additional security measures specifically to house RAF militants. The German state instituted extraordinary security measures and antiterror laws designed to limit the ability of defense lawyers to defend their clients and to more easily prosecute those suspected of radical political activity, drawing criticism from a range of German and European intellectuals and creating a sense of threat for radical movements. The RAF defendants were convicted and sentenced to life in prison, but they were involved in one more drama. In 1976 Meinhof was found dead in her prison cell, and the following year Baader, Ensslin, and Jan-Carl Raspe, another RAF member, died in custody. The authorities insisted that all the deaths were suicides (which appears likely to be true), but, given the extreme actions of the state, many at the time understandably questioned whether the suicides had been faked and the RAF militants assassinated by authorities.

The arrests and deaths of the founding group, however, were not the end of the RAF. When one set of militants was arrested, a new set stepped forward and the RAF's actions continued, conducting similarly symbolic campaigns with increasingly lethal means. The actions of the second generation of the RAF culminated in the 1977 "German Autumn," which included the assassination of the attorney general of West Germany, Siegfried Buback, who had been a member of the Nazi Party during the war and who as attorney general had sought to prosecute members of the RAF; the assassination of the director of the Dresdner Bank, Jürgen Ponto; and the hijacking of a Lufthansa flight in collaboration with the Popular Front for the Liberation of Palestine. The pinnacle of this series of actions was the kidnapping of Hanns Martin Schleyer, the president of the Confederation of German Employers' Associations, known for his intransigent opposition to workers' struggles as well as for inflammatory television appearances denouncing the

Left. Schleyer had been a member of Hitler Youth, a Nazi student leader, a member of the Nazi Party, and eventually an *Untersturmführer* in the SS. His biography thus perfectly illustrated the continuity between Germany's Nazi past and its reactionary capitalist class. After kidnapping Schleyer, and in the process killing his driver and three members of his police escort, the RAF team, led by Birgitte Mohnhaupt, demanded the release from prison of RAF members (Baader, Ensslin, and Raspe were still alive in Stammheim Prison at this point). The West German government, however, refused to release the prisoners. Then, when the news broke of the deaths in custody of Baader, Ensslin, and Raspe, the RAF team executed Schleyer.

From the first to the second half of the 1970s, then, and from the first to the second generation of militants, as the RAF's tactics became increasingly lethal and introduced targeted assassinations, their strategy shifted significantly: their actions continued to construct a map of the injustices committed by those in power, but they also increasingly focused attention on their own relation with the state. They attacked judges who had ruled against their members, took hostages in order to negotiate the release of their imprisoned comrades, and sought retaliation against the state when it acted against them. The RAF sought to become a direct interlocutor, in direct combat with the state.

The developments in Italy were parallel in many respects. By the mid-seventies most of the original leaders of the BR had been arrested. (Renato Curcio was arrested in 1974, freed in a dramatic prison break in 1975, and rearrested in 1976.) Like the RAF, the BR was repopulated with new militants and its activities continued unabated. The new "generation" acted with more violent and deadlier tactics, including kneecapping, bombing, kidnapping, and targeted assassination, all of which were conducted with extraordinary discipline and professional efficiency. At the same time, the state's repressive apparatuses became more severe. Italy passed a series of security measures designed to repress not just the armed groups but the radical Left as a whole. The 1975 Legge Reale, for instance, outlawed wearing helmets or face coverings at demonstrations, allowed for preventive detention of activists, and authorized the police to use weapons against demonstrators as they deemed necessary. From a certain perspective, the violence of the BR and the other clandestine armed groups and the violence of the state grew correspondingly in an expanding spiral.

The BR's direct military confrontation with the state culminated in their most theatrical and widely viewed spectacle, the 1978 kidnaping of Aldo

Moro, president of the Christian Democratic Party and a former prime minister.[8] Moro was a moderate within his own party and by no means the worst of the Italian political class. He was certainly not a symbol of the fascist past or reactionary violence (as was, for example, Hanns Martin Schleyer). He was taken, presumably, for crimes committed not by him specifically but by the government he stood for. The BR captured Moro from his car in Rome while killing the three members of his security team in a firefight. They held him hostage in secret locations around the city for fifty-five days, eluding capture despite an extensive manhunt.

Part of the spectacle involved the BR demonstrating their operational and logistical superiority over the police. While the police were searching furiously for the three vehicles used in the kidnapping, for instance, one of the cars suddenly appeared on a highly guarded street; the next day another of the cars appeared on the same street; the third day, the third car appeared. During the hostage crisis the BR appeared able to go head-to-head with the state even in military terms. The spectacle of the Moro kidnapping was also directed at constructing a political drama: during Moro's captivity, the BR interrogated him in a "people's trial" and made demands to the government in exchange for his release.

Finally, after the government refused to negotiate (with significant disagreements within each political party and among the parties), the Brigadists (with bitter disagreements, too, among themselves) decided to assassinate Moro. In one final act of theatrical bravura, Moro's corpse was left in the trunk of a car in Via Caetani equidistant from the Christian Democratic headquarters and the Communist Party headquarters, symbolizing the equal guilt of both parties, especially for their "historic compromise" to collaborate in government. For the entire period of Moro's captivity and long afterward, the affair dominated political debates and completely transfixed the national and international media.

The Political Isolation of Clandestine Life

Up to this point I have tried to present in relatively neutral fashion the actions of a selection of clandestine armed organizations, which demonstrate their strategy to construct a cognitive map of or a political narrative about the injustices of those in power. From this basic account, however, it is clear that the clandestine life of these militants posed a serious obstacle. Obviously, they were forced into an underground existence to avoid detection and capture. For some, fugitive life meant simply adopting false identities and keeping their political activities secret. The threat of arrest and interrogation led other groups to adopt military structures in which, for example, each cell of the organization had little or no communication with others. In this way the interrogation of one captured militant would not disclose the whereabouts of others. In all cases—and this is the immovable obstacle— the clandestine armed groups were by necessity isolated from the political terrain of the movements. Their ability to interact with and be informed by the debates and developments of the movements was extremely limited. As I have tried to demonstrate in the chapters of this book, political movements in the seventies were constantly engaged in collective discussions aimed at transforming themselves in response to both the changing political landscape and internal challenges and pressures. The clandestine groups were deprived of the benefits of these political dynamics.

One can imagine that, after a long period of clandestine existence, some of these militants were like those emigrants who assume their country of origin has remained frozen in time, just the way it was when they left it years earlier. This kind of temporal disjunction is suggested, for example, by the way that Mario Moretti, primary organizer of the BR's kidnapping and assassination of Moro, remained mystified by the developments of the Italian movements in the late 1970s: "For me, but not only for me, that movement [the movement of '77] will remain an unknown object until the end. It is my own limitation, I don't understand it, it is not a factory movement, it is new, what produced it and what it produced or left behind, I still don't know even now" (quoted in Saccoman 2013, 117). As I detailed in Chapter 10, at the opening of the decade Italian movements were primarily dedicated to the struggles of industrial workers, but by the middle of the seventies many activists had begun to register "the end of the centrality of the industrial worker" and thus develop movements of multiple subjectivities, including waged and unwaged workers in various sectors, the unemployed, feminists, gay and lesbian activists, students, and others. The movement of '77 was, in many respects, the blossoming of this new political phase. It is easy to imagine that years of clandestine existence and isolation from the movements had deprived Moretti and others like him of the means to understand and participate in this political transformation.[9]

Their political isolation thwarted the clandestine groups' aspirations for a politics of representation in two senses. First, the strategy of aesthetic representation, that is, the staging of the injustices of power to create an in-structive political narrative or theater, was thwarted by their isolation. In this light, my earlier comparison between the pedagogical dramas of the urban guerrilla groups and Brecht's learning-plays was clearly off the mark. Learning-plays are meant not to teach truths but instead to provide the platform or framework for exchanges and debates. "The text and its perfor-mance," Fredric Jameson writes about Brecht's *Lehrstück*, "slowly blur and disappear into enlarged discussions, into fights about interpretation and the proposing of all kinds of alternative gestures and stage business" (1998, 64). This kind of open interaction and debate, which Brecht advocated and which was taking place in movements in the seventies, is exactly what was missing from the kinds of theater that the clandestine armed groups constructed—and, really, given their isolation, it could not be otherwise.

Second, most of these groups sought a position of political representation, as a vanguard speaking for the people or the proletariat. By the late seventies in Italy, however, the BR and the other clandestine armed groups were widely seen by other revolutionary movements as incapable of representing others. I Volsci, for example, a Rome collective in the "area" of Autonomia, maintained that the isolation of the clandestine groups precluded effective representation: "terrorist action is the form of representation that is the most external and superficial to the real movement of the masses" (I Volsci 1980, 195). The journal *Rosso* similarly portrayed the BR's claim to representation as a paradox: "a vanguardist form of representation that does not represent anything" (*Rosso* 1980, 193). The militants in clandestine groups, because un-able to interact effectively with the wide terrain of movement activity and de-bate, were deprived of the mechanisms necessary for political representation.

Finally, isolation from the movements was part and parcel of the image, promoted by the groups themselves, that the clandestine organizations stood on par with the state, not only as direct interlocutors and antagonists but also as quasi-sovereign formations, reproducing the state's model of justice and its military methods. This "*morbid dramatization*," declared Félix Guattari in 1979, was "spawned by the altogether absurd confrontation between a mon-strous state power and pitiful politico-military machines" (1979, 112). It is easy to imagine that being more embedded in the movements and influenced by their political debates could have prevented some of the worst decisions of the clandestine organizations, such as the murders of Schleyer and Moro. In order to do that, of course, they would have had to abandon the polit-ical mode they had developed of acting as if they were a sovereign power.

"Precisely because we owe our comrades in the underground solidarity," wrote an anonymous German activist in the late 1970s, "because we are closely tied to them, we challenge them now to stop their death trip, to come out of their self-imposed 'armed isolation,' to discard their bombs, and to recommit themselves to a resistance for another kind of life" ("To Have Done with Armed Isolation" 1982, 133). The only way to reenter political life was to abandon their isolation.

Coda: Affective Intensities

Although I have explored the strategies and actions of some of the armed clandestine groups as well as the obstacles they faced, I have not yet accounted for what is, in some respects, their most salient feature: their generation of affective intensities among both those who supported them and those who opposed them. This power of fascination and the mystique surrounding these groups is at once the most obvious and the most difficult thing to explain. The sense of power created by weapons, highly disciplined organization, and the ability to strike directly at the highest levels of the state undoubtedly contributed to the fascination. It could appear as an antidote to the sense of powerlessness many on the Left felt, especially in the face of rising levels of repression and the sense that protest had lost its effectiveness. Also spellbinding, certainly, was the absolute conviction and unalloyed dedication of the armed militants themselves, who threw themselves without reserve into the struggle, risking their lives in the most daring exploits. This fascination was accompanied by fear and loathing in some and admiration and excitement in others—and, indeed, all of these affects sometimes commingled.

The fascination with the clandestine armed groups, however, far exceeded such easily comprehensible reactions, especially among the media, which seemed to be completely mesmerized by them. It is true, of course, that segments of the media often use coverage of the most radical leftist groups to condemn the Left as a whole, but that only partially accounts for the media reaction. "The intense emotional charge associated with the 'terrorist phenomenon,'" affirms Félix Guattari, "has become a fundamental given of current political strategies. Like it or not, politics today has become inseparable from the collective affects molded and transmitted by the media, which constitutes a means of subjectivation . . . at the heart of which it is very difficult to separate the manipulated fantasies from socioeconomic realities" (1979, 109).

One example that indicated the level of fascination and affective manipulation is the gender panic the media promoted in reaction to images of women with guns and to the fact that many women occupied prominent leadership positions, including Bernardine Dohrn of the Weather Underground, Shigenobu Fusako of the Japanese Red Army, Ulrike Meinhof of the RAF, and Mara Cagol of the BR.[10] The German media subjected women in the RAF to especially intense and bizarre treatment, frequently portraying them in erotic terms—alternately as frigid or oversexed, as incapable of affection and intimacy, or as libertines who seduce young men and women into a life of brutal sex and violence.[11] Such media gender panic is likely a symptom of some deeper cultural and political anxiety, but instead of excavating that complex topic, allow me to curtail this discussion and proceed in Chapter 17 to explore a very different usage of arms among other movements in the seventies.

17

Dual Strategy and Double Organization

The Breakfast for Children Program ... represents the best and most
influential activity going for the BPP [Black Panther Party] and, as
such, is potentially the greatest threat to efforts by authorities ... to
neutralize the BPP and destroy what it stands for.
                            —J. Edgar Hoover, director of the FBI, May 15, 1969

I identified in Chapter 15 two general strategies that progressive and liberation movements pursued in response to rising political repression and
decreasing political responsiveness to protests. One strategy was to create
autonomous political projects on various scales, from the small collective
to national networks. These projects risked being destroyed, however, if
they could not defend themselves and the broader community from a host
of threats, including police violence, government surveillance and infiltration, fascist gangs and death squads, right-wing terrorism, imprisonment,
and more. At the same time, as I argued in Chapter 16, the organizations
that chose the second strategy became militarized and, especially, when
forced into clandestinity, became increasingly isolated from the terrain of
the movements, unable to participate in their debates and dynamics. Either
way, their organizational projects of social and political liberation were
undermined.

To avoid this double bind, some liberation groups in the 1970s deployed a
dual strategy and created a double organization that held together, in tension,
two relatively separate initiatives: a defensive, militarized structure and an
autonomous democratic social project. The strategy allowed them to avoid
the isolation that was so destructive for the clandestine armed groups. Said
another way, although the actions of these organizations were much less theatrical than those of the clandestine groups, their internal political dynamics
more closely approximated Brecht's *Lehrstück* insofar as they maintained
open spaces for debate and dissent.

Breakfast Programs and Guns

The meteoric rise to fame of the Black Panther Party (BPP) in 1967 and 1968 was due in large part to the audacity and effectiveness of its tactics of armed self-defense for the Black community and, subsequently, to the brutality of police and state repression it suffered. Party members with shotguns at the Sacramento statehouse, the Free Angela and Free Bobby campaigns, the assassinations of Bobby Hutton, Fred Hampton, and others: spectacular images and slogans around these events thrust the BPP almost immediately onto center stage of the national and international political consciousness in a way that few revolutionary organizations in the United States have ever achieved. The first and most powerful message communicated was that there was a civil war going on in the United States, a war against Black people— which did not begin with the Panthers, of course, and had, indeed, been going in various guises for hundreds of years. In addition to the overt violence of the police, the covert repression mounted by the FBI against the BPP reached extraordinary levels that were only fully revealed years later (Spencer 2016, 88–90). In this context, the mere presence of the BPP and their defiant stance seemed to serve as a catalyst to refine people's political vision, allowing them finally to see the war that had long been right in front of them. The actions served, too, as a demonstration that Black people can fight back. In this first guise, then, "at the center of their politics," as Bloom and Martin maintain, "was the practice of armed self-defense against the police," and for this the BPP necessarily adopted a militarized figure, through its rhetoric, style, organization, and actions (2012, 13).

In subsequent years, however, primarily between 1969 and 1970, emerged a second guise or aspect of the BPP, which did not supplant but rather supplemented the first: the establishment of a host of community service and political education programs, which demonstrated some degree of independence from the state. The Free Breakfast for Children program began in Oakland in January 1969 and by April, after the program had spread to several other cities, the party was reported to be feeding twelve hundred children per day. The breakfast program worked something like this: party members solicited food donations from local businesses (sometimes with mild coercion), prepared meals, and often picked up the children from their homes, and while the children ate they provided liberation lessons on Black history and other topics (Bloom and Martin 2012, 184–185). In these years, the Panthers initiated in cities across the country an extraordinary array of community programs, including free health and dental clinics, sickle-cell anemia research, freedom schools, bus transport to visit prison inmates, and housing cooperatives (Spencer 2016, 131). Internal FBI documents reveal that FBI director J. Edgar Hoover considered the children's breakfast program, in particular, an extremely dangerous threat and thus a primary target of FBI actions (Bloom and Martin 2012, 211). One should not rely on Hoover, of course, for political judgments about the importance of these activities, but his fears and anxieties are indications of how much attention the social programs received. This second face of the party thus constituted a relatively autonomous community welfare structure (Pope and Flanigan 2013).

These two coexisting faces of party strategy were certainly coherent at an ideological level, insofar as they both defended the Black community and asserted autonomy, but they did occupy very separate social spheres, were generally conducted by different groups of party members, and required different, even conflicting forms of organization. Although there were exceptions, the gender division between these two parts of the party generally mapped to the dominant gender division of labor: the military face of the party was male-dominated, especially in the early years, whereas the welfare face was largely conducted by women (Bloom and Martin 2012, 193). Furthermore, military strategy tends to require centralized organization, discipline, and a chain of command. The extraordinary FBI repression tactics, including massive infiltration of the BPP, required a centralization of party structures and led to a widespread practice of expelling members who failed to follow party directives and discipline (Spencer 2016, 89–95). Welfare strategy, in contrast, requires widely distributed structures of accountability, allowing those responsible for a specific social service or task substantial latitude in organizing and fulfilling the tasks.

By highlighting this bifurcation—the distance in terms of strategy between the military and welfare aspects of the party, and, moreover, the tension between the forms of organization that each required, centralized versus decentralized—I do not intend to criticize the party as internally contradictory or incoherent. On the contrary: it was a great accomplishment for the Panthers to be able to keep this tension alive and to hold together this dual strategy and double organization as long as they did. A major factional dispute within the BPP, which came to a head in 1971, highlighted how difficult this was. Reducing the complexities of the positions a great deal, one faction associated with Eldridge Cleaver advocated that the party emphasize its military vocation and insurrectional strategy, lamenting the party's turn toward social programs, whereas the faction around David Hilliard and, after his prison release, Huey Newton advocated emphasis on social programs over the military (Bloom and Martin 2012, 367–371; Spencer 2016, 91–92; Jacobs 1997, 132). Cleaver left the party in April 1971, and in the subsequent years (due more to external forces than to these internal disputes) the BPP experienced a rapid decline.

It would have been disastrous, in my view, for the party to abandon either strategy. On the one hand, given the state of violent repression in the late 1960s and early 1970s, especially against Black liberation movements, and the Panthers most of all, it is no exaggeration to say that they were thrust unwillingly into a civil war. One can certainly question whether their tactics were the most effective; whether arms should have deployed and, if so, what kind and how; if their engagements with the police were effective; and so forth. But there can be no doubt that some structures of defense and resistance were necessary.

On the other hand, if the BPP had developed as exclusively or even predominantly a military formation, it would have inevitably been isolated from the movements and grassroots organizing. The emergence of the Black Liberation Army (BLA) in the early 1970s and its differences from the BPP illustrate this point. The BLA was dedicated explicitly to armed struggle (although its organization was relatively decentralized, with no established chain of command) and, because it was a clandestine organization, it did not have the opportunity to create social programs or any such political projects in the community. Although the BLA conducted bank robberies and airline hijackings (primarily to raise funds), its central focus was directed against the police, most often as retaliation either for actions by specific officers or for large-scale events such as the attacks on prisoners during the 1971 Attica prison uprising. Many Panthers and former Panthers, Bloom and Martin report, admired the heroics of the BLA guerrillas, as did many others on the Left. But in political terms, Bloom and Martin continue, the BLA's "direct organization of guerilla warfare was a world apart from the politics of armed self-defense upon which the Black Panther Party had thrived" (2012, 388–389). As a consequence of their dedication to guerrilla warfare and their military organization, the BLA was, one might say, unburdened of the tensions created by the dual strategy that characterized the Panthers. But this means, too, that they were relatively isolated from the terrain of the movements and prohibited from creating social and political community projects.

Civil War in Italy

All the Italian political developments of the 1970s that I analyzed in Chapter 10 took place against the backdrop of extreme fear, tension, and violence. (Italians often refer to the seventies as *gli anni di piombo*, "the years of lead.") The decisions made by the movements, the obstacles they faced, how their aims were distorted, and the causes of their defeat cannot be understood without situating them in that atmosphere. For many radical Italian activists in the seventies, like for the Black Panthers, violence versus nonviolence was not the primary debate. Instead, the more pressing issue was to decide what kind of force to deploy and how best to organize it.

To understand this attitude, one needs to appreciate the intensity of violence that activists had to confront. In the late 1960s and early 1970s, social and revolutionary movements in Italy, as in many other countries, were battered by increasing waves of repression from the police and the state, at times in league with fascist groups: violence (sometimes deadly) against protests and strikes, disinformation campaigns, layoffs of activist workers, provocations and entrapment, targeted assassinations of leaders, preventive detention and illegal arrest, and much more. The Italian government, or elements within it, conducted a "strategy of tension" that fostered political violence (on the Left and on the Right) in order to create a chaotic situation that would subsequently justify police and state repression and command.[1] Italian activists, along with activists in many other countries, recognized that protest alone was no longer effective and that, faced with such violence and repression, revolutionary movements required strategic innovations. Some activists, of course, chose to withstand the repression passively as best they could or to retire from activism altogether, but many developed strategies of self-defense and, eventually, armed combat in various forms. The militarization of the movements was much criticized and hotly debated at the time, but by the second half of the decade, Italy was in a state of low-intensity civil war, punctuated with flashes of high intensity.

The repression came first, and to give some indication of it, let me focus on a single event, which quickly became iconic and charged with political significance in Italy: on December 12, 1969, a bomb planted at a bank at Piazza Fontana in Milan killed seventeen and injured eighty-eight. The developments after the attack seem like a Hollywood movie script, but one sure to be rejected by producers for being too absurd.[2] Later on the same day of the bombing police arrested and accused two well-known anarchists, Pietro Valpreda and Giuseppe Pinelli, despite the fact, which many remarked upon at the time, that such a deadly bombing was completely outside the repertoire of practices of the anarchists and other Far Left groups. Anarchists had a tradition of exploding small bombs at symbolic locations where they could guarantee there would be no injuries. The Piazza Fontana bombing instead was designed to create mass casualties. Three days after the explosion, the Milan police reported that one of the arrested anarchists, Pinelli, had died in custody, claiming, quite implausibly, that he had committed suicide by jumping out a fourth-story window of the police station.

Gradually, over the course of months and years, what those on the Left suspected immediately was confirmed: the arrested anarchists had nothing to do with the bombing, and the police were directly responsible for Pinelli's death. But more alarming evidence emerged, too: fascist activists were, in fact, the perpetrators of the bombing, and they had been aided in its planning and realization by elements of the police and the secret service, with connections going all the way to top government officials.[3] Details remain murky to this day, as they often do in such cases, but the broad, confirmed outlines of the event are enough to be shocking: an attack planned and carried out through the collaboration of police, state, and fascist forces, designed to inculpate leftist activists, resulted directly and intentionally in scores of dead and injured as collateral damage. This was the first in a series of 1970s political attacks that came to be called "state massacres" (*stragi di stato*), conducted with almost complete impunity.

Lotta Continua, the revolutionary political party I discuss briefly in Chapter 10, launched immediately after the bombing an extensive public campaign to denounce the real perpetrators in the Piazza Fontana attack and its aftermath, highlighting the culpability and complicity of the police and the state. The campaign was a defining project for the party and gained great admiration from others on the left. Lotta Continua mobilized to make certain that the bombing and Pinelli's death were not covered up or silenced (Bobbio 1988, 61–63). In particular, the party led a sustained denunciation of the Milan police official Luigi Calabresi, who not only was responsible for Pinelli's interrogation but also in previous years had led police surveillance and investigation of leftist activism. It came to light later that Calabresi had, indeed, prior to Piazza Fontana, entrapped, falsely accused, and imprisoned other anarchists for smaller bombings. In other words, the Piazza Fontana bombing was a rehearsed police strategy.[4]

One might say, in retrospect, that the Piazza Fontana massacre, the violence and impunity of the police and the state in collaboration with fascist groups, set the stage for the escalating and increasingly violent repression of the subsequent decade. Violence by police and factory security squads against demonstrations and strikers became more intense. There were repeated incidents of police firing weapons on demonstrators in the street, on several occasions killing them. Fascist squads not only conducted small attacks against leftist demonstrations and social centers but also carried out terrorist actions that intentionally resulted in mass deaths, including the 1974 bombing of an antifascist demonstration in Brescia (8 dead, 102 wounded); the 1974 Italicus Express train bombing (12 dead, 48 injured); and the 1980 Bologna train station bombing (85 dead, over 200 wounded). There were even credible reports of the danger of a right-wing coup d'état in Italy in the mid-1970s, which seemed even more plausible after the September 1973 coup in Chile. It remains unclear how close those fears of a coup came to reality, but it was certainly reasonable at the time to question, at the very least, whether Italy's not-too-distant fascist past was really past at all.

In reaction to the escalating violence and repression, all the radical leftist movements felt the pressure to construct some means of self-defense. Factory workers were among the first on the Left to arm themselves. Organized workers used weapons not only to defend themselves against factory guards and police but also to carry out sabotage in the factory and, increasingly as the decade went on, to conduct reprisals against guards, foremen, and bosses guilty of abuse (Berardi 1980, 151). At the massive 1973 Fiat strike in Turin, for instance, workers defended the occupied factory with arms, and in the surrounding years armed worker cells were formed in other factories, too. The Italian radical workers were not alone in this regard. I described briefly in Chapter 8 the armed self-defense of US autoworkers in the early 1970s. In Germany, too, armed industrial workers emerged on the scene. Karl-Heinz Roth, writing after a 1973 wave of strikes and repression in factories in Mannheim, Bremen, Lippstadt, and Köln, proclaimed that since the owners had marshaled armed guards and thugs together with the police to wage war on workers, "the only possible response was to make the factory into a worker fortress, the point of departure from which workers could dismantle the entire social machine. The state of emergency of the daily lives of workers will lead to workers' guerrilla war" (1974, 241). It is difficult to know how many workers were actually armed and with what weapons, but it is clear that the image of the armed worker became a symbol of resistance for many on the Left (as well as a locus of fear for management and bosses).

By the mid-1970s most of the major Italian movements recognized the need for self-defense and deployed force in some way. Every worker or student demonstration, of course, at least since the late sixties, organized a security team (*servizio d'ordine*) to protect demonstrators and, if attacked by police or fascists, to respond in self-defense, often with sticks or metal bars. In the course of the seventies, especially in the years when police shot and killed an increasing number of demonstrators, guns were deployed by the movements at demonstrations. In Autonomia, as in other groups, a military wing to manage the needs of self-defense developed in parallel to the political structures that I analyzed in Chapter 10: the network of relatively independent collectives focused on different structures of oppression, including waged, unwaged, precarious, and unemployed workers; feminists; gay liberation activists; students; and so forth.

In practice, however, the military and political wings of Autonomia were, in some respects, not as separate as this description makes it seem. Autonomia's mass deployment of violence at demonstrations in the late 1970s intersected with its mass practices of illegality that I mentioned in Chapter 10, including housing occupations, the self-reduction of transport fares, and the organization of "proletarian shopping." Furthermore, as Emilio Quadrelli attests, Autonomia's armed structures and practices shared, to some extent, the plural, decentralized nature of its political organization (Quadrelli 2008, 111). That said, however, all military formations, including those of Autonomia, are necessarily shaped by pressures toward central control, for obvious reasons. First, the acquisition and deployment of arms as well as planning for military operations have to maintain secrecy in the interests of protection from legal prosecution. Second, some sort of oversight is required to ensure that activists acting independently do not conduct armed actions that are irresponsible and politically counterproductive. Finally, some structure of coordination is required to guarantee that armed actions will be politically effective. Even though Autonomia's military structures echoed some aspects of its political organization, then, there was significant disjunction between its democratic, inclusive efforts in the political sphere and the demands of effectiveness and discipline in the military. Indeed, the ways in which activists in Autonomia and the broader Left criticized the militarization of the movements—for its distraction from the political work, its distortion of political organization, its masculinist bravura, and more—is indicative of the difficulties of bridging the gap between the two modes of organization.

Autonomia's experiment in double organization, however, was not allowed much time to develop. A new and dramatically intensified wave of repression in the second half of the 1970s defeated the revolutionary movements in Italy, including Autonomia. The state targeted both terrorist and nonterrorist movements. As I mentioned in Chapter 16, special laws were passed that gave the police and prosecutors expanded powers, allowing preventive detention of political activists for extended periods without charging them, imprisonment for years before coming to trial, highly irregular legal charges, and conviction on the basis of dubious testimony of those turned state's evidence, despite the protestations of Amnesty International and other human rights organizations. A network of special political prisons was constructed to house the activists and to keep them separate from the criminal prison population. As Patrick Cuninghame claims, this was "the largest round up of political activists in Western Europe since 1945" (2002, 145). Forty thousand activists were charged with crimes, fifteen thousand were arrested, four thousand were convicted and sentenced to terms long and short, and thousands of others fled in exile (Balestrini and Moroni 2021, 540). Although the numbers of dead, tortured, and imprisoned in Italy did not reach the levels of some other countries, such as Argentina, Chile, or Turkey—each country's repressive history contains unique horrors—the repression in Italy put an end to the long period of revolutionary activity and experimentation that culminated in the seventies. Despite the travails of civil war, however, these activists were able to hold together for a time, as the Panthers did, a dual strategy to keep alive their democratic political projects.

From Resistance Committees to People's Committees: Devrimci Yol and the Fatsa Commune

At the end of the 1970s in Fatsa, a small city on Turkey's Black Sea coast, three hundred miles northeast of Ankara, an innovative democratic experiment took place, against all odds, that resonated with the dual strategies of the Black Panther Party and Autonomia. Fikri Sönmez, popularly known as "Fikri the Tailor," was elected mayor in 1979 and, together with the leftist movement Devrimci Yol (Revolutionary Path), he created people's committees to run many facets of the city government, notably developing and implementing infrastructure projects. In early 1980, Sönmez declared that his position of authority had been turned over to the democratic process: "Today, rather than a mayor, the public is in the administration of the municipality. The people of Fatsa manage themselves" (quoted in Türkmen 2006, 117). A few months later, however, after a mere nine months in office, the mayor was arrested and tortured. At his trial the military prosecutor alleged that Sönmez had created a "Fatsa Commune," reminiscent of the Paris Commune, a damning (if rather erudite) charge in such an anticommunist context. The former mayor maintained in his defense that giving people a voice and making them decision-makers in government, as he had done, was merely a basic requirement of democracy (Türkmen 2006, 96). Sönmez died in prison five years later.

To understand how the fortunes of Fatsa and its mayor were reversed so radically and so rapidly, and, moreover, how the improbable democratic experience came about in the first place, we have to back up and take account of the complex political situation of Turkey and the Turkish Left in the 1970s. The Fatsa experience was an anomaly in the political scene of 1970s Turkey, but it helps illuminate two facts. First, the brief "Fatsa Commune" was a manifestation of a profound desire for democratic participation on the revolutionary Left, a symptom of what could have been more prevalent if the constant threat and reality of fascist violence had not been so intense. Second, without the dual strategy and double organization of Devrimci Yol, such a democratic experiment amid the resistance struggles against fascists would not have been possible.

In the second half of the seventies the Turkish revolutionary Left was vibrant but extraordinarily fractured and sectarian. A 1974 amnesty had freed many imprisoned leftist militants, who flowed into myriad conflicting groups. A major division pitted those following the Soviet line against adherents of the Chinese line, but some organizations refused both sides of that divide. Among them was Devrimci Yol, the largest movement in the 1970s and the one with the most popular support (Bozkurt 2008, 52–53). Antifascist struggle was the central pillar of Devrimci Yol's program, and, indeed, fascist violence was an extraordinarily widespread and pressing threat in Turkey.[5] The Nationalist Movement Party (Milliyetçi Hareket Partisi) was a fascist presence in parliament, and the paramilitary Grey Wolves (Bozkurtlar) were violent action squads that targeted leftists along with ethnic and religious minorities, including Kurds and Alevis. Fascist violence, led primarily by the Grey Wolves, accounted for over five thousand deaths in this period (Benlisoy 2018). "In these areas of the fiercest fascist terror," Ahmet Samim claims, "it was primarily the militants of Devrimci-Yol who had to bear the brunt of the anti-fascist struggle and local self-defense. In some towns . . . half of the community was literally under fascist control, while the other half was defended by revolutionaries" (1981, 80). The state, which had murky connections to the fascist groups, clearly could not be counted on for protection. In fact, as in Italy, the Turkish state pursued a "strategy of tension" in the 1970s: along with the army, it allowed and even encouraged violent unrest so as to be able to justify its subsequent intervention to restore order and counter the purported communist threat.

To defend communities against fascists, Devrimci Yol created throughout the country "resistance committees" (*direniş komiteleri*) that were open to all (except fascists, of course), and these committees constituted the widest base and most outward-looking structures of the party. The party did not have formal membership but, in particular through the resistance committees, built a very large following. Devrimci Yol's organizational structure was designed to be narrow at the top and wide at the bottom: "to create the narrowest cadre," according to the movement's slogan, "within the widest mass" (Bozkurt 2008, 65). At the top, Devrimci Yol's seven-member central committee determined the political line and made strategic decisions; below them was a general committee with an advisory role that included regional leaders and other key militants; and the base, including the resistance committees, was meant to be as large and open as possible (Bozkurt 2008, 55). In addition to these different levels of political organization, Devrimci Yol developed two levels of armed organizations. The "armed resistance forces," which were composed of resistance committees, were relatively decentralized and operated at the local level, whereas the "revolutionary war forces," composed of professional revolutionaries, formed something like a guerrilla army and reported directly to the central committee (Bozkurt 2008, 56).

Devrimci Yol's most innovative political developments took place in its wide base. The military prosecutor facing Mayor Sönmez was not the only one to see foreign ideas at work. Some Turkish leftists also viewed the democratic experiments operating in the committees of Devrimci Yol as out of place and un-Turkish. Militants who broke with Devrimci Yol in the late seventies and formed Devrimci Sol (Revolutionary Left), for instance, accused it of creating a "horizontal" organization that they thought was better suited to the dominant capitalist countries (Bozkurt 2008, 105). The practices of Devrimci Yol were not, in fact, derived from other countries, but I interpret this impression of "foreignness," whether welcomed or not, as a mark of their originality. And these innovations came not from the narrow summit of Devrimci Yol but from its wide and open, "horizontal" base.

To appreciate the nature of this base and the political dynamic created there, one has to look more closely at the antifascist resistance committees. In addition to combating fascists, the committees functioned as recruitment tools and "hubs of organization and theoretical education" (Acaroglu 2019, 416). Ultimately, when the fascist threat could be held in check, the resistance committees were intended to be transformed into democratic political projects. Specifically, Devrimci Yol used resistance committees as the basis for participatory institutions of self-governance, including neighborhood or municipal people's committees (*halk komiteleri*), as well as factory committees and student committees.[6] The resistance committees were a gateway, in other words, that opened to democratic participation. Defending against fascists was, of course, essential—without that, nothing else could be done—but the experience of participation and cooperation in the resistance committees also served as a training in self-governance and created desire for it.

This is the political context that made possible the election of Fikri Sönmez and the Fatsa experiment in participatory democracy. Sönmez, a veteran leftist activist closely allied with Devrimci Yol, ran for mayor as an independent. For years before the election, Devrimci Yol had been active and gained popularity in the Fatsa area, in particular by leading one campaign to aid hazelnut growers (a major economic sector in the region) who were exploited by merchants offering low prices and usurious loans and a second campaign to combat exploitation and hoarding in the black-market economy (Türkmen 2006, 64, 70). The key factor was that fascists, although still a real threat, were less powerful in Fatsa and the nearby region than in other parts of the country. Less energy required for antifascist defense meant more for constituting new democratic forms. Resistance committees could thus be transformed into people's committees (Türkmen 2006, 64).

Upon his election in October 1979, Sönmez established in each of the eleven districts of the city a people's committee with frequent meetings open to all residents (Morgül 2019, 289; Ersan 2013, 291). The committees were designed to allow people to participate actively in government decision-making, but they also had other important effects. By giving people a direct role in governance, the committees effectively broke long-standing traditional patronage relations and served as an instrument for politicization and mobilization, leading to greater participation (Türkmen 2006, 102–103).

The major accomplishments of the Fatsa people's committees were relatively mundane and primarily concerned with city infrastructure. The "end the mud" campaign, for example, focused on repairing sewage and drainage systems while paving and constructing roads. The campaign was claimed to have been much more efficient and successful due to the guidance and active engagement of the people through the committees. Road construction that was previously thought to require years was accomplished with the participation of hundreds of citizens in a remarkably short time.[7] Fatsa also successfully organized a Popular Culture Festival in February 1980 with leftist intellectuals and artists from other parts of the country, in part as celebration and showcase of its accomplishments (Türkmen 2006, 106–115). Despite its small size and distance from metropolitan centers, Fatsa quickly become renowned as a success of the Left.

These democratic experiments in Fatsa, however, were not given much room to breathe or time to grow. Turkish military troops entered Fatsa and took control of the city in July 1980, and Mayor Sönmez was arrested the following month (Türkmen 2006, 138–139). The crackdown in Fatsa was in some sense a prelude. Soon afterward, on September 12, 1980, Turkey suffered the third coup d'état in the history of the republic: the military claimed it had overthrown the government in order to put an end to political violence and "restore order," and in the process it executed dozens and imprisoned hundreds of thousands. The strategy of tension had served its purpose.

In the end, perhaps the military prosecutor's charge that Mayor Sönmez together with Devrimci Yol militants had created a Paris Commune on the Black Sea was not completely off the mark. Yes, little provincial Fatsa is a far cry from metropolitan Paris, and the practical municipal improvements they made were modest. But the essence of the Paris Commune, as Marx asserted shortly after its fall, was its working existence, that is, its participatory governance structures that opened the possibility of a government of the people and by the people. The people's committees of Fatsa were precisely that. The real question is, what would the people of Fatsa have been able to create if their experiment had been given more than nine months to develop? Or, perhaps more importantly, what kinds of participatory governance structures would Devrimci Yol and other revolutionary groups have been able to establish elsewhere in Turkey if they did not have to dedicate so much of their energies to defending against fascist attacks? After all, the relatively low threat from fascists is what set Fatsa apart and made its experiments possible. What if all of the resistance committees could have been transformed into people's committees as institutions of participatory democracy?

Such contrapositive conjecture may not be useful, because the fascist threat in Turkey in the 1970s inside the state and out was an ineluctable reality. What is certain, however, is that Devrimci Yol's multiple organizational structures allowed it, even in such an unfavorable environment, to organize participatory democratic experiences while accomplishing the necessary tasks of armed resistance. The "Fatsa Commune," although a small and brief experiment, is a significant demonstration of the political potentials opened by such dual strategy.

Mass Armed Struggle Within the Movements

The fact that the BPP, Autonomia, and Devrimci Yol were all defeated by the end of the 1970s does not negate the importance of the dual strategy they pursued. Instead of choosing either the construction of autonomous democratic projects or clandestine armed struggle, they found the means to combine the two. In the context of extreme repression, including police and fascist violence, which characterized so many countries in that decade, it was absolutely necessary to develop political and military organizational structures that were separate but held together in the same overall project. Such double organization held open a space, albeit for a limited time, to advance democratic experiments. Moreover, they demonstrated a mode of armed self-defense that did not lead to isolation from the movements.

Several recent and contemporary struggles might be considered inheritors of these 1970s efforts at dual strategy and double organization. The Zapatista communities in Chiapas, Mexico, for example, have since 1994 maintained a military structure, the Zapatista Army of National Liberation (EZLN), to protect against forces of the Mexican state while developing novel democratic social and political relations. The innovative self-governed Kurdish communities of Rojava, in northern Syria, have similarly maintained a dynamic between autonomous democratic governance structures and people's protection units, along with other military structures. A third example is the decades-long Naxalite insurrection together with Adivasi populations in large portions of eastern India (Shah 2018). Each of these struggles is complex and there are important differences among them—and, furthermore, none of them was directly influenced by the 1970s movements I analyzed above. And yet each has carried further in inspiring ways the development of the dual strategy that in the face of violence can deploy armed self-defense while forging new democratic forms.

18

Conclusion

The 1970s and Us

Nothing takes longer to solve than a problem that does not exist or
has been poorly posed.

—Louis Althusser

In the preceding chapters I have generally approached struggles separately,
with the assumption that they cannot be understood without engaging
their specific local and national political conditions. Whereas Kwangju
rebels combated a military dictatorship, liberation fighters in Guinea-Bissau
battled a colonial Portuguese regime, and US and Italian industrial workers
challenged capitalist command, Nicaraguan revolutionaries overthrew
an authoritarian regime. And yet, as the developments unfolded, echoes
among the movements continually emerged. Despite disparate geographical
locations, cultural traditions, and political circumstances, the reverberations
became stronger as the struggles accumulated. Their repertoires of practices,
political vocabularies, and aspirations resonated with each other like the
strings of musical instruments that oscillate in sympathetic vibration to a
sound of the same frequency.

There is nothing mystical, of course, about these resonances. Activists,
after all, were keenly aware of revolutionary advances and setbacks in other
parts of the world, often translating their lessons so as to be applicable to
their own circumstances. Reports of Allende's election in Chile, for example,
generated hope for novel revolutionary possibilities across the globe, just as
Allende's overthrow sent a warning. In addition to news reports, of course,
activists traveled, and they learned directly from the experiences of others,
creating friendships and material solidarities. Representatives from Black
revolutionary workers in Detroit traveled to Italy, for instance, to speak to
radical workers' collectives; in turn, Lotta Continua, the revolutionary Italian
party, rented a house in Lisbon in order to follow directly the developments

of the Portuguese Revolution; as one further link, progressive Portuguese soldiers are rumored to have learned the strategies of "popular power" from the anticolonial struggles they were supposed to be combating in Portugal's African colonies and then applied them back home. The complex set of international connections and correspondences among the movements of the seventies mapped uncharted patterns across the globe, as if the stars had aligned to form new constellations.[1]

Equally important to these international networks are the transversal connections among different streams of movements, which generated new bonds and inspiration. The Clamshell Alliance, for instance, in its struggle against the construction of the Seabrook nuclear power plant, adopted the democratic organizing practices of affinity groups and consensus decision-making used in feminist organizations. Activists occupying territory on the Larzac plateau in France to prevent the expansion of a military base, similarly, learned practices of forming democratic committees from workers who were occupying the Lip watch factory in Besançon.

Finally, along with international and transversal connections, genealogical relations are essential and formative for each movement. Because of the temporal frame of this book, I have not generally emphasized the ways in which the revolutionary struggles of the 1970s continued and built on the organizational forms and political objectives of previous movements, but many such genealogical relations were readily apparent. It should be no surprise, for instance, that the Paris Commune of 1871 served as a reference point for revolutionaries and their adversaries in such varied cities as Lisbon, Kwangju, and Fatsa. The commune's experiments in participatory democratic governance structures, its opposition to capitalist rule, and its armed defense against the forces of reaction were all developed in novel forms by the movements of the 1970s.

Investigating such international, transversal, and genealogical connections is a powerful method to begin study of social and political movements.[2] Each individual struggle gives a slightly different angle or perspective from which to view their shared characteristics and aspirations, something like a parallax technique, resulting in a richer vision of the whole. The multiple viewpoints and the connections among movements, moreover, bring into focus the concepts that I have followed as guides through investigations of the different movements—concepts that, too, resonate with the problematics of our contemporary political situation.

The Working Class Is Dead, Long Live the Working Class!

Focusing on concepts in my investigations has allowed me at the same time to recognize the heterogeneity of the different movements and to identify their coherence. In the Introduction I suggested autonomy, multiplicity, democracy, and liberation as concepts to follow in the various narratives, but in the course of the book many others have played central roles, such as popular power, self-management, and mediation.

I want to dwell briefly on the concept of class, which appeared primarily in the middle chapters of the book. I do this not in order to recenter the narrative, as if class were somehow the master concept that unifies all the movements, but rather because the crisis and reorientation of the concept of class in the seventies served as a precondition for the flourishing of the heterogeneous set of movements. I realize this is a large topic, so I will focus here simply on how recognizing the transformations of the notion of working class in the seventies helps us address some conceptual and political difficulties and confusions that persist today.

Exactly what do people mean today when they say "working class"? Is it only those with blue collars, who work with their hands? Does it include affective and intellectual work, informal or precarious labor, production and reproduction, the unwaged and the unemployed? There is a great deal of confusion, too, about its political status: some take for granted that the working class remains the bedrock and leading force of the Left, whereas others judge it to be an unreliable partner in progressive politics or even the primary base of the extreme Right. The 1970s is the origin point of many of these lasting misconceptions, and returning to the debates of that era allows us, if we can untangle some of the snarled threads, not only to formulate clearly the concept of class but also reveal some of the real political problems it continues to pose today.

The first knot to be unraveled poses a seeming paradox: the industrial workers' movement reached extraordinary heights in the 1970s, not only making major factories in many countries all but ungovernable but also threatening the governability of society as a whole, and yet, in the same decade, its power was radically undermined, leading many to declare farewell to the working class. When addressing the height of industrial worker militancy in Part III, I highlighted the double battle that radical industrial workers fought. On the one side, they conducted a sustained assault against the capitalist industrial system through combinations of strikes, slowdowns, absenteeism, sabotage, and other creative means. On the other, radical workers challenged the control of the dominant, established unions, insisting on their own autonomy to organize, make strategic decisions, and conduct their struggle. The two sides of the battle overlapped, of course, since without the established unions to discipline workers and guarantee the industrial order, management and ownership were deprived of their most reliable weapons. Most important was the fact that, especially when factory struggles spilled out onto the social terrain, industrial workers were often considered to be the central protagonists of progressive and revolutionary movements as a whole. Just when industrial workers in various countries appeared poised to realize a decades-long project and lead a revolutionary process, however, as I said, their power was destroyed. Industrial unions began a long process of decline in terms of numbers and power, and factory jobs were progressively eliminated in the dominant countries through automation and the shifting of production to subordinated countries.

It is really no paradox, however, or even coincidence that the same decade of the height of industrial workers' power was also that of its destruction. Various levels of capitalist authorities, from plant managers to owners and from right-wing intellectuals to political elites, recognized that the health of the industrial system was seriously compromised. Increasingly intense repression and violence against militant workers was only a temporary cure. The real remedy required major surgery. New management strategies and neoliberal economic policies were designed to respond to the threat of the industrial workers' movement and undermine its power. Capital's defeat of this worker offensive was accomplished in part, one could say in very summary terms, by radically transforming over an extended period the composition of the working class.

Something died in this process, but we need to be clear exactly what, and this is the second knot to be unraveled. One thing that died was the political centrality of industrial workers to progressive and revolutionary movements. The industrial workers' movement, in other words, could no longer be positioned as the vanguard or primary protagonist, to which other movements and social forces should direct their energies. This death, however, offers great potential benefits for the Left since, previously, the political primacy granted to the industrial workers' movement had effectively subordinated other liberation movements. The elimination of the assumption of priority opened the possibility for an articulation among diverse struggles, to which I will return momentarily.

Also dead, and this too is potentially advantageous, is the figure of the industrial worker as representation of the working class as a whole. According to the dominant image, the working class was composed of men with callused hands (and, indeed, the image was most often gendered). Although many workers were employed in nonindustrial sectors, industrial labor had for decades been considered representative, not necessarily in numerical terms but in terms of political significance. The various affirmations of the lumpenproletariat in the 1960s and 1970s, from Frantz Fanon and the Black Panthers to the East Asian Anti-Japan Armed Front, can be read, in this respect, as an objection to an exclusive, industrial representation of the class (Weeks 2023; Knaudt 2020). Once the figure of the industrial worker could no longer stand in for the class as a whole, then, a reckoning was required to discover what the class really consists of.

It makes no sense, obviously, to say that in this process the working class itself died—unless, of course, one stubbornly holds on to the belief that industrial workers represent the class as a whole. The working class was undoubtedly transformed by the processes of capitalist restructuring and neoliberal policies that began in the seventies, but it was already different from what it appeared to be. The first step is to conduct new investigations of the composition of the working class. Who works? What do they do? Under what conditions? Such investigations reveal the multiplicity of forms and conditions of labor, including industrial workers, of course, but also a variety of waged workers producing goods that are largely immaterial in various service and technological contexts, new and newly expanded realms of precarious, informal, and part-time employment, migrant and undocumented workers, and (as feminists have been insisting at least since the 1970s) diverse forms of social reproductive labor, often unwaged and usually gendered. Only on the basis of understanding that empirical composition are we able to talk about the political composition and political powers of the class.

Finally, class struggle did not die, either, but its methods and weapons have had to be reinvented. What studying the labor militancy of the seventies reveals most clearly, in fact, is the need for a sea change in labor organizing. When radical workers fought the established unions and the "official" workers' movement, they were not rejecting labor organizing as such, of course, but attempting to organize labor differently. The demand for workers' autonomy, while refusing centralized and bureaucratic decision-making structures, created the means for more democratic participation of the workers themselves.

The problem that emerges is thus double and doubly difficult, since demands for more autonomous and more democratic organizing have to be coupled with the need to recognize and embrace an expanded concept of the working class: how to invent new organizational forms that allow for the democratic participation of a wide range of laboring subjects, waged and unwaged, in production and in social reproduction? But there is even more. Labor organizing must recognize, in addition to the internal multiplicity of labor, the fact that anticapitalist struggle is only one among multiple liberation struggles. It is not sufficient simply to highlight and attack gender and racial divisions of labor or affirm the role of women and people of color in the working-class struggle, if that means maintaining capitalist domination as the master narrative. It is necessary, instead, to find the means to articulate together multiple relatively autonomous liberation struggles, such that class struggle cannot take place without feminist struggle and antiracist struggle and queer struggle and more. (To this issue of articulation, as I said, I will return shortly.) These are real political problems for working class politics that emerged in the 1970s. Since then and still today many workers' groups, labor organizers, theorists, and political organizations have engaged and made great progress on these issues. But these problems remain and continue to pose the contours of our central political challenges and possibilities.

Before leaving this topic, I want to return to the question of why there persist both in common parlance and political discourse, sometimes merely as implicit assumptions, so many anachronisms and confusions regarding the concept of the working class. Some of this may involve a combination of confusing the dead with the living or, rather, trying in vain to solve nonexistent or poorly posed problems. My sense, though, is that also at play is a powerful nostalgia—nostalgia not only for a strong industrial working class per se but in addition, and more importantly, for the political clarity that for many decades it provided. "Whose side are you on?" "We're on the side of the workers," meaning, primarily, the industrial working class represented by its unions and parties, whose interests are undeniably progressive. The political situation and the concept of class that emerge from the seventies, however, do not allow for simple solutions. Answering the question "Whose side are you on?" now requires a multipart, nuanced response. The seventies is undoubtedly a troubling decade, but it is good for us to be forced to stay with the trouble and learn to navigate the seas of political complexity.

Real Political Problems

I want now to suggest another method for reading the movements—or, rather, a slightly different angle on the conceptual approach—that highlights political problems. Philosophers insist that a core task of philosophy is to distinguish between poorly posed and well-posed problems. Whereas non-existent and poorly posed problems are extremely difficult to solve, they tell us, a well-posed problem already, in some sense, contains the conditions for its solution (Deleuze 1988, 15–17; Althusser 1970, 184). A central task of political theory, then, including the theory done collectively in movements, is to cast aside problems that do not exist or are poorly conceived and to formulate real ones clearly.

Many such political problems were engaged productively by the movements I have investigated. In the previous section, for instance, I described how in the course of the seventies it became clear to many in labor movements that the real problem is to discover the current composition of the class itself; to invent effective forms of labor organizing that address workers' demands for democratic participation; and to articulate labor struggle with other social justice and liberation movements. In addition, the constitution of a revolutionary democracy and the creation of participatory institutions to support it were posed as a problem in a wide range of movements. The movements I investigated in Part VI, to give yet another example, recognized that legitimation, which had been up until the 1960s a central preoccupation for those in power and essential for creating stable and lasting authority, no longer held a central role. The real problem that emerged, then, was how to act and organize politically when negotiation and reform are increasingly replaced by explicitly undemocratic rule, when "no one is listening" to the protests, and thus when command and violence are becoming primary strategies of power.

I want to consider a bit more deeply another cluster of problems that emerged in the seventies and which seem to me particularly pressing today. It has become a cliché to say that the seventies was an age of fracture that unleashed forces that continue today to undermine the unity of the Left. From the beginning of the decade, demands arose within the movements to recognize and examine difference, division, and hierarchy, with frequent calls for separatism. As the lines of fracture proliferated, the story goes, especially through developments of identity politics and new social movements, the Left became riven with internal divisions. It was falling apart, destroying itself, squandering the effectiveness it once had. In general, advocates of unity were not defending a vision of the Left as homogeneous, of course; rather, they conceived the heterogeneity of actors and demands as being previously contained under the hegemony of one central protagonist (as, for instance, the industrial working class in my account above). For many others, of course, overthrowing the hierarchies of both the traditional Left and the New Left was by the seventies long overdue, and to exit an oppressive unity, separatism appeared as a necessary path.[3]

Many 1970s movements, however, recognized that both unity and separatism led to dead ends, that they were poorly posed problems. As I elaborated in Chapter 11, especially in light of developments in feminist theory, multiplicity became key to the analysis of power and the strategies of struggle. On the one hand, multiple structures of domination were recognized as relatively autonomous and yet as interwoven and mutually constitutive, without any one holding priority over others. In the 1970s the set of powers often included capital, patriarchy, white supremacy, imperialism, and nationalism, but the content of that list is open and depends on the political education of the movement, that is, which forms of domination they have been able to recognize. Correspondingly, activists saw that multiple movements for liberation must remain relatively autonomous and yet discover the means to articulate together in a common struggle without priority among them.

The real political problem that emerged was thus not unity (or separation) but articulation. Note that while the analytical recognition that multiple structures of domination are interwoven is an important basis, it does not lead automatically to the articulation of struggles. That requires political work. One particularly difficult challenge facing strategies of articulation, as we saw in some of the chapters above, is to maintain the lack of priority among struggles, even while recognizing real differences among structures of domination, historically and in the present, and diverse pressures on each movement.

It is easy to recognize the aspiration to multiplicity among today's most powerful and inspiring movements. Black Lives Matter, for instance, was born in opposition to white supremacy and anti-Black violence, but at every demonstration that opposition is combined with affirmations of a feminist and anticapitalist program along with a celebration of Black trans lives. For the Ni Una Menos movement in Argentina, similarly, although it emerged to combat femicide and patriarchal oppression, the battles against coloniality, racism, transphobia, and capitalist domination are central to its agenda.

Likewise, labor organizing efforts—from the great union confederations to the smallest picket of striking Starbucks workers—increasingly today proclaim their agenda also in terms of feminist, trans, queer, decolonial, antiableist, and antiracist demands. Now, if each of these movements was to maintain one struggle as primary—antiracist, feminist, or anticapitalist, respectively—while attempting to link with other struggles in a secondary way, no real articulation would be possible (and, understandably, activists long engaged in those other struggles would be wary or dismissive of such efforts). Required, instead, is a strategic effort to create solidarity and a form of struggle in common without priority, even though, of course, in daily experiences the movements are confronted by real differences and real hierarchies.

I am not saying that any of these movements has discovered the solution. Their efforts demonstrate, instead, that confronting the problem of strategic articulations among struggles, which emerged from the seventies, remains today one of the unavoidable challenges that all progressive and revolutionary movements must face.

* * *

One reason we should be interested in the movements investigated in this book, as I claimed in the Introduction, is that the 1970s is when our era began. The primary forms of neoliberal discipline and control that rule over us today originated in that decade; correspondingly, the progressive and revolutionary movements of the 1970s tested that terrain for the first time and discovered there the means to further the struggle for liberation. One way to verify this shared political terrain is to recognize, as I just tried to demonstrate, that the political problems they identified are still our own. Karl Marx, for one, was confident that once we can clearly formulate real political problems we are already halfway to resolving them. Humanity, he proclaimed, poses itself a problem "only when the material conditions for its solution are already present or at least in the course of formation" (1975, 426).

I hope that both those who remember the seventies movements and those encountering them for the first time have experienced, while reading these chapters, an uncanny sense of recognition: they are so like us, with so many of the same dreams and problems. In some instances, we can now recognize clearly the mistakes they made; in others, their struggles constituted the larval stage of something that is now reaching maturity; and in still other respects, the seventies were actually more advanced politically than our times today are. The point, of course, is not either to disavow them because of their errors or to emulate them, but to take on their achievements as support for moving forward. I think of our relation to them as being like that of runners in a relay race. They were able to carry the baton only so far. Now it's up to us to complete the next leg of the journey.

Timeline

Events of Particular Relevance to the Movements
Discussed in This Book

1968

January—**Czechoslovakia**: Alexander Dubcek is elected first secretary and begins implementing reforms to create "socialism with a human face."

January—**Vietnam**: North Vietnamese military begins the Tet Offensive.

March—**Vietnam**: Mass murder of South Vietnamese civilians by US soldiers at My Lai.

April—**United States**: Martin Luther King Jr. is assassinated in Memphis; Bobby Hutton, Black Panther Party member, is killed by Oakland police.

April—**West Germany**: Rudi Dutschke is shot by an assailant with neo-Nazi ties. Dutschke sustained serious brain injuries and died of complications from the attack in 1979.

April—**United States**: Columbia University student strike begins.

May—**France**: Worker and student revolts paralyze the country.

June—**United States**: Robert F. Kennedy is assassinated after a presidential campaign speech in Los Angeles.

August—**Czechoslovakia**: Soviet bloc troops invade Prague to put down the reform movement.

August—**United States**: Chicago police attack protestors outside the Democratic National Convention.

September—**United States**: Ron March, cofounder of the Dodge Revolutionary Union Movement, wins the first round of an election for representative in a United Auto Workers local, but later loses a runoff election, which DRUM members claim was rigged.

September—**Portugal**: Prime Minister António de Oliveira Salazar suffers a massive stroke, but the fascist Estado Novo regime maintains rule for six more years.

October—**Mexico**: The armed forces open fire on a student demonstration protesting the upcoming Summer Olympics in the Tlatelolco neighborhood of Mexico City, leaving hundreds dead.

November—**United States**: The Third World Revolutionary Front at San Francisco State College begins a strike to demand the creation of an ethnic studies program and to admit more nonwhite students. Similar student strikes erupt at UC Berkeley and City College of New York in the following months.

December—**United States**: The Third World Women's Alliance is formed in New York.

1969

January—**United States**: The Black Panther Party initiates its Free Breakfast for Children Program.

February—**Uruguay**: The Tupamaros conduct their first major actions, raiding a bank to reveal corrupt books and robbing a casino.

March—**United States**: The Chicago 8 (later Chicago 7) are charged with conspiracy to incite a riot at the Democratic National Convention.

May—**United States**: Chicago police shoot and kill Manuel Ramos, member of the Young Lords Organization.

June—**United States**: In debates at the Students for a Democratic Society national convention in Chicago, the faction that emerges victorious eventually leads to the creation of the Weather Underground.

June—**United States**: Members of the New York gay community battle police at the Stonewall Inn in Greenwich Village. The New York section of the Gay Liberation Front is formed the following month.

June—**United States**: The League of Revolutionary Black Workers is formed in Detroit.

July—**South Africa**: Inaugural conference of the South African Students' Organisation, which elected Steve Biko as its first president.

July—**Italy**: At the pinnacle of Italy's "hot autumn," striking Fiat workers in Turin march outside the factory and, after uniting with community members, battle the police.

July—**South Africa**: The South African Students' Organisation, which plays a major role in the Black Consciousness Movement, hosts its inaugural conference.

October—**United States**: "Days of Rage" street demonstrations and direct action in Chicago are organized by the emerging Weathermen faction.

December—**United States**: Fred Hampton, chair of the Illinois chapter of the Black Panther Party, is murdered in his bed by Chicago police.

December—**Italy**: Fascists, supported by the police, bomb a bank at Piazza Fontana in Turin, killing seventeen and injuring eighty-eight, initiating a long season of "state massacres."

December—**United States**: In an election for union president widely recognized as rigged, the United Mine Workers of America declares W. A. Boyle victor over Jack Yablonski. On the thirty-first of the same month, assassins hired by Boyle murder Yablonski and his family.

1970

March—**United States**: In a New York City Greenwich Village townhouse, three members of the Weather Underground are killed when a bomb they are preparing explodes accidentally.

May—**United States**: The National Guard fires on antiwar protesters at Kent State University, Ohio, leaving four dead and nine injured.

May—**West Germany**: Andreas Baader, later member of the Red Army Faction, is freed from prison with the aid of then-journalist Ulrike Meinhof.

August—**United States**: Huey Newton, Black Panther Party leader, is cleared of charges and released from jail in California.

September—**Chile**: Salvador Allende and his Popular Unity alliance win the presidential election, establishing a model for the electoral path to socialism.

September—**Jordan**: After clashes between the Jordanian armed forces and the Palestine Liberation Organization, the PLO is expelled from Jordan.

October—**United States**: Angela Davis is arrested in New York on the charge that weapons she owned were used in an attempted prison break. "Free Angela" campaigns are subsequently launched in countries throughout the world. Davis was acquitted of all charges in June 1972.

October—**United Kingdom**: The first meeting of the UK Gay Liberation Front is held in the basement of the London School of Economics.

November—**West Germany**: Large antinuclear protests are held in Hamburg and other German cities.

December—**United States**: The Black Workers' Congress is formed in Detroit and, in 1971, holds its first national conference in Gary, Indiana.

1971

February—**Japan**: In one of many clashes, twenty thousand activists defend improvised fortresses against the police to block construction of Narita Airport. The resistance movement began in 1966 and lasted with periods of intense conflict until the opening of the airport in 1978.

March—**United States**: The Citizens' Commission to Investigate the FBI, a small, secret group of activists, breaks into a regional FBI office in Media, Pennsylvania, and steals documents, which lead to revelations of the FBI's COINTELPRO, a pattern of illegal activity against leftist organizations.

April—**Chile**: Workers occupy and self-manage the Tarur cotton factory in Santiago against the wishes of the government. Such occupations (or *tomas*) were a common practice of activists and an expression of "popular power" during the revolutionary period.

March—**France**: The Front Homosexuel d'Action Révolutionnaire is created.

June—**Italy**: The feminist organization Lotta Femminista is created, in part by women who had left the revolutionary workers' party Potere Operaio.

August—**United States**: Black intellectual and activist George Jackson is killed during an attempt to escape from San Quentin Prison in California.

September—**United States**: Inmates at Attica State Prison in New York take control of the prison to demand better conditions and political rights. While suppressing the revolt, police kill thirty-three inmates and ten correctional officers.

October—**France**: The government announces plans to expand the Larzac military base, setting off an occupation of the land to block construction that attracted activists from the entire country. The encampment lasted until 1981, when the government abandoned its plans.

December—**Japan**: In its first action, the East Asian Anti-Japan Armed Front bombs the Kōa Kannon monument, which celebrates imperial Japan's World War II heroes. The front bombs several symbolic sites of Japanese war crimes and the country's imperial past in the following years.

1972

January—**Northern Ireland**: On "Bloody Sunday," British soldiers fire on a peaceful demonstration in Derry to protest mass arrests, killing fourteen. The attack served as a turning point toward armed struggle against British rule.

March—**Italy**: In one of its early actions, the Red Brigades kidnap Idalgo Macchiarini, director of the Siemens plant, conducts a "political trial," and releases him.

March—**United States**: The strike at the GM auto plant in Lordstown, Ohio, is a sign of workers' increasing autonomy and refusal to accept factory discipline. The number and intensity of industrial strikes in the early 1970s was among the highest in US history.

May—**West Germany**: The Red Army Faction conducts its "May Offensive," with bombings in six cities leaving three dead. By the next month, the original core leaders of the group, including Andreas Baader and Ulrike Meinhof, are all arrested.

July—**Northern Ireland**: The Provisional Irish Republican Army explodes twenty-one car bombs in Belfast.

July—**Chile**: A "People's Assembly" in Concepción emphasizes the divergent conceptions of "popular power" held by the political parties and the popular movements.

July—**United States**: Members of the Black Liberation Army, which was formed in 1970 by former members of the Black Panther Party, hijack a Delta Airlines flight and collect $1 million in ransom.

September—**Germany**: The Black September Organization, which emerged from the Fatah movement after the PLO was expelled from Jordan in 1970, takes Israeli athletes hostage at the Summer Olympics in Munich and eventually kills eleven.

1973

January—**South Africa**: A three-month strike wave in Durban marks an increased intensity of Black resistance.

January—**Guinea-Bissau**: Amilcar Cabral is assassinated in Conakry by rival revolutionaries.

February—**United States**: Members of the American Indian Movement occupy the town of Wounded Knee, South Dakota, and hold off federal agents for over two months.

May—**United States**: After a traffic stop on the New Jersey Turnpike, Black Liberation Army members are engaged in a shoot-out with state troopers, one of whom is killed. BLA member Assata Shakur is arrested and given a life sentence but escapes from prison in 1979 and flees to Cuba.

March—**Italy**: Tens of thousands of autoworkers occupy the Fiat plant in Turin for three days but do not emerge from the factory gates to engage with other social struggles. Despite the extent and intensity of the strike, some activists interpret it as a sign that industrial workers can no longer be considered the vanguard of the revolutionary movements.

May—**Italy**: At its national conference, the revolutionary party Potere Operaio decides to dissolve. Many of the former members subsequently become part of the "area" of Autonomia.

June—**France**: Workers at the Lip watch factory in Besançon occupy the factory and vote to restart self-managed production.

June—**Uruguay**: A coup d'état installs a "civic-military" dictatorship that rules the country until 1985. One rationale given for the coup is the danger posed by the Tupamaros.

August—**France**: The "March to Larzac" of students, workers, and farmers from throughout the country supports the occupation blocking the expansion of the military base.

August: **West Germany**: A wave of wildcat strikes threatens major industries.

September—**Chile**: A coup d'état aided by the CIA overthrows the Allende government and installs the military dictatorship of Augusto Pinochet.

September—**France**: A national demonstration held in Besançon supports the Lip workers' strike.

September—**Guinea-Bissau**: The country declares independence from Portugal.

October—**Israel**: Egyptian and Syrian attacks begin the Arab-Israeli War.

October—**Thailand**: The largest protest in Thai history overthrows the military dictatorship, but dictator Thanom returns to power shortly afterward.

October—**Middle East**: Arab oil ministers announce an embargo against states that support the Israeli war effort, initiating a global oil crisis.

1974

January—**France**: Workers at the Lip factory agree to an accord with owners and abandon self-management. The plant is closed three years later.

February—**United States**: The Symbionese Liberation Army kidnaps Patty Hearst.

February—**Grenada**: The country declares independence from the United Kingdom.

March—**Argentina**: A wave of industrial strikes begins in Villa Constitucíon in which coordinating structures are created among many different factories.

April—**Portugal**: A military coup led by colonels who were members of the Armed Forces Movement overthrows the fascist government and begins the Carnation Revolution.

May—**Italy**: A national referendum to legalize divorce passes.

May—**Turkey**: The national parliament passes an amnesty law that frees many imprisoned leftist militants.

May—**Italy**: Fascists bomb an antifascist demonstration in Brescia, leaving eight dead.

July—**Greece**: The right-wing military dictatorship, which had ruled since 1967, collapses after the Turkish invasion of Cyprus.

August—**Italy**: Fascists bomb the Italicus Express train, leaving twelve dead.

August—**Portugal**: Workers occupy and self-manage the Sogantal sportswear factory—one among hundreds of worker factory occupations during the revolutionary period.

August—**Japan**: The East Asian Anti-Japan Armed Front bombs the Mitsubishi Heavy Industries headquarters in Tokyo, but its warning to evacuate the building is late, resulting in eight dead and hundreds injured.

December—**Nicaragua**: FSLN militants kidnap government officials at a holiday party, greatly increasing the visibility of the revolutionary movement.

1975

February—**West Germany**: After the government announces plans to build a nuclear reactor in Wyhl, activists occupy the site and block construction.

March—**Portugal**: A failed right-wing coup initiates a more radical phase of revolutionary developments.

March—**Iran**: Members of the Marxist guerrilla organization Fadai assassinate Abbas Shahriari, a notorious agent of SAVAK (the secret service of the shah's regime). A series of operations by Marxist and Islamic guerrilla organizations throughout the 1970s led to the insurrection.

April—**Vietnam**: The fall of Saigon marks the victory of the North Vietnamese army.

May—**Italy**: The Italian parliament passes the Legge Reale, which imposes harsh conditions on leftist movements, allowing for extended preventive detention of suspected activists, outlawing the wearing of face coverings and helmets at demonstrations, and granting police wide authority for the use of force.

June—**Argentina**: General strikes in the greater Buenos Aires area expand the wave of industrial rebellion that began in Villa Constitución the previous year.

June—**Mozambique**: The country declares independence from Portugal.

July—**Cape Verde**: The country declares independence from Portugal.

September—**Portugal**: The Struggle Committee (Comité de Luta) in Setúbal is formed to bring together the various worker and neighborhood commissions at a citywide level.

November—**Angola**: The country declares independence from Portugal.

November—**Spain**: The dictator Generalissimo Francisco Franco dies. In the subsequent years Spain goes through a "transition to democracy."

November—**Portugal**: After a failed coup attempt linked to the Communist Party, a successful right-wing coup puts an end to the revolutionary process.

1976

March—**Argentina**: A right-wing coup d'état establishes a military junta that rules the country until 1983.

May—**West Germany**: Ulrike Meinhof is found dead in her cell in Stammheim Prison. Authorities pronounce it a suicide but activists suspect she was assassinated.

June—**South Africa**: In the Soweto Uprising, tens of thousands of young students protest the introduction of Africaans-language instruction in Black schools. Police fire on protesters, killing hundreds.

June—**United States**: The Clamshell Alliance is formed to block construction of a nuclear power plant in Seabrook, New Hampshire.

September—**China**: Mao Zedong, president of the People's Republic, dies.

October—**Italy**: At its second national congress in Rimini, the revolutionary party Lotta Continua decides to dissolve.

1977

January—**Italy**: The parliament approves a law to legalize abortion.

April—**Argentina**: The Madres de la Plaza de Mayo conduct their first demonstration to protest those "disappeared" by the dictatorship.

April—**United States**: The Combahee River Collective drafts its "Statement." The group was formed in Boston in 1974.

May—**Turkey**: The revolutionary party Devrimci Yol (Revolutionary Path) publishes a manifesto to announce its formation.

May—**United States**: A total of 1,444 Clamshell Alliance activists are arrested after the group unsuccessfully attempts to occupy the Seabrook construction site.

May—**South Africa**: Steve Biko, in court testimony at the trial of fellow SASO members, gives the judges an extended lesson in the ideology and actions of the Black Consciousness Movement.

June—**Iran**: Ali Shari'ati, important intellectual influence of the revolutionary movement, dies in Southampton, England. Although he died of heart failure, many revolutionaries believe he was martyred by the regime.

July—**France**: During a protest against the construction of a nuclear plant at Malville, a demonstrator is killed by police.

September—**South Africa**: Steve Biko dies in police custody in Port Elizabeth. His funeral two weeks later is attended by tens of thousands.

September—**Italy**: A "convention against repression" is held in a sports arena in Bologna, with over a hundred thousand participants from groups across the radical Left.

September—**West Germany**: As part of its "German Autumn" actions, the Red Army Faction kidnaps industrialist and former Nazi Hanns Martin Schleyer. After the news in October that Baader, Ensslin, and Raspe were found dead in their cells in Stammheim Prison, they murder Schleyer.

October—**Iran**: Ten nights of poetry reading at the Goethe Institute in Tehran with over five thousand in attendance is viewed as a precursor to the insurrection.

1978

January—**Nicaragua**: Pedro Chamorro, newspaper owner and prominent centrist critique of the Somoza regime, is assassinated in Managua by the government.

March—**Italy**: The Red Brigades kidnap Aldo Moro, hold him captive for almost two months, and then murder him.

March—**Japan**: In one final action to protest the opening of Narita Airport, activists attack and briefly take charge of the airport control tower.

August—**Nicaragua**: FLSN militants capture the National Palace and hold the Congress hostage, leading to the final phase of the insurrection.

September—**Iran**: In the Black Friday massacre, army troops fire on antigovernment protestors in Jalal Square in Tehran, killing hundreds or thousands. Two days later, Michel Foucault arrives in Tehran for the first of two visits on assignment from the Italian newspaper *Corriere della Sera*.

1979

January—**Iran**: The shah flees to Egypt, Ayatollah Khomeini returns to the country two weeks later, and the regime falls in February.

April—**Italy**: In a coordinated police operation, hundreds of activists in the "area" of Autonomia are arrested, including the most prominent national figures. In the surrounding years, tens of thousands of leftist activists were imprisoned and thousands more fled into exile.

July—**Nicaragua**: The Somoza regime falls, giving full control to the revolutionary movement.

October—**Turkey**: Fikri Sönmez is elected mayor of Fatsa, creating what prosecutors eventually call the "Fatsa Commune."

October—**South Korea**: The assassination of President Park Chung-hee ends his civilian authoritarian regime but is followed by a military dictatorship led by General Chun Doo Hwan.

1980

April—**Zimbabwe**: The country declares independence.

May—**South Korea**: In the city of Kwangju, after protests against the military dictatorship and the imposition of martial law, armed citizens expel the military and briefly establish democratic governance structures, known as the "Kwangju Commune."

July—**Turkey**: Military troops take control of Fatsa and arrest Mayor Fikri Sönmez.

August—**Italy**: Fascists bomb the Bologna train station, leaving eighty-five dead and hundreds wounded.

September—**Turkey**: In a coup d'état, the armed forces take control of the government.

Acknowledgments

Many friends provided valuable suggestions that guided my research and helped me understand the specific struggles and the larger national political contexts for the different chapters of this book. I am grateful, in particular, to Jim Ferguson regarding southern Africa; Hamid Dabashi and Iman Ganji regarding Iran; Philip Wohlstetter regarding Chile; José Manuel Viegas Neves regarding Portugal; Alisa Del Re regarding Italy; Ahmed Veriava regarding South Africa; Gavin Walker and Pio D'Emilia regarding Japan; and Serhat Ururkulak and the Otonom collective for Turkey. None of them are responsible, of course, for errors I have made.

I presented an early draft of Chapter 17 as the David Graeber Memorial Lecture in April 2022. I am grateful to Andrej Grubacic for inviting me and to the participants for useful feedback. Parts of chapters 12 and 13 were presented as a Plenary Address at the 2022 meeting of the Society for Phenomenology and Existential Philosophy and appeared in slightly different form in "The Politics of Articulation and Strategic Multiplicities," published in the *Journal of Speculative Philosophy*. I thank the editors of the journal and the Penn State University Press for permission to include it here.

Regarding revolutionary movements in Italy in the 1970s, I have a particularly large debt, and I would like to thank for innumerable conversations over the course of many years, among others, Giuseppe Cocco, Leo Elicio, Maurizio Lazzarato, Christian Marazzi, Carlo Vercellone, and Paolo Virno.

I am especially grateful to those who read part or all of the manuscript and gave me encouragement and guidance, including Ben Crais, Fredric Jameson, Sandro Mezzadra, Antonio Negri, Raúl Sanchez Cedillo, Alberto Toscano, Ahmed Veriava, and Kathi Weeks, as well as the anonymous reviewers.

I dedicate this book to the memory of two dear friends, Lauren Berlant and Robert Adelman.

Works Cited

Chapter 1: Introduction

Balestrini, Nanni, and Primo Moroni, eds. 2021. *The Golden Horde*. Translated by Richard Braude. Seagull Books.

Berger, Dan. 2010. "Introduction: Exploding Limits in the 70s." In *The Hidden 1970s: Histories of Radicalism*, edited by Dan Berger, 1–17. Rutgers University Press.

Breines, Winifred. 1988. "Whose New Left?" *Journal of American History* 75, no. 2: 528–545.

Buhle, Paul. 1993. "Madison Revisited." *Radical History Review* 57: 242–249.

Cowie, Jefferson. 2010. *Stayin' Alive: The 1970s and the Last Days of the Working Class*. New Press.

Deleuze, Gilles, and Félix Guattari. 1987. *A Thousand Plateaus*. Translated by Brian Massumi. University of Minnesota Press.

Deleuze, Gilles, and Félix Guattari. 1993. *Anti-Oedipus*. Translated by Robert Hurley, Mark Seem, and Helen Lane. University of Minnesota Press.

Dreyfus-Armand, Geneviève, Robert Frank, Marie-Françoise Lévy, and Michelle Zancarini-Fournel, eds. 2000. *Les années 68*. Éditions Complexe.

Elbaum, Max. 2002. *Revolution in the Air: Sixties Radicals Turn to Lenin, Mao and Che*. Verso.

Firestone, Shulamith. 1970. *The Dialectic of Sex*. William Morrow.

Gitlin, Todd. 1987. *The Sixties: Years of Hope, Days of Rage*. Bantam.

Hamon, Hervé, and Patrick Rotman. 1987. *Génération*, vol. 1, *Les années de rêve*. Seuil.

Hamon, Hervé, and Patrick Rotman. 1988. *Génération*, vol. 2, *Les années de poudre*. Seuil.

Hardt, Michael, and Antonio Negri. 2017. *Assembly*. Oxford University Press.

Hernández, Roberto. 2015. "1968: On Social, Epistemic, and Historiographic (?) Revolutions." *Kalfou* 2, no. 1: 135–146.

Jameson, Fredric. 1984. "Periodizing the 60s." *Social Text* 9/10: 178–209.

Kelley, Robin D. G. 2002. *Freedom Dreams*. Beacon Press.

Kissack, Terence. 1995. "Freaking Fag Revolutionaries: New York's Gay Liberation Front, 1969–1971." *Radical History Review* 62: 104–134.

Kruse, Kevin M., and Julian E. Zelizer. 2019. *Fault Lines: A History of the United States Since 1974*. Norton.

Lewis, Paul H. 2002. *Guerillas and Generals*. Praeger.

Pensado, Jaime M., and Enrique C. Ochoa. 2018. "Introduction: México Beyond 1968." In *México Beyond 1968: Revolutionaries, Radical, and Repression During the Global Sixties and Subversive Seventies*, edited by Jaime M. Pensado and Enrique C. Ochoa, 3–16. University of Arizona Press.

Reagon, Bernice Johnson. 1983. "Coalition Politics: Turning the Century." In *Home Girls: A Black Feminist Anthology*, edited by Barbara Smith, 356–368. Kitchen Table Press.

Rodgers, Daniel T. 2011. *Age of Fracture*. Harvard University Press.

Ross, Kristin. 2004. *May '68 and Its Afterlives*. University of Chicago Press.

Wallerstein, Immanuel. 1989. "1968, Revolution in the World-System." *Theory and Society* 18, no. 4: 431–449.

Windham, Lane. 2017. *Knocking on Labor's Door: Union Organizing in the 1970s and the Roots of a New Economic Divide*. University of North Carolina Press.

Zaretsky, Natasha. 2018. *Radiation Nation: Three Mile Island and the Political Transformation of the 1970s*. Columbia University Press.

Chapter 2: Revolutionary Democracy

Blackburn, Robin. 1974. "The Test of Portugal." *New Left Review* 87–88: 5–46.

Borges, Sónia Vaz. 2019. *Militant Education, Liberation Struggle, Consciousness: The PAIGC Education in Guinea-Bissau 1963–1978*. Peter Lang.

Cabral, Amilcar. 1980a. "General Watchwords." In *Unity and Struggle: Speeches and Writings*, 224–250. Translated by Michael Wolfers. Heinemann.

Cabral, Amilcar. 1980b. "The Weapon of Theory." In *Unity and Struggle: Speeches and Writings*, 119–137. Translated by Michael Wolfers. Heinemann.

Cahen, Michel. 1987. *Mozambique: La révolution implosée*. L'Harmattan.

Davidson, Basil. 1974. *Growing from Grass Roots: The State of Guinea-Bissau*. Committee for Freedom in Mozambique, Angola and Guinea.

Davidson, Basil. 1976a. "Angola: A Success That Changes History." *Race and Class* 18, no. 1: 23–37.

Davidson, Basil. 1976b. "The Angolans Themselves." *New Society*, January 15, 1976, 102–103.

Davidson, Basil. 1976c. "The Politics of Armed Struggle: National Liberation in the African Colonies of Portugal." In Basil Davidson, Joe Slovo, and Anthony Wilkinson, *Southern Africa: The New Politics of Revolution*, 15–102. Penguin.

Davidson, Basil. 1979. "The Revolution of People's Power: Notes on Mozambique 1979." *Race and Class* 21, no. 2: 127–143.

Davidson, Basil. 1980. "Introduction." In Amilcar Cabral, *Unity and Struggle: Speeches and Writings*, ix–xvii. Heinemann.

Davidson, Basil. 1981. *The People's Cause: A History of Guerrillas in Africa*. Longman.

Davidson, Basil. 2009. "Mozambique Diary" [1980]. *Race and Class* 51, no. 2: 104–108.

Ferguson, James. 2006. *Global Shadows: Africa in the Neoliberal World Order*. Duke University Press.

La lutte de libération dans les colonies portugaises. 1973. La Brèche. [Basil Davidson says that this was written by Cabral, but the text gives no indication.]

Machel, Samora. 1974. "A libertação da mulher é uma necessidade da revolução" [1973]. In *A luta continua*, edited by José Salvador, 55–72. Afrontamento.

Machel, Samora. 1975. *O processo da revoluçao democrática popular em Moçambique*. Slemes.

Machel, Samora. 1985a. "Defining Woman's Enemy" [1976]. In *Samora Machel: An African Revolutionary*, edited by Barry Munslow, translated by Michael Wolfers, 169–178. Zed Books.

Machel, Samora. 1985b. "Establishing People's Power to Serve the Masses" [1974]. In *Samora Machel: An African Revolutionary*, edited by Barry Munslow, translated by Michael Wolfers, 1–33. Zed Books.

Munslow, Barry. 1983. *Mozambique: The Revolution and Its Origins*. Longman.

Munslow, Barry, and Phil O'Keefe. 1984. "Rethinking the Revolution in Mozambique." *Race and Class* 26, no. 2: 15–31.

Newitt, Malyn. 2017. *A Short History of Mozambique*. Oxford University Press.

O'Keefe, Phil. 1983. "Review of Munslow, *Mozambique: The Revolution and Its Origins*." *Journal of Modern African Studies* 21, no. 2: 347–349.

Poblet, Maria. 2013. "Revolutionary Democracy, Class-Consciousness, and Cross-Class Movement Building." In *Claim No Easy Victories: The Legacy of Amilcar Cabral*, edited by Firoze Manji and Bill Fletcher Jr., 239–247. CODESRIA.

Robinson, Cedric. 1981. "Amilcar Cabral and the Dialectic of Portuguese Colonialism." *Radical America* 15, no. 3: 39–57.

Santos, Boaventura de Sousa. 1982. "Law and Revolution: The Experiences of Popular Justice After the 25th of April 1974." In *The Politics of Informal Justice*, edited by Richard Abel, 251–280. Academic Press.

Sweezy, Paul. 1975. "Class Struggles in Portugal, part 1." *Monthly Review* 4: 1–26.

Trotsky, Leon. 1977. *The History of the Russian Revolution*. Translated by Max Eastman. Pluto Press.

Chapter 3: Gay Liberation

Berlant, Lauren, and Michael Warner. 1998. "Sex in Public." *Critical Inquiry* 24, no. 2: 547–566.

Bloom, Joshua, and Waldo Martin. 2012. *Black Against Empire: The History and Politics of the Black Panther Party*. University of California Press.

Delany, Samuel. 1990. *Times Square Red, Times Square Blue*. New York University Press.

Downs, Jim. 2016. *Stand by Me: The Forgotten History of Gay Liberation*. Basic Books.

Foucault, Michel. 1997. "Friendship as a Way of Life" [1981]. In *Ethics*, edited by Paul Rabinow, 135–140. New Press.

Gay Liberation Front. 1978. "Manifesto" [1971]. https://sourcebooks.fordham.edu/pwh/glf-london.asp.

Girard, Jacques. 1981. *Le mouvement homosexuel en France 1945–1980*. Syros.

Hobson, Emily. 2016. *Lavender and Red: Liberation and Solidarity in the Gay and Lesbian Left*. University of California Press.

Kissack, Terence. 1995. "Freaking Fag Revolutionaries: New York's Gay Liberation Front, 1969–1971." *Radical History Review* 62: 104–134.

Lovett, Joseph, dir. 2005. *Gay Sex in the 70s* [film].

Marx, Karl. 1975. "Economic and Philosophical Manuscripts." In *Early Writings*, 279–400. Penguin Books.

Muñoz, José Esteban. 2009. *Cruising Utopia: The Then and There of Queer Futurity*. New York University Press.

Third World Gay Revolution. 1970. "Sixteen Point Platform and Program." https://pinko.online/pinko-1/third-world-gay-revolution-archive.

Walter, Aubrey, ed. 1980. *Come Together: The Years of Gay Liberation (1970–1973)*. Gay Men's Press.

Weeks, Jeffrey. 1990. *Coming Out: Homosexual Politics in Britain from the Nineteenth Century to the Present*. Revised ed. Quartet Books.

Chapter 4: Liberation Theologies

Abrahamian, Ervand. 1982. *Iran: Between Two Revolutions*. Princeton University Press.

Bayat, Assef. 1987. *Workers and Revolution in Iran*. Zed Books.

Behrooz, Maziar. 1999. *Rebels with a Cause: The Failure of the Left in Iran*. I. B. Tauris.

Borge, Tomás. 1987. *Christianity and Revolution*. Edited and translated by Andrew Reding. Orbis Books.

Bradstock, Andrew. 1987. *Saints and Sandinistas: The Catholic Church in Nicaragua and Its Response to the Revolution*. Epworth Press.

Cardenal, Ernesto. 1976. *The Gospel in Solentiname*. Translated by Donald D. Walsh. Orbis Books.

Cardenal, Ernesto. 1979. "Solentiname—the End." *Index on Censorship* 1: 11–13.

Clos, Ryne. 2012. "In the Name of the God Who Will Be: The Mobilization of Radical Christians in the Sandinista Revolution." *Journal for the Study of Radicalism* 6, no. 2: 1–51.

Dodson, Michael. 1986. "The Politics of Religion in Revolutionary Nicaragua." *Annals* (AAPSS) 483: 36–49.

Foroohar, Manzar. 1989. *The Catholic Church and Social Change in Nicaragua*. State University of New York Press.

Foucault, Michel. 2005a. "Dialogue Between Michel Foucault and Baqir Parham." In *Foucault and the Iranian Revolution*, edited by Janet Afary and Kevin Anderson, 183–188. University of Chicago Press.

Foucault, Michel. 2005b. "Iran: The Spirit of a World Without Spirit." With Claire Brière and Pierre Blanchet. In *Foucault and the Iranian Revolution*, edited by Janet Afary and Kevin Anderson, 250–260. University of Chicago Press.

Foucault, Michel. 2005c. "Tehran: Faith Against the Shah." In *Foucault and the Iranian Revolution*, edited by Janet Afary and Kevin Anderson, 198–203. University of Chicago Press.

Foucault, Michel. 2020. "Political Spirituality as the Will for Alterity: An Interview with the *Nouvel Observateur*." Translated by Sabina Vaccarino Bremner. *Critical Inquiry* 47: 121–134.

Ghamari-Tabrizi, Behrooz. 2000. "Review of Ali Rahnema, *An Islamic Utopian*." *Critique: Critical Middle Eastern Studies* 9, no. 16: 105–111.

Ghamari-Tabrizi, Behrooz. 2004. "Contentious Public Religion: Two Conceptions of Islam in Revolutionary Iran." *International Sociology* 19, no. 4: 504–523.

Ghamari-Tabrizi, Behrooz. 2016. *Foucault in Iran: Islamic Revolution After the Enlightenment*. University of Minnesota Press.

Grandin, Greg. 2011. *The Last Colonial Massacre: Latin America in the Cold War*. 2nd ed. University of Chicago Press.

Hodges, Donald. 1986. *Intellectual Foundations of the Nicaraguan Revolution*. University of Texas Press.

Jafari, Peyman. 2019. "Linkages of Oil and Politics: Oil Strikes and Dual Power in the Iranian Revolution." *Labor History* 60, no. 1: 24–43.

Kanaaneh, Abed. 2021. "Ali Shari'ati: Islamizing Socialism and Socializing Islam." *Left History* 24, no. 1: 45–64.

Kinzer, Stephen. 2003. *All the Shah's Men*. Wiley and Sons.

Kirk, John M. 1992. *Politics and the Catholic Church in Nicaragua*. University of Florida Press.

Moghadam, Val. 1987. "Socialism or Anti-Imperialism? The Left and Revolution in Iran." *New Left Review* 166: 5–28.

O'Shaughnessy, Laura Nuzzi. 1986. "The Conflicts of Class and Worldview: Theology in Revolutionary Nicaragua." In *The Church and Revolution in Nicaragua*, edited by Laura Nuzzi O'Shaughnessy and Luis H. Serra, 1–42. Ohio University Center for International Studies.

Rahnema, Ali. 1998. *An Islamic Utopian: A Political Biography of Ali Shari'ati*. I. B. Tauris.

Randall, Margaret. 1983. *Christians in the Nicaraguan Revolution*. Translated by Mariana Valverde. New Star Books.

Reding, Andrew. 1987. "Introduction." In Tomás Borge, *Christianity and Revolution*, edited and translated by Andrew Reding, 1–12. Orbis Books.

Rossa, Alberto, ed. 1986. *The Theology of Liberation*. Historical Conservation Society.

Saffari, Siavash. 2017. *Beyond Shariati*. Cambridge University Press.

Sassine, Farès, and Michel Foucault. 2018. "There Can't Be Societies Without Uprisings." Translated by Alex J. Feldman. *Foucault Studies* 25: 324–350.

Vahabzadeh, Peyman. 2019. *A Guerrilla Odyssey*. Syracuse University Press.

Weber, Henri. 1981. *Nicaragua: The Sandinista Revolution*. Translated by Patrick Camiller. Verso

Chapter 5: Two Versions of Popular Power

Allende, Salvador. 2000a. "Address to the United Nations General Assembly" (December 4, 1972). In *Salvador Allende Reader*, edited by James Cockcroft, 200–221. Ocean Press.

Allende, Salvador. 2000b. "First Annual Message to the National Congress" (May 21, 1971). In *Salvador Allende Reader*, edited by James Cockcroft, 89–113. Ocean Press.

Berlinguer, Enrico. 1973. "Riflessioni sull'Italia dopo i fatti del Cile." *Rinascita*, October 12, 1973, 3–5.

Cárcamo Hernández, Ovidio. 2016. "Movimiento campesino revolucionario y consejos comunales campesinos de base." *Desacatos* 52: 94–111.

Cury, Márcia. 2018. *El protagonismo popular chileno*. LOM Ediciones.

Debray, Régis. 1971. *Conversations with Allende*. New Left Books.

Gaudichaud, Franck. 2013. *Chili 1970–1973: Mille jours qui ébranlèrent le monde*. Presses Universitaires de Rennes.

Gerhardt, Christina. 2018. *Screening the Red Army Faction: Historical and Cultural Memory*. Bloomsbury.

Grandin, Greg. 2006. *Empire's Workshop*. Metropolitan Books.

Grandin, Greg. 2015. *Kissinger's Shadow*. Metropolitan Books.

Hardt, Michael, and Antonio Negri. 2017. *Assembly*. Oxford University Press.

Pérez Suárez, Miguel Ángel. 2020. "A autogestão no processo revoluciónario português de 1974–75." In *História do Movimento Operário e Conflitos Sociais em Portugal*, edited by Pamela Peres Cabreira, 201–224. Livros IHC.

Santos, Boaventura de Sousa. 1982. "Law and Revolution: The Experiences of Popular Justice After the 25th of April 1974." In *The Politics of Informal Justice*, edited by Richard Abel, 251–280. Academic Press.

Schlotterbeck, Marian. 2018. *Beyond the Vanguard*. University of California Press.

Weisz, Eduardo. 2004. "El PRT-ERP: Nueva izquierda e izquierda tradicional." Cuaderno de Trabajo no. 30. Ediciones del Instituto Movilizador de Fondos Cooperativos.

Winn, Peter. 1986. *Weavers of Revolution*. Oxford University Press.

Chapter 6: Commission Democracy

Barca, Stefania, and Ana Delicado. 2016. "Anti-Nuclear Mobilization and Environmentalism in Europe: A View from Portugal (1976–1986)." *Environment and History* 22: 497–520.

Bermeo, Nancy. 1986. *The Revolution Within the Revolution: Workers' Control in Rural Portugal*. Princeton University Press.

Blackburn, Robin. 1974. "The Test of Portugal." *New Left Review* 87–88: 5–46.

d'Arthuys, Béatrice, and Marielle Christine Gros. 1976. "Les commissions de 'Moradores': Organisation ou pouvoir populaire." *Autogestion et socialisme* 33–34: 35–53.

Del Pero, Mario. 2011. "'Which Chile, Allende?' Henry Kissinger and the Portuguese Revolution." *Cold War History* 11, no. 4: 625–657.

de Sousa, Antónia, and Maria Antóna Palla. 1975. *Nome mulher: O caso Sogantal* [film].

Downs, Charles. 1983. "Residents' Commissions and Urban Struggles in Revolutionary Portugal." In *In Search of Modern Portugal*, edited by Lawrence Graham and Douglas Wheeler, 151–179. University of Wisconsin Press.

Downs, Charles. 1989. *Revolution at the Grassroots: Community Organizations in the Portuguese Revolution*. State University of New York Press.

Hammond, John. 1980. "Portugal's Communists and the Revolution." *Radical History Review*, Spring 1980, 140–161.

Hammond, John. 1984. "The Portuguese Revolution: Two Models of Socialist Transition." *Insurgent Sociologist* 12, no. 1: 83–100.

Hammond, John. 1985. "Popular Power and the Portuguese Far Left." *European Journal of Political Research* 13: 207–225.

Hammond, John. 1988. *Building Popular Power: Workers' and Neighborhood Movements in the Portuguese Revolution*. Monthly Review Press.

Harlan, Thomas, dir. 1975. *Torre Bela* [film].

Kramer, Robert, dir. 1977. *Scenes from the Class Struggle in Portugal* [film].

Mailer, Phil. 1977. *Portugal: The Impossible Revolution*. Solidarity Books.

Margarido, Alfredo. 1976. "Fin de partie au Portugal." *Esprit*, February 1976, 330–333.

Margarido, Alfredo. 1980. "Review of Jean-Pierre Faye, *Portugal 1974-1975: Regards sur une tentative de pouvoir populaire*." *Esprit*, February 1980, 180–181.

Noronha, Ricardo. 2019. "A Real State of Exception: Class Composition and Social Conflict During Portugal's Carnation Revolution, 1974–1975." *Critical Historical Studies*, Spring 2019, 93–123.

Pérez Suárez, Miguel Ángel. 2020. "A autogestão no processo revoluciónario português de 1974–75." In *História do Movimento Operário e Conflitos Sociais em Portugal*, edited by Pamela Peres Cabreira, 201–224. Livros IHC.

Ramos Pinto, Pedro. 2008. "Urban Social Movements and the Transition to Democracy in Portugal, 1974–1976." *Historical Journal* 51, no. 4: 1025–1046.

Robinson, Peter. 2011. "Workers' Councils in Portugal, 1974–1975." In *Ours to Master and to Own: Workers' Control from the Commune to the Present*, edited by Dario Azzellini and Immanuel Ness, 263–281. Haymarket Books.

Santos, Boaventura de Sousa. 1979. "Popular Justice, Dual Power and Socialist Strategy." In *Capitalism and the Rule of Law*, edited by Bob Fine, Richard Kinsey, John Lea, Sol Picciotto, and Jock Young, 151–163. Hutchinson.

Santos, Boaventura de Sousa. 1982. "Law and Revolution: The Experiences of Popular Justice After the 25th of April 1974." In *The Politics of Informal Justice*, edited by Richard Abel, 251–280. Academic Press.

Sweezy, Paul. 1975. "Class Struggles in Portugal, Part 1." *Monthly Review* 4: 1–26.
Thibaud, Paul. 1976. "A propos du pouvoir populaire." *Esprit* 44, no. 2: 333–334.
Varela, Raquel. 2019. *A People's History of the Portuguese Revolution*. Translated by Sean Purdy. Pluto Press.

Chapter 7: Promise of Another Democracy

Chang, Paul Y. 2015. *Protest Dialectics: State Repression and South Korea's Democracy Movement, 1970–1979*. Stanford University Press.
Choi, Jung-woon. 2003. "The Formation of an 'Absolute Community.'" In *Contentious Kwangju: The May 18 Uprising in Korea's Past and Present*, edited by Gi-Wook Shin and Kyung Moon Hwang, 3–10. Rowman & Littlefield.
Cummings, Bruce. 1999. "Introduction." In Jae-eui Lee, *Kwangju Diary: Beyond Death, Beyond the Darkness of the Age*, 17–36. UCLA Asian Pacific Monograph Series.
Katsiaficas, Georgy. 2006a. "Comparing the Paris Commune and the Gwangju Uprising." In *South Korean Democracy: Legacy of the Gwangju Uprising*, edited by Georgy Katsiaficas and Na Kahn-chae, 184–195. Routledge.
Katsiaficas, Georgy. 2006b. "Remembering the Gwangju Uprising." In *South Korean Democracy: Legacy of the Gwangju Uprising*, edited by Georgy Katsiaficas and Na Kahn-chae, 1–23. Routledge.
Lee, Jae-eui. 1999. *Kwangju Diary: Beyond Death, Beyond the Darkness of the Age*. Translated by Kap Su Seol and Nick Mamatas. UCLA Asian Pacific Monograph Series.
Na, Kahn-chae. 2006. "A New Perspective on the Gwangju People's Resistance Struggle." In *South Korean Democracy: Legacy of the Gwangju Uprising*, edited by Georgy Katsiaficas and Na Kahn-chae, 165–183. Routledge.
Shin, Gi-Wook. 2003. "Introduction." In *Contentious Kwangju: The May 18 Uprising in Korea's Past and Present*, edited by Gi-Wook Shin and Kyung Moon Hwang, xi–xxxi. Rowman & Littlefield.
Shorrock, Tim. 2015. "The Gwangju Uprising and American Hypocrisy." *The Nation*, June 5, 2015. https://www.thenation.com/article/world/kwangju-uprising-and-american-hypocrisy-one-reporters-quest-truth-and-justice-korea/.

Chapter 8: Ungovernable Factories

Aronowitz, Stanley. 1973. *False Promises*. McGraw-Hill.
Aronowitz, Stanley. 1990. "Writing Labor's History." *Social Text* 25–26: 171–195.
Bird, Stewart, Rene Lichtman, and Peter Gessner, dirs. 1970. *Finally Got the News* [film].
Chamayou, Grégoire. 2021. *The Ungovernable Society*. Translated by Andrew Brown. Polity Press.
Cotarelo, María Celia, and Fabián Fernández. 1998. "Lucha del movimiento obrero en un momento de crisis de la sociedad: Argentina, 1975–1976." *Revista RyR* 4, https://razonyrevolucion.org/lucha-del-movimiento-obrero-en-un-momento-de-crisis-de-la-sociedad-argentina-1975-1976/.
Cowie, Jefferson. 2010. *Stayin' Alive: The 1970s and the Last Days of the Working Class*. New Press.
Davis, Mike. 1986. *Prisoners of the American Dream*. Verso.

Glaberman, Martin. 1972. "Unions vs. Workers in the Seventies: The Rise of Militancy in the Auto Industry." *Society*, November–December 1972, 85–89.

Georgakas, Dan, and Marvin Surkin. 1975. *Detroit, I Do Mind Dying*. South End Press.

Gorz, André (Michel Bosquet, pseud.). 1972. "Les patrons découvrent 'l'usine-bagne,'" part 3. *Le Nouvel Observateur* 384 (March 20, 1972). https://www.nouvelobs.com/opini ons/00024209.EDI0001/les-patrons-decouvrent-l-usine-bagne-iii.html.

Gorz, André (Michel Bosquet, pseud.). 1976. "The Tyranny of the Factory: Today and Tomorrow" [1972]. In André Gorz, *The Division of Labor: The Labor Process and Class Struggle in Modern Capitalism*, 55–61. Harvester Press.

Huntington, Samuel. 1975. "The Crisis of Democracy." In Michel Crozier, Samuel Huntington, and Joji Watanuki, *The Crisis of Democracy*, 59–118. New York University Press.

James, Daniel. 1988. *Resistance and Integration: Peronism and the Argentine Working Class, 1946–1976*. Cambridge University Press.

Kopple, Barbara, dir. 1976. *Harlan County, USA* [film].

Lewis-Colman, David. 2008. *Race Against Liberalism: Black Workers and the UAW in Detroit*. University of Illinois Press.

Linebaugh, Peter, and Bruno Ramirez. 1975. "Crisis in the Auto Sector." *Zero Work* 1: 61–85.

Löbbe, Héctor. 2006. *La guerrilla fabril*. Ediciones RyR.

Moody, Kim. 1997. *Workers in a Lean World*. Verso.

Moody, Kim. 2000. "The Rank and File Strategy." Solidarity working paper.

National Archives. n.d. "Vietnam War U.S. Military Fatal Casualty Statistics." https:// www.archives.gov/research/military/vietnam-war/casualty-statistics (accessed July 25, 2022).

Roth, Karl-Heinz. 1974. *Die "andere" Arbeiterbewegung und die Entwicklung der kapitalistischen Repression von 1880 bis zur Gegenwart*. Trikont Verlag.

Stein, Judith. 2010. *Pivotal Decade*. Yale University Press.

Tripp, Luke. 1994. "Black Working Class Radicalism in Detroit, 1960–1970." Ethnic and Women's Studies Working Papers 7, St. Cloud State University. https://repository.stclo udstate.edu/ews_wps/7.

Tronti, Mario. 2019. *Workers and Capital* [1966, 1971]. Translated by David Broder. Verso.

Watson, Bill. 1971. "Counter-Planning on the Shop Floor." *Radical America* 5, no. 3: 77–85.

Werner, Ruth, and Facundo Aguirre. 2007. *Insurgencia obrera en la Argentina 1969–1976*. Ediciones IPS.

Windham, Lane. 2017. *Knocking on Labor's Door: Union Organizing in the 1970s and the Roots of a New Economic Divide*. University of North Carolina Press.

Winslow, Cal. 2021. "The 1970s: Decade of the Rank and File." *Jacobin Magazine*, January 23, 2021. https://www.jacobinmag.com/2021/01/1970s-decade-strike-workers-labor-history.

Chapter 9: Self-Management in the Watch Factory

Berger, Claude. 1973. "Lip et après." *Les temps modernes* 327: 559–564.

Gourgues, Guillaume, and Claude Neuschwander. 2018. *Pourquoi ont-ils tué Lip? De la victoire ouvrière au tournant libéral*. Raisons d'Agir.

Hamon, Hervé, and Patrick Rotman. 1988. *Génération*, vol. 2, *Les années de poudre*. Seuil.

Piaget, Charles. 2018. "Mai 68 chez Lip à Besançon." *Les Utopique Solidaires* 7. https://www.lesutopiques.org/mai-68-chez-lip-a-besancon/.

Reid, Donald. 2018. *Opening the Gates: The Lip Affair, 1968–1981*. Verso.

Rosanvallon, Pierre. 1976. *L'âge de l'autogestion*. Seuil.

Rosanvallon, Pierre. 1979. "Sur l'autogestion, l'expérimentation, les mouvements sociaux" (interview with Jacques Caroux and Olivier Mongin). *Esprit*, September–October 1979, 98–109.

Vigna, Xavier. 2015. *L'insubordination ouvrière dans les années 68*. Presses Universitaires de Rennes.

Chapter 10: Laboratory Italy

Balestrini, Nanni. 1989. *The Unseen* [1987]. Translated by Liz Heron. Verso.

Balestrini, Nanni. 2016. *We Want Everything* [1971]. Translated by Matt Holden. Verso.

Balestrini, Nanni, and Primo Moroni, eds. 2021. *The Golden Horde*. Translated by Richard Braude. Seagull Books.

Berardi, Franco (Bifo, pseud.). 1980. "Anatomy of Autonomy." In "Autonomia: Post-Political Politics," special issue edited by Sylvère Lotringer and Christian Marazzi. *Semiotext(e)* 3, no. 3: 148–171.

Berardi, Franco. 2007. "Genesi e significato del termine 'autonomia.'" In *Gli autonomi*, vol. 1, edited by Sergio Bianchi and Lanfranco Caminiti, 40–54. DeriveApprodi.

Bianchi, Sergio, and Lanfranco Caminiti, eds. 2007. *Gli autonomi*, vol. 2. DeriveApprodi.

Bobbio, Luigi. 1988. *Storia di Lotta Continua*. Feltrinelli.

Castellano, Lucio. 1980. "Introduzione." In *Aut. Op.*, edited by Lucio Castellano, 7–21. Savelli Editori.

Castellano, Lucio, et al. 1996. "Do You Remember Revolution?" In *Radical Thought in Italy*, edited by Michael Hardt and Paolo Virno, 225–238. University of Minnesota Press.

Ceri, Paolo. 2001. "L'autonomia operaia tra organizzazione del lavoro and sistema politico (1977)." *Quaderni di sociologia* 26–27: 287–306.

Cherki, Eddy, and Michel Wieviorka. 1980. "Autoreduction Movements in Turin." In "Autonomia: Post-Political Politics," special issue edited by Sylvère Lotringer and Christian Marazzi. *Semiotext(e)* 3, no. 3: 72–78.

Ciuferri, Nicholas. 2014. "A/traverso: Franco 'Bifo' Berardi in movimento, 1964–1978." PhD thesis, National University of Ireland.

Comitati autonomi operai, Via dei Volsci, 6. 2007. "Introduzione al libro, *Autonomia Operaia*" [1976]. In *Gli autonomi*, vol. 2, edited by Sergio Bianchi and Lanfranco Caminiti, 31–39. DeriveApprodi.

Cuninghame, Patrick Gun. 2002. "*Autonomia*: A Movement of Refusal." PhD thesis, Middlesex University.

Dalla Costa, Mariarosa. 2017. "The Door to the Flower and the Vegetable Garden." *Viewpoint*, June 20, 2017. https://viewpointmag.com/2017/06/20/the-door-to-the-flower-and-the-vegetable-garden-2002/.

Dalla Costa, Mariarosa, and Selma James. 1972. *The Power of Women and the Subversion of Community*. Falling Wall Press.

Fortunati, Leapoldina. 2013. "Learning to Struggle: My Story Between Workerism and Feminism." *Viewpoint*, September 15, 2013. https://viewpointmag.com/2013/09/15/learning-to-struggle-my-story-between-workerism-and-feminism/.

Giachetti, Diego, and Marco Scavino. 1999. *La Fiat in mano agli operai: L'autunno caldo del 1969.* Biblioteca Franco Serantini.

Gorz, André (Michel Bosquet, pseud.). 1972. "Les patrons découvrent 'l'usine-bagne,'" part 3. *Le Nouvel Observateur* 384. https://www.nouvelobs.com/opinions/00024209. EDI0001/les-patrons-decouvrent-l-usine-bagne-iii.html.

Gorz, André. 1976. "The Tyranny of the Factory: Today and Tomorrow" [1972]. In André Gorz, *The Division of Labor: The Labor Process and Class Struggle in Modern Capitalism*, 55–61. Harvester Press.

Gray, Neil. 2018. "Beyond the Right to the City: Territorial Autogestion and the Take over the City Movement in 1970s Italy." *Antipode* 50, no. 2: 319–339.

Gruppo Gramsci. 1980. "Una proposta per un diverso modo di fare politica" [1973]. In *Aut. Op.*, edited by Lucio Castellano, 88–98. Savelli Editori.

Hardt, Michael. 1996. "Introduction: Laboratory Italy." In *Radical Thought in Italy*, edited by Michael Hardt and Paolo Virno, 1–10. University of Minnesota Press.

Kushner, Rachel. 2013. *The Flamethrowers.* Scribner.

Lanzardo, Dario. 1979. *La rivolta di Piazza Statuto.* Feltrinelli.

Mezzadra, Sandro. 2021. "Postfazione." In *Gli Autonomi: Autonomia operaia a Genova e in Liguria*, edited by Roberto Demontis and Giorgio Moroni, 325–333. DeriveApprodi.

Moroni, Primo. 2021. "Preface to the Second Edition." In *The Golden Horde*, edited by Nanni Balestrini and Primo Moroni, 28–36. Translated by Richard Braude. Seagull Books.

Negri, Antonio. 1979. *Dall'operaio massa al operaio sociale* (interview with Paolo Possi and Roberta Tommasini). Multhipia Edizioni.

Negri, Antonio. 2005. "Domination and Sabotage." In Antonio Negri, *Books for Burning: Between Civil War and Democracy in 1970s Italy*, translated by Timothy Murphy, 231–290. Verso.

Negri, Antonio. 2007. "Articolazioni organizzative e organizzazione complessiva: il partito di Mirafiori" [1973]. In *Gli autonomi*, vol. 2, edited by Sergio Bologna and Lanfranco Caminiti, 80–84. DeriveApprodi.

Negri, Antonio. 2021a. "The Defeat of '77." In *The Golden Horde*, edited by Nanni Balestrini and Primo Moroni, 633–638. Translated by Richard Braude. Seagull Books.

Negri, Antonio. 2021b. "One Step Forward, Two Steps Back: The End of the Groups" [1974]. In *The Golden Horde*, edited by Nanni Balestrini and Primo Moroni, 446–456. Translated by Richard Braude. Seagull Books.

Palazzo, David. 2014. "The 'Social Factory' in Postwar Italian Radical Thought from Operaismo to Autonomia." PhD thesis, CUNY Graduate Center.

Pizzolato, Nicola. 2017. "A New Revolutionary Practice: *Operaisti* and the 'Refusal of Work' in 1970s Italy." *Estudos Históricos* 30, no. 61: 449–464.

Quadrelli, Emilio. 2008. *Autonomia operaia: Scienza della politica e arte della guerra dal '68 ai movimenti globali.* NdA Press.

Ramirez, Bruno. 1975. "The Working Class Struggle Against the Crisis: Self-Reduction of Prices in Italy." *Zero Work* 1: 143–150.

Soresina, Marco. 2020. "The Housing Struggle in Milan in the 1970s." *Journal of Urban History* 46, no. 6: 1386–1406.

Tronti, Mario. 2019. *Workers and Capital.* Translated by David Broder. Verso.

Virno, Paolo. 2021. "Work Doesn't Set You Free." In *The Golden Horde*, edited by Nanni Balestrini and Primo Moroni, 324–342. Translated by Richard Braude. Seagull Books.

Weeks, Kathi. 2011. *The Problem with Work.* Duke University Press.

Wright, Steve. 2002. *Storming Heaven: Class Composition and Struggle in Italian Autonomist Marxism*. Pluto Press.

Chapter 11: Feminist Articulations

Borden, Lizzie, dir. 1983. *Born in Flames* [film].

Collins, Patricia Hill. 1990. *Black Feminist Thought: Knowledge, Consciousness and the Politics of Empowerment*. Hyman.

Combahee River Collective. 2017. "The Combahee River Collective Statement" [1977]. In *How We Get Free*, ed. Keeanga-Yamahtta Taylor, 15–27. Haymarket Books.

Dalla Costa, Mariarosa, and Selma James. 1972. *The Power of Women and the Subversion of Community*. Falling Wall Press.

Da Silva, Denise Ferreira. 2022. *Unpayable Debt*. Sternberg Press.

Davis, Angela. 1981. *Women, Race and Class*. Vintage.

Davis, Angela. 2016. *Freedom Is a Constant Struggle*. Haymarket.

Eisenstein, Zillah, ed. 1979a. *Capitalist Patriarchy and the Case for Socialist Feminism*. Monthly Review Press.

Eisenstein, Zillah. 1979b. "Developing a Theory of Capitalist Patriarchy and Socialist Feminism." In *Capitalist Patriarchy and the Case for Socialist Feminism*, edited by Zillah Eisenstein, 5–40. Monthly Review Press.

Federici, Silvia. 2021. *Patriarchy of the Wage: Notes on Marx, Gender, and Feminism*. PM Press.

Foucault, Michel. 1978. *The History of Sexuality, Volume 1*. Translated by Robert Hurley. Random House.

Foucault, Michel. 2003. *"Society Must Be Defended": Lectures at the Collège de France, 1975–1976*. Edited by Mauro Bertani and Alessandro Fontana, translated by David Macey. Picador.

Gago, Verónica. 2020. *Feminist International: How to Change Everything*. Translated by Liz Mason-Deese. Verso.

Hall, Stuart. 2019. "Race, Articulation, and Societies Structured in Dominance" [1980]. In Stuart Hall, *Essential Essays*, vol. 1, *Foundations of Cultural Studies*, edited by David Morley, 172–221. Duke University Press.

Hall, Stuart. 2021. "Pluralism, Race and Class in Caribbean Society" [1977]. In Stuart Hall, *Selected Writings on Race and Difference*, edited by Paul Gilroy and Ruth Wilson Gilmore, 136–160. Duke University Press.

Haraway, Donna. 1985. "A Manifesto for Cyborgs: Science, Technology and Socialist Feminism in the 1980s." *Socialist Review* 15: 65–107.

Hartmann, Heidi. 1981. "The Unhappy Marriage of Marxism and Feminism." In *Women and Revolution*, edited by Lydia Sargent, 1–41. Black Rose Books.

Hartsock, Nancy. 1983. *Money, Sex, and Power*. Northeastern University Press.

Hilderbrand, Lucas. 2013. "In the Heat of the Moment: Notes on the Past, Present, and Future of *Born in Flames*." *Women and Performance* 23, no. 1: 6–16.

hooks, bell. 1984. *Feminist Theory: From Margin to Center*. South End Press.

Kelley, Robin D. G. 2021. "Foreword." In Cedric Robinson, *Black Marxism*, 3rd ed., xi–xxvi. University of North Carolina Press.

Laclau, Ernesto. 2005. *On Populist Reason*. Verso.

Lorde, Audre. 1984. *Sister Outsider: Essays and Speeches*. Crossing Press.

Lorde, Audre. 2000. "There Is No Hierarchy of Oppression." In *Women's Health: Readings on Social, Economic, and Political Issues*, edited by Nancy Worcester and Marianne Whatley, 89–90. Kendall/Hunt.

McDuffie, Erik. 2011. *Sojourning for Freedom: Black Women, American Communism, and the Making of Black Left Feminism*. Duke University Press.

Robinson, Cedric. 2021. *Black Marxism*. 3rd ed. University of North Carolina Press.

Rowbotham, Sheila. 1973. *Woman's Consciousness, Man's World*. Penguin.

Sargent, Lydia, ed. 1981. *Women and Revolution*. Black Rose Books.

Smith, Barbara. 2017. "Interview." In *How We Get Free*, edited by Keeanga-Yamahtta Taylor, 71–109. Haymarket Books.

Spillers, Hortense. 1981. "Mama's Baby, Papa's Maybe: An American Grammar Book." *Diacritics* 17, no. 2: 64–81.

Sussler, Betsy. 1983. "Born in Flames." *Bomb* 7: 27–29.

Szczesniak, Magda. 2020. "Blowing Glitter Through Straws: Revolutionary Moods in Lizzie Borden's 'Born in Flames' and Jill Godmilow's 'Far from Poland.'" *View: Theories and Practices of Visual Culture* 26, https://doi.org/10.36854/widok/2020.26.2135.

Taylor, Keeanga-Yamahtta. 2019. "Black Feminism and the Combahee River Collective." *Monthly Review* 70, no. 8: 20–28.

Tronti, Mario. 2019. *Workers and Capital* [1966, 1971]. Translated by David Broder. Verso.

Wallace, Michele. 1979. *Black Macho and the Myth of the Superwoman*. Dial Press.

Weeks, Kathi. 2011. *The Problem with Work: Feminism, Marxism, and Antiwork Politics, and Postwork Imaginaries*. Duke University Press.

Weeks, Kathi. 2018. *Constituting Feminist Subjects*. Reprint ed. Verso.

Wilderson, Frank B., III. 2020. *Afropessimism*. Norton.

Willse, Craig, and Dean Spade. 2013. "We Are *Born in Flames*." *Women and Performance* 23, no. 1: 1–5.

Young, Iris. 1981. "Beyond the Unhappy Marriage." In *Women and Revolution*, edited by Lydia Sargent, 43–70. Black Rose Books.

Chapter 12: Strategic Racial Multiplicities

Ali, Yasmin. 1991. "Echoes of Empire: Towards a Politics of Representation." In *Enterprise and Heritage*, edited by John Corner and Sylvia Harvey, 194–211. Routledge.

Anzaldúa, Gloria. 2021a. "Foreword to the Second Edition." In *This Bridge Called My Back: Writings by Radical Women of Color*, edited by Cherríe Moraga and Gloria Anzaldúa, 253–254. State University of New York Press.

Anzaldúa, Gloria. 2021b. "La Prieta." In *This Bridge Called My Back: Writings by Radical Women of Color*, edited by Cherríe Moraga and Gloria Anzaldúa, 198–209. State University of New York Press.

Beins, Agatha. 2015. "Radical Others: Women of Color and Revolutionary Feminism." *Feminist Studies* 41, no. 1: 150–183.

Biko, Steve. 1978. *The Testimony of Steve Biko*. Edited by Millard Arnold. Grafton Books.

Biko, Steve. 1987. "Fear—an Important Determinant in South African Politics." In Steve Biko, *I Write What I Like*, edited by Aelred Stubbs, 73–79. Heinemann.

Bloom, Joshua, and Waldo Martin. 2012. *Black Against Empire: The History and Politics of the Black Panther Party*. University of California Press.

Brixton Black Women's Group. 1984. "Black Women Organizing." *Feminist Review* 17: 84–89.

Davis, Angela. 2018. "The Past, Present, and Future of Assata's Message." *Women's Studies Quarterly* 46, nos. 3–4: 232–234.

Epstein, Brian. 2018. "Biko on *Non-White* and *Black.*" In *Debating African Philosophy*, edited by George Hull, 97–117. Routledge.

Farmer, Ashley. 2019. *Remaking Black Power: How Black Women Transformed an Era.* University of North Carolina Press.

Gilroy, Paul. 1987. *There Ain't No Black in the Union Jack: The Cultural Politics of Race and Nation.* University of Chicago Press.

Hall, Stuart. 1996. "New Ethnicities." In *Stuart Hall: Critical Dialogues in Cultural Studies*, edited by David Morley and Kuan-Hsing Chen, 223–227. Routledge.

Hernández, Roberto. 2015. "1968: On Social, Epistemic, and Historiographic (?) Revolutions." *Kalfou* 2, no. 1: 135–146.

Lorde, Audre. 2000. "There Is No Hierarchy of Oppression." In *Women's Health: Readings on Social, Economic, and Political Issues*, edited by Nancy Worcester and Marianne Whatley, 89–90. Kendall/Hunt.

Modood, Tariq. 1994. "Political Blackness and British Asians." *Sociology* 28, no. 4: 859–876.

Moraga, Cherríe. 2021. "La Jornada: Preface, 1981." In *This Bridge Called My Back: Writings by Radical Women of Color*, edited by Cherríe Moraga and Gloria Anzaldúa, xliii–xlix. State University of New York Press.

Olcott, Jocelyn. 2017. *International Women's Year: The Greatest Consciousness-Raising Event in History.* Oxford University Press.

Pulido, Laura. 2006. *Black, Brown, Yellow, and Left.* University of California Press.

Ross, Loretta. 2011. "The Origin of the Phrase 'Women of Color.'" YouTube, posted by Western States Center, February 15, 2011. https://www.youtube.com/watch?v=82vl34mi4Iw.

Ryan, Angela. 2010. "Education for the People: The Third World Student Movement at San Francisco State College and City College of New York." PhD thesis, Ohio State University.

Safire, William. 1988. "On Language: People of Color." *New York Times Magazine*, November 20, 1988, 18, 20.

Sandoval, Chela. 1991. "U.S. Third World Feminism: The Theory and Method of Oppositional Consciousness in the Postmodern World." *Genders* 10: 1–24.

Spira, Tamara Lee. 2014. "Intimate Internationalisms." *Feminist Theory* 15, no. 2: 119–140.

"The Third World." 1976. *The Black Scholar* 7, no. 9: 1.

Uyematsu, Amy. 1969. "The Emergence of Yellow Power." *Gidra* 1, no. 7: 8–11.

Veriava, Ahmed. n.d. "Frank-Talking." Unpublished manuscript.

"Women in the Struggle." 1971. *Triple Jeopardy* (published by Third World Women's Alliance), September–October 1971, 8–9.

Young, Cynthia. 2006. *Soul Power.* Duke University Press.

Chapter 13: New Alliances Against the State

Andrews, William. 2016. *Dissenting Japan.* Hurst.

Apter, David, and Nagayo Sawa. 1984. *Against the State.* Harvard University Press.

Bowen, Roger Wilson. 1975. "The Narita Conflict." *Asian Survey* 15, no. 7: 598–615.

Colombel, Jeannette. 1977. "Présentation: Résistance du Larzac (1971–1977)." *Les temps modernes* 371: 1971–1977.

Franquemagne, Gaël. 2007. "From Larzac to the Altermondialist Mobilization." *Environmental Politics* 16, no. 5: 826–843.

Gildea, Robert, and Andrew Tompkins. 2015. "The Transnational in the Local: The Larzac Plateau as a Site of Transnational Activism Since 1970." *Journal of Contemporary History* 50, no. 3: 581–605.

Nornes, Abé Mark. 2007. *Forest of Pressure: Ogawa Shinsuke and Postwar Japanese Documentary*. University of Minnesota Press.

Reid, Donald. 2014. "Larzac in the Broad 1968 and After." *French Politics, Culture and Society* 32, no. 2: 99–122.

Ross, Kristin. 2018. "The Long 1960s and 'The Wind from the West.'" *Crisis and Critique* 5, no. 2: 319–335.

Rouaud, Christian, dir. 2011. *Tous au Larzac* [film].

Ogawa, Shinsuke, dir. 1971. *Sanrizuka: Peasants of the Second Fortress* [film].

Chapter 14: Antinuclear Democratizations

Avenell, Simon. 2016. "Antinuclear Radicals." *Science, Technology and Society* 21, no. 1: 88–109.

Brulle, Robert. 2009. "Science, Democracy, and the Environment: The Contributions of Barry Commoner." *Organization and Environment* 22, no. 1: 3–5.

Downey, Gary. 1986. "Ideology and the Clamshell Identity: Organizational Dilemmas in the Anti-Nuclear Power Movement." *Social Problems* 33, no. 5: 357–373.

Epstein, Barbara. 1991. *Political Protest and Cultural Revolution*. University of California Press.

Epstein, Steven. 1991. "Democratic Science? AIDS Activism and the Contested Construction of Knowledge." *Socialist Review* 21, no. 2: 35–64.

Gainesville Women's Liberation. 2000. "What We Do at Meetings." In *Dear Sisters: Dispatches from the Women's Liberation Movement*, edited by Rosalyn Baxandall and Linda Gordon, 70–72. Basic Books.

Hager, Carol. 1993. "Citizen Movements and Technological Policymaking in Germany." *Annals* (AAPSS) 528 : 42–55.

Karapin, Roger. 2007. *Protest Politics in Germany: Movements on the Left and Right Since the 1960s*. Pennsylvania State University Press.

Kauffman, L. A. 2017. *Direct Action: Protest and the Reinvention of American Radicalism*. Verso.

McCormick, Sabrina. 2007. "Democratizing Science Movements: A New Framework for Mobilization and Contestation." *Social Studies of Science* 37, no. 4: 609–623.

McCormick, Sabrina. 2009. "From 'Politico-Scientists' to Democratizing Science Movements." *Organization and Environment* 22, no. 1: 34–51.

Milder, Stephen. 2017. *Greening Democracy*. Cambridge University Press.

Sarachild, Kathie. 1978. "Consciousness-Raising: A Radical Weapon." In *Feminist Revolution*, edited by Redstockings, 144–150. Random House.

Sarkar, Saral. 1986. "The Green Movement in West Germany." *Alternatives* 11: 219–254.

Sheehan, Joanne, and Eric Bachman. n.d. "Seabrook—Wyhl—Marckolsheim: Transnational Links in a Chain of Campaigns." *Empowering Nonviolence* (blog), https://www.nonviolence.wri-irg.org/en/resources/2008/seabrook-wyhl-marckolsheim-transnational-links-chain-campaigns (accessed July 22, 2022).

Tomkins, Andrew. 2016. "Grassroots Transnationalism(s): Franco-German Opposition to Nuclear Energy in the 1970s." *Contemporary European History* 25, no. 1: 117–142.

Zelko, Frank. 2013. *Make It a Green Peace! The Rise of Countercultural Environmentalism.* Oxford University Press.

Zelko, Frank. 2017. "Scaling Greenpeace." *Historical Social Research* 42, no. 2: 318–342.

Chapter 15: The End of Mediation

Bologna, Sergio. 1980. "The Tribe of Moles." In "Autonomia: Post-Political Politics," special issue edited by Sylvère Lotringer and Christian Marazzi. *Semiotext(e)* 3, no. 3: 36–61.

Brown, Wendy. 2017. *Undoing the Demos.* Zone Books.

Brown, Wendy. 2019. *In the Ruins of Neoliberalism.* Columbia University Press.

Buchanan, James, and Richard Wagner. 1977. *Democracy in Deficit.* Academic Press.

Chamayou, Grégoire. 2021. *The Ungovernable Society.* Translated by Andrew Brown. Polity Press.

Clausewitz, Carl von. 1976. *On War.* Translated by Michael Howard and Peter Paret. Princeton University Press.

Cohen, Jean, and Andrew Arato. 1992. *Civil Society and Political Theory.* MIT Press.

Dahl, Robert. 1971. *Polyarchy: Participation and Opposition.* Yale University Press.

Finn, Daniel. 2019. *One Man's Terrorist.* Verso.

Foucault, Michel. 2003. *"Society Must Be Defended": Lectures at the Collège de France, 1975–1976.* Edited by Mauro Bertani and Alessandro Fontana, translated by David Macey. Picador.

Foucault, Michel. 2015. *The Punitive Society.* Edited by Barnard Harcourt, translated by Graham Burchell. Palgrave.

Green, Sam, and Bill Seigel, dir. 1983. *The Weather Underground* [film].

Habermas, Jürgen. 1976. *Legitimation Crisis.* Translated by Thomas McCarthy. Polity Press.

Harvey, David. 2007. *A Brief History of Neoliberalism.* Oxford University Press.

Horn, Eva. 2012. "Machine Learning: Friedrich Kittler (1943–2011)." *Art Forum,* September 2012, 476–479.

Huntington, Samuel. 1975. "The Crisis of Democracy." In Michel Crozier, Samuel Huntington, and Joji Watanuki, *The Crisis of Democracy,* 59–118. New York University Press.

Khalidi, Rashid. 2020. *The Hundred Years' War on Palestine.* Metropolitan Books.

Lessin, Tia, and Emma Pildes, dir. 2022. *The Janes* [film].

McLuhan, Marshall. 1964. *Understanding Media.* McGraw-Hill.

Meinhof, Ulrike. 2008. "From Protest to Resistance." In *Everybody Talks About the Weather . . . We Don't: The Writings of Ulrike Meinhof,* edited by Karin Bauer, 239–243. Seven Stories Press.

Mitchell, W. J. T., and Mark Hansen. 2010. "Introduction." In *Critical Terms for Media Studies,* edited by W. J. T. Mitchell and Mark Hansen, vii–xxii. University of Chicago Press.

Negri, Antonio. 2005a. "Domination and Sabotage." In Antonio Negri, *Books for Burning: Between Civil War and Democracy in 1970s Italy,* translated by Timothy Murphy, 231–290. Verso.

Negri, Antonio. 2005b. "Workers' Party Against Work" [1973]. In Antonio Negri, *Books for Burning: Between Civil War and Democracy in 1970s Italy,* translated by Timothy Murphy, 51–117. Verso.

Peters, John Durham. 2015. *The Marvelous Clouds: Towards a Philosophy of Elemental Media*. University of Chicago Press.

Roth, Karl-Heinz. 1974. *Die "andere" Arbeiterbewegung und die Entwicklung der kapitalistischen Repression von 1880 bis zur Gegenwart*. Trikont Verlag.

Tuschling, Anna. 2015. "Historical, Technological and Medial A Priori: On the Belatedness of Media." *Cultural Studies* 30, no. 4: 680–703.

Varon, Jeremy. 2004. *Bringing the War Home*. University of California Press.

Zwerman, Gilda, Patricia Steinhoff, and Donatella della Porta. 2000. "Disappearing Social Movements: Clandestinity in the Cycle of New Left Protests in the U.S., Japan, Germany, and Italy." *Mobilization* 5, no. 1: 85–104.

Chapter 16: Theaters of Injustice

Andrews, William. 2016. *Dissenting Japan*. Hurst.

Ayers, Bill. 2000. *Fugitive Days*. Beacon.

Bauer, Karin. 2008. "In Search of Ulrike Meinhof." In *Everybody Talks About the Weather... We Don't: The Writings of Ulrike Meinhof*, edited by Karin Bauer, 12–99. Seven Stories Press.

Berger, Dan. 2006. *Outlaws of America*. AK Press.

Bielby, Clare. 2012. *Violent Women in Print: Representations in the West German Print Media of the 1960s and 1970s*. Boydell & Brewer.

Blum, Pablo. 2014. "Revisiting Urban Guerrillas: Armed Propaganda and the Insurgency of Uruguay's MLN-Tupamaros, 1969–1970." *Studies in Conflict and Terrorism* 37, no. 5: 387–404.

Caula, Nelson, and Alberto Silva. 2009. *Alto el fuego: La obra completa*. Ediciones B Uruguay.

Cavallini, Massimo. 1978. *Il terrorismo in fabbrica*. Editori Riuniti.

Dohrn, Zayd. 2022. "Mother Country Radicals: A Family History of the Weather Underground" [podcast].

Drake, Richard. 2021. *The Revolutionary Mystique and Terrorism in Contemporary Italy*. 2nd ed. Indiana University Press.

Guattari, Félix. 1979. "Comme un echo de la mélancholie collective." *Les temps modernes*, special issue on Germany, July–August 1979, 413–420. (English translation: "Like the Echo of a Collective Melancholia," in Félix Guattari, *Soft Subversions*, 106–112. Semiotext(e), 2009.)

Hamilton, Johanna, dir. 2014. *1971* [film].

I Volsci. 1980. "Il metodo di combattimento della Autonomia operaia." In *Aut. Op.*, edited by Lucio Castellano, 194–197. Savelli Editori.

Jacobs, Ron. 1997. *The Way the Wind Blew: A History of the Weather Underground*. Verso.

Jameson, Fredric. 1998. *Brecht and Method*. Verso.

Knaudt, Till. 2020. "A Farewell to Class: The Japanese New Left, the Colonial Landscape of Kamagasaki, and the Anti-Japanese Front (1970–75)." *Journal of Japanese Studies* 46, no. 2: 395–422.

Marighella, Carlos. 1985. *Manual of the Urban Guerrilla*. Translated by Gene Hanrahan. Documentary Publications.

Medsger, Betty. 2014. *The Burglary: The Discovery of J. Edgar Hoover's Secret FBI*. Knopf.

Orsini, Alessandro. 2011. *Anatomy of the Red Brigades: The Religious Mind-Set of Modern Terrorists*. Translated by Sarah Nodes. Cornell University Press.

Passmore, Leith. 2011. *Ulrike Meinhof and the Red Army Faction: Performing Terrorism*. Palgrave Macmillan.

Rocha, Mona. 2020. *The Weatherwomen: Militant Feminists of the Weather Underground*. McFarland.

Rosso. 1980. "L'autonomia organizzata di fronte al 'dopo Moro.' " In *Aut. Op.*, edited by Lucio Castellano, 190–194. Savelli Editori.

Saccoman, Andrea. 2013. *Le Brigate Rosso a Milano*. Edizioni Unicopli.

Schieder, Chelsea Szendi. 2019. "East Asian Anti-Japan Armed Front: A Tale for These Times." *The Funambulist* 25: 36–41.

Scribner, Charity. 2014. *After the Red Army Faction: Gender, Culture, and Militancy*. Columbia University Press.

Steiner, Anne, and Loïc Debray. 1987. *La faction armée rouge : Guérilla urbaine en Europe occidentale*. Méridiens Klincksieck.

Tarì, Marcello. 2015. *Autonomie! Italie, les années 1970*. Translated by Étienne Dobenesque. La Fabrique Editions.

"To Have Done with Armed Isolation." 1982. In *The German Issue*, edited by Sylvère Lotringer, 130–133. Semiotext(e) Foreign Agents Series. Sternberg Press.

Varon, Jeremy. 2004. *Bringing the War Home*. University of California Press.

Wagner-Pacifici, Robin. 1986. *The Moro Morality Play: Terrorism as Social Drama*. University of Chicago Press.

Chapter 17: Dual Strategy and Double Organization

Acaroglu, Onur. 2019. "Paris 1871 and Fatsa 1979: Revisiting the Transition Problem." *Globalizations* 16, no. 4: 404–423.

Balestrini, Nanni, and Primo Moroni, eds. 2021. *The Golden Horde*. Translated by Richard Braude. Seagull Books.

Benlisoy, Foti. 2018. "A Brief History of the Turkish Left, Part I: From the Origins to the 1980 Coup." *LEFTEAST*, May 22, 2018. https://lefteast.org/turk-euro-left-history/.

Berardi, Franco (Bifo, pseud.). 1980. "Anatomy of Autonomy." In "Autonomia: Post-Political Politics," special issue edited by Sylvère Lotringer and Christian Marazzi. *Semiotext(e)* 3, no. 3: 148–171.

Bloom, Joshua, and Waldo Martin. 2012. *Black Against Empire: The History and Politics of the Black Panther Party*. University of California Press.

Bobbio, Luigi. 1988. *Storia di Lotta Continua*. Feltrinelli.

Bozkurt, Sümercan. 2008. "The Resistance Committees: Devrimci Yol and the Question of Revolutionary Organization in Turkey in the Late 1970s." MA thesis, Middle East Technical University.

Castellano, Lucio, et al. 1996. "Do You Remember Revolution?" In *Radical Thought in Italy*, edited by Michael Hardt and Paolo Virno, 225–238. University of Minnesota Press.

Cuninghame, Patrick Gun. 2002. "*Autonomia*: A Movement of Refusal." PhD thesis, Middlesex University.

Ersan, Vehbi. 2013. *1970'lerde Türkiye Solu*. Iletisim Yayinlari.

Fo, Dario. 1994. *Accidental Death of an Anarchist*. Adapted by Gavin Richards from a translation by Gillian Hanna. Methuen Drama.

Gotor, Miguel. 2021. "Due presidenti e una strage." *L'Espresso*, May 9, 2021, 58–63.

I Volsci. 1980. "Il metodo di combattimento della Autonomia operaia." In *Aut. Op.*, edited by Lucio Castellano, 194–197. Savelli Editori.

Jacobs, Ron. 1997. *The Way the Wind Blew: A History of the Weather Underground*. Verso.

Morando, Paolo. 2019. *Prima di Piazza Fontana: La prova generale*. Laterza.

Morgül, Kerem. 2019. "Performing Revolutionary Populism: The Revolutionary Path Movement in Turkey." *Qualitative Sociology* 42: 273–297.

Pope, Ricky J., and Shawn T. Flanigan. 2013. "Revolution for Breakfast: Intersections of Activism, Service, and Violence in the Black Panther Party's Community Service Programs." *Social Justice Research* 26, no. 4: 445–470.

Quadrelli, Emilio. 2008. *Autonomia operaia: Scienza della politica e arte della guerra dal '68 ai movimenti globali*. NdA Press.

Rosso. 1980. "L'autonomia organizzata di fronte al 'dopo Moro'" [1978]. In *Aut. Op.*, edited by Lucio Castellano, 190–194. Savelli Editori.

Roth, Karl-Heinz. 1974. *Die "andere" Arbeiterbewegung und die Entwicklung der kapitalistischen Repression von 1880 bis zur Gegenwart*. Trikont Verlag.

Samim, Ahmet. 1981. "The Tragedy of the Turkish Left." *New Left Review* 126: 60–85.

Shah, Alpa. 2018. *Nightmarch: Among India's Revolutionary Guerrillas*. New ed. Hurst.

Spencer, Robyn C. 2016. *The Revolution Has Come: Black Power, Gender, and the Black Panther Party in Oakland*. Duke University Press.

Türkmen, Hade. 2006. "Radicalisation of Politics at the Local Level: The Case of Fatsa During the Late 1970s." MA thesis, Middle East Technical University.

Chapter 18: Conclusion

Althusser, Louis. 1970. "The Object of Capital." In Louis Althusser and Étienne Balibar, *Reading Capital*, translated by Ben Brewster, 71–198. New Left Books.

Deleuze, Gilles. 1988. *Bergsonism*. Translated by Hugh Tomlinson and Barbara Habberjam. Zone Books.

Hayden, Tom, ed. 2016. *Inspiring Participatory Democracy: Student Movements from Port Huron to Today*. Routledge.

Knaudt, Till. 2020. "A Farewell to Class: The Japanese New Left, the Colonial Landscape of Kamagasaki, and the Anti-Japanese Front (1970–75)." *Journal of Japanese Studies* 46, no. 2: 395–422.

Marx, Karl. 1975. "Preface to A Contribution to the Critique of Political Economy." In Karl Marx, *Early Writings*, translated by Rodney Livingstone and Gregor Benton, 424–428. Penguin.

Morgan, Robin. 2003. "Goodbye to All That." In *Takin' It to the Streets: A Sixties Reader*, edited by Alexander Bloom and Wini Breines, 418–421. Oxford University Press.

Traverso, Enzo. 2021. *Revolution: An Intellectual History*. Verso.

Weeks, Kathi. 2023. "The Lumpenproletariat and the Politics of Class." Forthcoming in *Crisis and Critique*.

Notes

Chapter 1

1. The "dirty war" conducted by Argentina's military junta presents an extreme but nonetheless revealing example of the mindset of those on the hunt for subversives. Soon after the 1976 coup d'état, General Luciano Benjamín Menéndez reportedly warned that in order to restore order, "we are going to have to kill 50,000 people: 25,000 subversives, 20,000 sympathizers, and we will make 5,000 mistakes" (cited in Lewis 2002, 147). Preparing to kill subversives en masse is itself an outrage, and targeting sympathizers is even more barbaric, but the real key to the atrocities justified by this mentality is the acceptance of five thousand mistakes. Tragically, the general's projected figures proved to be not far from the mark.

2. In some national contexts, in fact, my exhortation to focus on the seventies can be translated to say: take 1968 not as the end of the road but as the point of departure.

3. I am attempting here for the 1970s what Fredric Jameson achieved for the previous decade in his remarkable essay "Periodizing the 60s." Jameson's argument highlights continuities or correspondences across distant and disparate social and political phenomena, but this does not imply homogeneous conditions or developments. "The 'period' in question is understood not as some omnipresent and uniform shared style or way of thinking and acting," Jameson claims, "but rather as the sharing of a common objective situation, to which a whole range of varied responses and creative innovations is then possible, but always within the situation's structural limits" (1984, 178). Discovering the common objective situation is thus, for Jameson, the first task of analysis, which then allows for positioning the diverse cultural, theoretical, social, and political phenomena in relation to it.

4. Many US historians have argued convincingly for the importance of focusing on the 1970s, breaking the negative image of the period as a vacant hiatus between the revolutionary 1960s and reactionary 1980s (for example, Zaretsky 2018). My sense, however, is that the negative image of the 1970s persists in the popular imagination in the United States and more so in many other countries.

5. The same accounts of the sixties that tend to hide the revolutionary activity of the seventies are often themselves distortions of what happened in the sixties. For one corrective account, see Ross 2004, which argues against the tendency to reduce 1968 in France to merely cultural effects and maintains instead that the actions should be understood politically (15).

6. A more sophisticated perspective, which effectively eclipses the seventies with respect to labor politics, views the decade "as half post-1960s and half pre-1980s" (Cowie 2010, 11), either leaving out the seventies or conceiving it as merely a bridge between

the more substantial decades. For an effective rebuttal to this claim, emphasizing the importance of labor organizing among women and people of color in the seventies, see Windham 2017.

7. Ross (2004, 19–27) confronts a similar mystification by those who claim that "nothing happened" in France in 1968.

8. In many national contexts—Japan and Italy are two examples—the process of "coming to terms with the seventies" has barely begun and the movements of the era continue to be demonized.

9. "These alternative, political communities [of the 1970s]," Dan Berger rightly insists, "were led by people whose voices or perspectives had often been unheard a few years earlier: women, indigenous peoples, gays, lesbians, bisexuals and transgender people, Puerto Ricans, environmentalists, people with disabilities, and others. More so than their 1960s counterparts, many of these groups were committed to addressing the ways power inequalities reproduced themselves within social movements and not just outside of them" (2010, 5). On how the good sixties/bad seventies paradigm eclipses especially movements of people of color, see also Breines 1988; Elbaum 2002, 35–37; Hernández 2015, 136. Regarding the blindness to gay liberation movements, see Kissack 1995, 104–107.

10. A symptom of Hamon and Rotman's blindness to radical political developments in the sixties and seventies, caused in part by the limited group of student and cultural figures they consider, is their claim that the 1968 generation brought about the end, among other things, of revolution as a goal and anticapitalism as a perspective. "It was, in all certainty, the final generation motivated by a revolutionary ideal" (Hamon and Rotman 1988, 666); and "What has collapsed, little by little, what has crumbled, is the keystone: anticapitalism" (668). The strength and variety of anticapitalist movements in many countries, especially since 2008, clearly disprove Hamon and Rotman's conclusions.

11. In reaction to Gitlin's argument, see, for example, Breines 1988, 533–535; Elbaum 2002, 8–9; Buhle 1993, 248.

12. In contrast to the "good sixties/bad seventies" historical arguments that pose a strong division between the decades, some historians, particularly in France, conceive of the two decades together as one extended period, "the long 1968" or *les années 68*, which stretches from the 1962 end of the French war in Algeria to the 1981 election of François Mitterrand (see Dreyfus-Armand et al. 2000). These arguments are beneficial in that they do not obscure or invalidate the political activities of the seventies, but in doing so they fail to appreciate, in my view, the historical shift that took place between the decades or, more precisely, in many national contexts, around 1968.

13. Several historians identify the 1970s as the origin of growing divisions and fracturing of US society, caused in large part by right-wing political developments, but also by these conflicts on the Left. "What society conjured up now was something smaller," claims Daniel Rodgers, "more voluntaristic, fractured, easy to exit, and more guarded from others" (2011, 220). See also Kruse and Zelizer 2019.

14. If one wanted to construct a balance sheet, however, one should not forget all of the victorious revolutions of the 1970s, even though the results of many of them

became in time ambiguous or downright tragic: Vietnam, Cambodia, Laos, Grenada, Nicaragua, Chile, Portugal, Afghanistan, Iran, Ethiopia, Mozambique, Angola, Guinea-Bissau, Cape Verde, São Tomé and Principe, and (in 1980) Zimbabwe.

15. One version of this dichotomy, which, although clichéd and superficial, nonetheless captures a prevalent sentiment, contrasts two US music festivals that took place four months apart: Woodstock, New York, in August 1969 (the culmination of the sixties, a celebration of life) and Altamont, California, in December 1969 (the preview of the seventies, in which the Hell's Angels, hired as security for the Rolling Stones, beat an unruly fan to death during the concert). See Gitlin 1987, 392–393.

16. The political and theoretical shifts between the two volumes of Deleuze and Guattari's *Capitalism and Schizophrenia* (1983, 1987) pose particularly clearly the virtues of political complexity in the 1970s. Just as *Anti-Oedipus* (originally published in 1972) was an expression of and critical reflection on the thought of 1968, *A Thousand Plateaus* (originally published in 1980), a great book of multiplicities, belongs to the 1970s and offers a distillation of its innovations, an accounting of its dangers and defeats, and a proposition for potential steps beyond.

17. Regarding the global 1968 as turning point, see Wallerstein 1989. For an argument that the restructuring of capitalist power in the 1970s was a response to the progressive and revolutionary initiatives that coalesced and came to a head in 1968, see, for example, the proposition that neoliberalism was such a reaction (Hardt and Negri 2017, 155–158).

Chapter 2

1. Phil O'Keefe (1983, 347) notes that the liberation struggle in Mozambique had to face two separate powers: Portuguese political power and South African capital. The former, he claims, proved much easier than the latter to break from. On the power of South African capital in Mozambique, see also Munslow 1983, 16–22.

2. The struggle against gender hierarchies and the liberation of women is part of the discourse regarding popular power and revolutionary democracy. See, for example, Machel 1985a, 1974. I have been unable, however, to verify efforts to implement gender equality in the movements.

3. "During 1971," Davidson reported, "village committees in each sector of the liberated areas elected sector committees. In 1972 a general election by direct and secret ballot elected a regional committee for each of the fifteen liberated regions. These regional committees then met and elected representatives to a National Assembly" (1974, 7).

4. In April 1974, the Portuguese Armed Forces Movement (MFA), led by midlevel officers who were exhausted by the seemingly pointless and unwinnable colonial wars, overthrew the Portuguese government, the longest-standing fascist regime, promising decolonization and democratization. Many have claimed, in fact, that the African struggles not only provided the spark for Portugal's revolution but also informed its content—in other words, that members of the Portuguese military learned the project of "popular power" in the colonies and then applied these lessons at home, specifically

as part of the commission structures that constituted an important stream of the revolutionary process. "Some of the most active of these officers [in the MFA]," Davidson claimed without citing evidence, "as they bore witness then or later, had learned their politics of liberation from the example of the PAIGC" (1980, xvi). Robin Blackburn echoes Davidson's claim: "The MFA is reputed to have adopted the cell structure of the African liberation movements they had been sent to fight" (1974, 13). Paul Sweezy, in contrast, after a brief visit to revolutionary Portugal, expressed his skepticism, with equally little evidence, that MFA soldiers were influenced by African liberation ideologies (1975, 9n). It is certainly plausible that there was some influence, given that "popular power" and the creation of democratic commission structures was a central demand in both contexts, but I have been unable to find convincing evidence of direct influence.

5. For one particularly illuminating example, see Ferguson 2006, which makes clear the relation between the political insufficiencies of postcolonial states and their continuing economic subordination in the global capitalist system. "A recent literature," Ferguson writes, "makes clear that most African states today are indeed 'failing' to perform most of the tasks that they are, in the terms of almost any normative political theory, 'supposed to do,' and that much of the continent suffers from levels of insecurity and violence (if not outright civil war) that Africans and Africanists alike regard as terrifying. At the same time, it is equally clear that the latest round of worldwide capitalist restructuring, with its frenzied construction of 'the global economy,' has left little or no place for Africa outside of its old colonial role as provider of raw materials (specifically mineral wealth)" (8).

6. Robinson 1981 emphasizes Cabral's focus on the revolutionary role of the petty bourgeoisie.

7. Michel Cahen, among others, emphasizes the lack of democracy and the state's centralization of political power: "I would say that 'Poder Popular,'" he claims with regard to Frelimo and Mozambique in the decade after independence, "was a complete ideological fiction" (1987, 141).

8. "The privilege," writes Trotsky, "of historical backwardness—and such a privilege exists—permits, or rather compels, the adoption of whatever is ready in advance of any specified date, skipping a whole series of intermediate stages. . . . The fact that Germany and the United States have now economically outstripped England was made possible by the very backwardness of their capitalist development. On the other hand, the conservative anarchy in the British coal industry . . . is a paying-up for the past when England played too long the role of capitalist pathfinder" (1977, 26–27).

Chapter 3

1. Lauren Berlant and Michael Warner, writing in the late 1990s, present the "radical aspirations of queer culture building" in similar terms: "not just a safe zone for queer sex but the changed possibilities of identity, intelligibility, publics, culture, and sex that appear when the heterosexual couple is no longer the referent or the privileged example of sexual culture" (1998, 548).

Chapter 4

1. An excellent source on the Tudeh Party is Abrahamian 1982, 281–415.
2. On granting the US companies oil rights, see Kinzer 2003.
3. Behrooz Ghamari-Tabrizi contests "the myth of the stolen revolution," whereby the Islamic clergy hijacked the revolution that leftist and democratic secular forces had begun, because it obscures "the constitutive significance of Shi'ism" in the uprising (2016, 19–20).
4. Shari'ati exchanged a few letters with Fanon on the role of Islam in the anticolonial war (Rahnema 1998, 127).
5. Rahnema maintains that "Shari'ati's emphasis on the importance of 'common objectives' and the dissimulation of differences in the face of the 'enemy,' was a call to the tactical alliance of the Muslim Mojahedin and the Marxist Feda'ian" (1998, 304–305), although he is clear that Shari'ati had not direct contact or relations with the organizations.
6. The fact that Ayatollah Khomeini managed after the revolution to win over the followers of Ali Shari'ati, despite the fact that Shari'ati had argued so vehemently against the clerics and a clerically defined concept of Islam (Abrahamian 1982, 534), should not somehow taint or disqualify the liberatory nature of Shari'ati's thought.
7. For the text of the Council of Latin American Bishops plus selections from Gutierrez, Boff, and other liberation theologians, see Rossa 1986.
8. Many controversies erupted following publication of Foucault's essays and interviews on Iran. Behrooz Ghamari-Tabrizi (2016) wonderfully responds to Foucault's critics, demonstrating their misunderstandings regarding both the Iranian Revolution and Foucault's philosophical project.

Chapter 5

1. "It is indisputable," maintains Miguel Ángel Pérez Suárez, "that the Chilean experience of 1970–73 weighed heavily on the imagination of Portuguese activism" (2020, 212). For an excellent comparison between the contexts of revolution in Chile and Portugal, see Santos 1982, 266–268.
2. For a helpful explanation of the traditional Left/New Left distinction in Latin America, see Weisz 2004.
3. Debray 1971, 52. Salvador Allende and Fidel Castro were indeed friends, and Castro visited Chile in November 1971 and stayed for over a month. Their friendship, however, did not disrupt the prevalent narrative that positioned them as representing competing strategies of revolutionary struggle.
4. For an analysis of the division between the UP and the MIR, affirming the MIR's relation to peasant movements, see Cárcamo Hernández 2016.
5. Schlotterbeck maintains that "grassroots social struggle often defied the ideological narratives held by the Old Left and the New Left" (2018, 165).

6. Cárcamo Hernández argues that the MIR was able, in contrast to the government, to develop a relation of popular power, especially with respect to peasant movements (2016, 107). Schlotterbeck, however, maintains that "despite close ties with radicalized grassroots movements, the MIR did not escape the same rigid internal hierarchies and top-down control that plagued other political parties" (2018, 91).

7. Winn reports the content of these meetings with Allende primarily on the basis of interviews he conducted with Jorge Varas, a Socialist labor leader who was present (Winn 1986, 182–186).

8. Winn makes a similar point when he claims this conflict poses "a question of whether the Chilean revolutionary process was of and by the workers or merely for the workers" (1986, 169).

9. For an analysis of the common in contrast to both private and public property, see Hardt and Negri 2017, 85–105.

10. Gaudichaud 2014, 74. Cury makes a similar point: "The implementation of a system of participation created an unexpected effect, leading many workers to question maintaining traditional vertical relations and to seek a more active participation in the control and direction of the sources of labor" (2018, 178).

Chapter 6

1. Popular power movements were allowed to flourish, in certain respects and in certain periods, due to the support of the MFA. Some historians, in fact, consider the military support essential, such that popular power itself is defined as "an alliance between the military and grassroots organizations, bypassing the political parties" (Ramos Pinto 2008, 1034).

2. Reports of the many leftist intellectuals who traveled to Portugal during the revolution or analyzed the developments from abroad invariably highlighted the role of the military. See, for example, Sweezy 1975 and Blackburn 1974. Documentary filmmakers from abroad were much more attuned to the popular power movements; see Kramer 1977 and Harlan 1975.

3. On the possibility that Portuguese troops took revolutionary lessons from the anticolonial guerrillas they were meant to fight and then employed what they learned by conducting revolution back in Portugal, see note 4 in Chapter 2.

4. John Hammond identifies the goal of the popular power movement as the formation of a society governed "by a direct democracy in which all would have the opportunity to participate directly in making the authoritative decisions by which they were governed" (1985, 213).

5. Recall that in Chapter 2 I analyzed similar commission structures in Guinea-Bissau, Mozambique, and Angola, and their role in the project for revolutionary democracy.

6. Soldiers' assemblies were also formed. On the growth of democracy in the barracks and regimental assemblies of soldiers, see Sweezy 1975, 20, 24.

7. Once again, refer to Chapter 2 for ways in which commissions in Guinea-Bissau, Mozambique, and Angola were able to scale up.

8. The film *Torre Bela* (Harlan 1975) follows a worker named Wilson whose passion and rhetorical skills gain him a prominent voice in the formation of a rural commission. There were, no doubt, numerous such local leaders in the popular power movement.

9. Ricardo Noronha argues that the increased worker militancy of the late sixties and early seventies was an essential preparation for the labor struggles and the actions of workers' commissions in the revolutionary period. "The transgressive repertoire of collective mobilization adopted during the Carnation Revolution is inseparable from the experiences accumulated by the working class during the final years of the Estado Novo" (2019, 122).

10. For a discussion of worker self-management and its challenges, see Chapter 9 on the 1973 occupation of the Lip watch factory in Besançon, France.

11. Bermeo provides a detailed argument regarding the autonomy of land occupations in a single county in southern Portugal (1986, 84–98). Varela similarly claims that whereas the PCP is often seen as having supported the agricultural movement and land occupations, "the fact is that the occupations were not led in the first place by the Communist Party. They were in essence autonomous; they came about from below, and were initiated by the labourers themselves" (2019, 192).

12. Margarido's assessment, for instance, that the MFA in the final analysis always harbored authoritarian tendencies is clearly exaggerated. "The support given to the popular forces, however," he claims, "was never free from a certain ambiguity. The military in no way wanted to give up their right to oversight, which often took the form of dictatorial type intervention" (1976, 330).

13. The alternative model for socialism provided by the Portuguese Revolution is a central theme of John Hammond's analysis. See Hammond 1984 and, more generally, Hammond 1988.

Chapter 7

1. For an excellent brief presentation of South Korean political history leading up to the Kwangju Uprising, see Cummings 1999.

2. Paul Chang argues that, although it is normally assumed that the seventies are a "dark age" for democracy in South Korea because of the authoritarian government, there were, in fact, important democratic social movements. Authoritarian government, he claims, decreases activism in some ways and increases it in others (2015, 3–8).

3. Na Kahn-chae gives an excellent account of the uprising in three stages, which I have adopted with slight modifications (2006, 166–168). For another useful, brief narrative of the events, see Shin 2003, xiv–xix. The best and most detailed account is Lee 1999.

Chapter 8

1. Cowie, for example, considers the established unions and their electoral power to be essential to the existence of the working class. The working class, he claims, "was a conceptual unity that could briefly but imperfectly be identifiable as a unionized voting block from the New Deal to the 1970s" (2010, 18).

2. Cowie provides a good account of the Yablonski murders and the UMWA leadership struggle (2010, 23–26). The aftermath of Yablonski's murder figures prominently in Barbara Kopple's classic documentary film *Harlan County USA* (1976).
3. Cowie cautions against exaggerating the strength and extent of worker antagonism to the unions: "The bureaucracy often did fail to respond to the rank and file, but to think that the entire working class was on the brink of fundamental transformation with or without the much-maligned 'union bureaucrats' was naive" (2010, 69). He is certainly right that not all workers fought the unions and that fundamental change was not imminent. But it seems to me a mistake to minimize the importance of the rank-and-file movement that contested union authority and circumvented union control. The historical decline of unions is, at least in part, a result of the unions' failure to respond to workers' demands for democratic transformation. Furthermore, the fact that these workers were able to articulate these political demands autonomously is itself extremely significant for understanding the history of the workers' movements and their potential futures.
4. The difficult relations in Detroit between the League of Revolutionary Black Workers and the Black Panther Party in the years around 1970 reveal tensions regarding this claim to an industrial worker vanguard. Georgakas and Surkin describe how the two organizations had strongly overlapping agendas and many militants were members of both, but ideological conflicts gradually created a rift (1975, 75, 119). Whereas the league was dedicated to the centrality of industrial workers, the BPP promoted a more expansive conception of class struggle, which included notably the lumpenproletariat.
5. On the "coordinadoras interfabriles," see also Löbbe 2006; Cotarelo and Fernández 1998. More generally, on the divisions within the Argentine working class and their relation to Peronism, see James 1998.
6. "At the level of socially developed capital," claimed Mario Tronti, when analyzing worker struggles in early 1960s Italy, "capitalist development is subordinate to working-class struggles; not only does it come after them, but it must make the political mechanism of capitalist production respond to them" (2019, 65).
7. There were, of course, examples of US radical organizations that attempted to rethink class struggle in these ways, albeit on a smaller scale. For one example, see the website of the Zerowork collective, zerowork.org.
8. Several authors and organizers in the seventies and in the subsequent years, such as Kim Moody (1997, 2000) and Stanley Aronowitz (1990), argued convincingly for the need to combine labor struggle and social movements in some form of social movement unionism.

Chapter 9

1. Charles Piaget, leader of the CFDT union at Lip, declared, "We didn't get there until 1973, but a big step forward was made possible by May 68. . . . There would never have been Lip 73 without May 68!" (2018, 3, 16). Pierre Rosanvallon also affirms that the widespread discourse of self-management began in France in 1968 (1976, 7).
2. On the initial events of the Lip occupation, see Reid 2018, 95–129; Hamon and Rotman 1988, 483–484; Gourgues and Neuschwander 2018, 43–53.

3. Vigna details how ransacking the administration offices and holding administrators hostage (*sequestration*) were increasingly widespread practices among militant French workers in the early 70s (2015, 100–107).

4. We will see in Chapter 13 that the protest movement in Larzac against the expansion of a military base learned from the Lip workers to form horizontal commissions in order to create a democratic governance structure.

Chapter 10

1. Many theorists, including me, have used the term "Laboratory Italy" to refer to the innovative atmosphere of the movements during these years. "Many in the Western world think, rightly," writes Moroni, "that the Italian case is one of the most revealing social and productive laboratories for deciphering the epoch-defining passage from one phase of capitalism to another" (2021, 34). See Hardt 1996.

2. It is easy to understand, writes Paolo Virno, "how the current decline of the line worker has been actively mistaken for the decline of the working class *tout court* (and it is not so important whether this claim is met with euphoria or dismay)" (2021, 325).

3. One of the best historical accounts of the battle of Corso Traiano and the events surrounding it is Nanni Balestrini's 1971 novel *We Want Everything*.

4. The tension between a narrow conception of worker centrality and a wider decentered view of social struggle runs through Lotta Continua up until the dissolution of the party in 1976. See Bobbio 1988, 175–176.

5. The term "refusal of work" was elaborated by Mario Tronti in an essay published in his 1966 book *Workers and Capital*, but the development of the concept in the movements was not restricted to Tronti's analysis.

6. One event in the early 1960s is often invoked on the Italian Far Left as the origin story for workers' autonomy and an illustration of the gap or antagonism between workers and the unions. In July 1962, during a strike of workers at the Fiat plant in Turin, the leadership of the most conservative of the major unions representing Fiat workers signed an agreement without the consent of its own membership or the support of the striking workers as a whole. When workers learned they had been betrayed, they descended on the union headquarters and battled police, who defended the union building for an entire day. Since that time, Piazza Statuto, the location of the union headquarters, has served as shorthand for workers' autonomy. For an excellent account of the events and their significance, see Lanzardo 1979.

7. Wright 2002 presents an account of "the collapse of workerism" and the end of the centrality of the industrial worker in Italy.

8. For a useful analysis of the concept of social factory, somewhat different from my own, see Palazzo 2014.

9. On the decision to dissolve Potere Operaio, see Castellano 1980, 17; Negri 1979, 119–121. Another tension that contributed to the dissolution of Potere Operaio had to do with the militarization of the party and the movements, and the development of a double organization. I will return to this issue in Chapter 17.

10. See Berardi 1980, esp. 155–160. On the composition of Autonomia, see also Castellano et al. 1996 and Balestrini 1989.

11. "The theoretical proposals of *autonomia operaia*," maintains Emilio Quadrelli, "tend to radiate out in all directions and thus the immediate effect is not to fill the ranks of a single organization in a disciplinary way, but rather to foster a cascading proliferation of innumerable groups, committees, and collectives loosely held together but opposed to any form of family discipline" (2008, 111).

12. Ballestrini 1989, 130. For another novelistic account of the "movement of '77" in Italy, see Kushner 2013.

13. The social centers were burdened, first of all, with a constant need to defend their space and frequent clashes with the police. Another constant problem, which became particularly severe in Italy in the late seventies, was the sale and use of drugs, particularly heroin. The social centers frequently became zones of the drug trade since police were forbidden entry. Many social centers were forced to engage in a battle on two fronts: to combat, on one side, drug prohibitions and police interventions and, on the other, the heroin epidemic.

14. The area of Autonomia was also deeply embedded in Italy's 1970s countercultural movement, in which the free radio stations and music concerts played central roles. For a brief, synthetic account of the cultural face of Autonomia, see Berardi 1980, 156–157; for an in-depth analysis of the "creative wing" of Autonomia, with a focus on Bifo's role, see Ciuferri 2014.

15. The PCI, which was focused on its "historic compromise" and on joining the governing coalition in these years, reacted particularly negatively to the social composition of Autonomia. Through the latter half of the seventies, in fact, the PCI spearheaded, even more than the centrist and right-wing parties, the most extreme repression (police violence, special laws, mass incarceration, and more) against Autonomia and the other movements of the Far Left. "The tragic demise of the unions and the Communist Party," according to Moroni, "lay in not having understood and taken up the extraordinary innovative charge of that revolutionary wave: instead, they fiercely repressed it, allying themselves with oligarchic capital and the repressive agents of the state. By doing so, they committed suicide" (2021, 33).

16. Many segments within Autonomia itself found the notion of an "area" and the image of a network too vague to constitute an effective organizational structure. For I Volsci, for example, the primary pole of Autonomia in Rome, which favored a more centralized organizational structure, "the term 'area' can, in fact, mean everything and nothing, once everyone is free to have and develop their own conception . . . of Autonomia operaia" (Comitati autonomi operai 2007, 38).

Chapter 11

1. The socialist feminist texts from the 1970s and 1980s that served as a starting point for me include Dalla Costa and James 1972; Davis 1981; Eisenstein 1979a; Haraway 1985; Hartsock 1983; Collins 1990; Rowbotham 1972; and Sargent 1981. For more

contemporary texts that reflect on and extend this tradition see Federici 2021; Weeks 2011, 2018.

2. There are certainly concepts of articulation that operate without this requirement of no priority. The most prominent is that of Ernesto Laclau (2005), which, in the conceptions of the relations among both power structures and liberation struggles, rests on the hegemony of one of the forces.

3. For an excellent, brief formulation of the concept of racial capitalism, see Kelley 2021.

4. Hall 1977 works through a similar problematic but does not develop the concept of articulation as fully.

5. The Black feminist theory texts of the 1970s and 1980s that served as a starting point for me include Davis 1981; hooks 1984; Collins 1990; 1984; Spillers 1981; and Wallace 1979.

6. For insightful analysis of the film and helpful information on its production, see Szczesniak 2020.

7. Hilderbrand notes that this passage from the Combahee River Collective Statement "seems to provide a pitch for the film's premise" (2013, 8).

8. In response to the charge that the film is antisocialist, Borden responds, "It's not anti-socialist at all. It criticizes an opportunistic manifestation of a government that calls itself a Social Democracy but which has not restructured at all its capitalist underpinning" (quoted in Sussler 1983, 29).

9. Craig Willse and Dean Spade admire the film's willingness in scenes like this "to portray political differences and debates among activists and its refusal to neatly resolve conflict" (2013, 5). Some of the organizational debates in the film certainly do resonate strongly with activist discussions that continue to be central today.

Chapter 12

1. For an illuminating analysis of direct connections made among feminists at the remarkable 1975 conference in Mexico City, sponsored by the United Nations, to celebrate "International Women's Year," see Olcott 2017.

2. In their account of the TWLF strike, Bloom and Martin emphasize even more strongly the directive role of the Black Panther Party (2012, 272–273).

Chapter 14

1. Andrew Tomkins emphasizes the transnational circulation of encampment strategies among antinuclear movements. The Wyhl occupation borrowed practices, such as the construction of a "friendship house," developed at the French encampment at Marckolsheim to protest construction of a chemical plant just across the Rhine. Later, the Clamshell Alliance attempted to reproduce aspects of the Wyhl experience (2016, 124–125).

2. The name of the alliance was chosen to emphasize that clams along with other species in the coastal area would, according to environmental researchers, be harmed by the

nuclear plant. Two US activists who visited Wyhl in summer 1975 reported back to the Clamshell Alliance news of the encampment and the tactics used (Sheehan and Bachman n.d.).

Chapter 15

1. For introductions to these theoretical frameworks, regarding pluralism, see Dahl 1971; regarding civil society, see Cohen and Arato 1992.
2. Mitchell and Hansen 2010, vii. John Durham Peters's (2005) notion of "elemental media," although different in many regards, similarly poses media as prior to and thus the condition of experience.
3. Foucault 2015, 13; see also 2003, 23. Foucault was also fascinated in this period with Carl von Clausewitz's famous proposition that "war is the continuation of politics by other means" (1976, 69). Clausewitz is really insisting on the continuing operations of mediation: whereas one normally assumes that the onset of armed confrontation means the end of political mediation, he proposes that political mediation continues, even if by other means. Foucault reverses the formula: "We can invert Clausewitz's proposition and say that politics is the continuation of war by other means" (2003, 15). Whereas for Clausewitz war is still "filled" with political mediation, for Foucault politics has been reduced to military-style confrontation, "emptied" of mechanisms of mediation. Although Foucault poses this inverted formula as a general analysis of power, it seems reasonable to me, especially given the fact that his courses were much more tied to current events than his books, to interpret it as a comment on the political transformations of the 1970s.
4. See, for instance, Santos's discussion in Chapter 6 of how the revolutionary movements in Portugal suggested but did not achieve a situation of dual power. The classic reference for the concept of dual power is Lenin's analysis of the brief period of transition when a parallel revolutionary government was formed in Russia between February and October 1917. In the context of the 1970s (and, indeed, contemporary political situations), however, it is more appropriate to think of dual power not as an immediate prelude to revolution but rather an accumulation of counterpowers and democratic social relations within the shell of the dominant order.
5. The dramatic increase of armed and terrorist operations of Palestinian organizations does not fit well in the narrative of "the end of mediation" I have constructed here, in part because they had not benefited previously from mediatory mechanisms. Instead, as Rashid Khalidi maintains, an important impulse toward renewed Palestinian militancy was, paradoxically, Israel's victory in the 1967 Six-Day War (2020, 112–117). After the defeat of Egypt and Syria, Palestinians were less reliant on Arab states to advance their interests and also less restrained by their control. Palestinian armed operations of the 1970s were some of the most widely publicized and most tragic.

Chapter 16

1. In the 1970s, Passmore writes, "understanding terrorism centered largely on finding psychological defects and a terrorist personality" (2011, 6). That sociopsychological pathology approach, unfortunately, continues to the present. For a recent example of that lamentable tradition, see, for example, Orsini 2011.

2. The account of the Citizens' Commission to Investigate the FBI in the following paragraphs is derived primarily from Medsger 2014 and Hamilton 2014.

3. In 1974, the front began calling itself "The Wolf Cell" in reference to the extinct Honshu wolf, "likening the oppressed masses," Chelsea Szendi Schieder explains, "to that eradicated beast" (2019, 36).

4. Although I focus here primarily on the anti-imperialist aspect of the Anti-Japanese Front, also important for the group was their affirmation of the needs of day laborers, supported by a theory of lumpenproletariat revolution (Knaudt 2020).

5. The most comprehensive and intelligent history of the Weather Underground is Dohrn 2022.

6. Rocha makes the case that, despite persistent sexism within the group, women in the Weather Underground developed an important feminist component: "The organization was more than just an anti-war, anti-racism group: it was also a militant feminist group, one with a varied and complex type of feminism that has been ignored in the literature up to now" (2020, 164–165). On the relation of the group to feminism, see also Berger 2006, 170–175, 290–293.

7. "The Red Brigades were born in Milan not Trento, and not in university classrooms but in the large factories and proletarian neighborhoods" (Saccoman 2013, 28). For interviews with workers that express the Communist Party viewpoint regarding the emergence of the BR at four large factories (Fiat, Sit-Siemens, Magneti Marelli, and Alfa Romeo), see Cavallini 1978.

8. On the theatrical nature of the Moro affair, see Wagner-Pacifici 1986.

9. "The Red Brigades," maintains Marcello Tarì, "shared equally with the PCI a blindness with respect to the gigantic social transformation that had been produced over the course of a few years" (2015, 139).

10. Steiner and Debray claim that that the RAF was composed of roughly equal numbers of men and women, and that it broke traditional gender roles within the organization more successfully than did other guerrilla groups and even the radical left movements of the time (1987, 82–85). "Faced with a high participation rate of women," Leith Passmore claims, "West German terrorism was considered a particularly female problem (2011, 8).

11. In 1972, the popular magazine *Quick* published a photo essay titled "Ulrike Meinhof and Her Savage Girls," including a bare-breasted image of Gudrun Ensslin (Bauer 2008, 71). Four years later, *Quick*'s coverage of the Ponto assassination, which included photos of four RAF women suspected of the attack, opened with an oblique reference to "blood-red" menstrual fluid, and added, "Whenever terrorism shows its filthy face here, girls [*Mädchen*] are involved in this senseless killing" (Bielby 2012,

152). Moreover, since several of them were mothers of young children, they were cast as violating the laws of maternal love and the norms of the family (Scribner 2014 , 4). "The real scandal," maintains Karin Bauer, "was thus not militant violence, but the rejection of a traditional female role" (2008, 72).

Chapter 17

1. "This policy [the strategy of tension] amounts to the artificial creation of moments of extreme tension through such means as incidents provoked by fascist groups or by agents that often have direct links to the government's Secret Service" (Berardi 1980, 150).
2. The events have, indeed, been subject of Italian films and plays, the best of which is Dario Fo's *Accidental Death of an Anarchist* (1994).
3. Miguel Gotor (2021) claims that there is strong evidence that Giuseppe Saragat, then president of the Republic, had approved of a strategy of fascist bombings (although it was supposed to avoid casualties) and that Aldo Moro, the leading Christian Democrat politician, although he had no knowledge before the Piazza Fontana massacre, agreed to the cover-up plan as part of a political compromise with Saragat to hide the responsibility of the fascists and blame the anarchists.
4. On Calabresi's previous false arrests of anarchists for bombings as dress rehearsals for Piazza Fontana, see Morando 2019. Less than three years after Piazza Fontana, in May 1972, Commissioner Calabresi was assassinated and the police were long unable to solve the crime. Decades later, at the end of the 1990s, Adriano Sofri, a central leader of Lotta Continua, and another party leader were convicted of having ordered the murder of Calabresi, despite maintaining their innocence. The sole basis of conviction was the testimony of the admitted killer in exchange for a lighter sentence.
5. "From 1973 onwards," Ahmet Samim wrote in the early 1980s, "fascism grew far more swiftly than the left" (1981, 80).
6. For an account of workers' committees of a radical miners' unions associated with Devrimci Yol that pressed for self-management, see Bozkurt 2008, 95–97.
7. Ersan 2013, 292. Acaroglu remarks that the practice of cooperative building and infrastructure projects like the "end the mud" campaign has deep roots in Turkey, specifically "the ancient Anatolian tradition of imece" (2019, 418).

Chapter 18

1. Enzo Traverso, referring to similar international connections, characterizes the global 1968 as "a constellation of events which were in dialogue with each other" (2021, 393). This is an apt description, too, of the movements of the seventies.

2. In the Social Movements Lab, Sandro Mezzadra and I have developed an effective method whereby we begin study of each movement by exploring its genealogical, transversal, and international connections.

3. "Goodbye," declared Robin Morgan, for instance, "goodbye forever, counterfeit Left, counterleft, male-dominated cracked-glass-mirror reflection of the Amerikan Nightmare. Women are the real left" (2003, 421).

Index

Groupe de Libération Homosexuelle, 26
Gorz, André, 90–1, 97, 98, 114
Greenpeace, 193–5
Guattari, Félix, 230, 231
Guinea-Bissau, 15–6, 19–20, 21, 29, 65
Gurvitch, George, 40
Gutierrez, Gustavo, 44

Habermas, Jürgen, 204
Hall, Stuart, 153–6, 177–8
Hager, Carol, 193
Hammond, John, 71, 74
Hamon, Hervé, 4
Hampton, Fred, 204, 213
Hansen, Mark, 206
Hantai Dōmei. *See* Narita Airport
    struggle
Harlan, Thomas, 72
Hartmann, Heidi, 151, 156, 159
Harvey, David, 210
Hilliard, David, 236
Hobson, Emily, 26, 27
Horn, Eva, 206
housing occupations, 60–2, 71–2, 74, 107, 122
Huntington, Samuel, 97–8, 208

intersectionality, 158–60, 163–4
Iran, 34–42, 46–9
Islamic revolutionary movements, 35, 39–42, 47–9
Italy, 3–4, 100–101
    armed struggle, 224–8, 230, 239–41
    feminism, 116–7, 119, 123
    repression, 237–9
    workers' movements, 109–24, 225, 229, 239–40

James, Selma, 116
Jameson, Fredric, 230
Japan, 183–6, 191, 194–5, 221–3
Jara, José de la, 45
John Paul II, Pope, 46

Katsiaficas, Georges, 83
Kauffman, L. A., 197
Kelley, D. G., 6, 21, 123–4

Kennedy, Flo, 162
Kent State University shootings, 204
Khomeini, Ruhollah (Ayatollah of Iran), 34, 38
Kissinger, Henry, 53, 73
Kittler, Friedrich, 206
Korea, 221–2
    See also South Korea

land occupations, 61–2, 71–2
    See also encampments
Lanza del Vasto, 187
Larzac military base struggle, 183–4, 187–90, 249
League of Revolutionary Black Workers, 95–6
Lee, Jai-eui, 82
legitimation crisis, 205, 209, 254
Lewis-Colman, David, 95
liberation, 2, 9, 11
Liberation Front of Mozambique (FRELIMO), 16, 18–9, 21
Linebaugh, Peter, 90, 94
Lip watch factory occupation, 102–6, 189, 249
Lorde, Audre, 152, 174
Lordstown General Motors strike, 89–90
Lotta Continua, 112–3, 116–7, 120, 122, 238, 248–9
Lovett, Joseph, 25
lumpenproletariat, 122, 252

Macchiarini, Idalgo, 225
March, Ron, 92–3
Marighella, Carlos, 224
Martin, Waldo, 234, 236
Marx, Karl, 30–1, 39, 160, 163, 245, 256
Machel, Samora, 18, 20, 21
Margarido, Alfredo, 72
McCormick, Sabrina, 195
McDuffie, Erik, 157
McLuhan, Marshall, 206
mediation, 204–8
    end of, 91, 93, 208–14
Meinhof, Ulrike, 161, 213–4, 226, 232
Mezzadra, Sandro, 117–8, 124
Mitchell, W. J. T., 206